Successive Thought and Fact of Indian Mythology

Successive Thought and Fact of Indian Mythology

Abhay Bajaj

2008

CYBER TECH PUBLICATIONS
4264/3, Ansari Road, Daryaganj, New Delhi-110002 (India)
Ph.: 011-23244078. Fax: 011-23280028
E-Mail: cyberpublicationsdelhi@yahoo.com

SUCCESSIVE THOUGHT AND FACT OF INDIAN MYTHOLOGY

Abhay Bajaj

First Edition 2008

Published by :

G.S. Rawat for **Cyber Tech Publications**
4264/3, Ansari Road, Daryaganj, New Delhi-110002 (India)
Ph.: 011-23244078. Fax: 011-23280028
E-Mail: cyberpublicationsdelhi@yahoo.com

Printed at : **Amit Enterprises**, Maujpur, Delhi, (9810878184)

Preface

Hindu mythology is a term used by modern scholarship for a large body of Indian literature that details the lives and times of legendary personalities, deities and divine incarnations on earth interspersed with often large sections of philosophical and ethical discourse. Despite connotations of fiction in common usage, the term *myth*, in theological and academic studies, does not necessarily imply that a narrative is untrue. The use of term mythology is a western construct applied primarily to non-Judeo-Christian religious literature. It is intellectually insincere to describe other religious literature as mythology while labelling the biblical literature as 'legends'. It must be noted that many of the topics that fall under the category of *Hindu mythology* are cherished beliefs of Hindus.

All ancient religions contain stories that are accepted as literal truth by some, and as philosophical or allegorical insights by others. Thus, the biblical stories may be similarly construed as Jewish/Christian mythology. The stories in Indian mythology vary from subtle maxim conveying tales of Panchatantra and Jataka-tales to subtle life paradigm defining stories from the Bhagavad-Gita, Ramayana and Mahabharata. A key point to note is that there are usually multiple stories explaining the same fact or occasion or festival. So each version is right in its own merit.

—*Author*

Contents

1

HINDU MYTHOLOGY AND COSMOLOGY

INTRODUCTION

Hindu mythology is a term used by modern scholarship for a large body of Indian literature that details the lives and times of legendary personalities, deities and divine incarnations on earth interspersed with often large sections of philosophical and ethical discourse. Despite connotations of fiction in common usage, the term *myth*, in theological and academic studies, does not necessarily imply that a narrative is untrue. The use of term mythology is a western construct applied primarily to non-Judeo-Christian religious literature. It is intellectually insincere to describe other religious literature as mythology while labelling the biblical literature as 'legends'. It must be noted that many of the topics that fall under the category of *Hindu mythology* are cherished beliefs of Hindus.

All ancient religions contain stories that are accepted as literal truth by some, and as philosophical or allegorical insights by others. Thus, the biblical stories may be similarly construed as Jewish/Christian mythology. The stories in Indian mythology vary from subtle maxim conveying tales of Panchatantra and Jataka-tales to subtle life paradigm defining stories from the Bhagavad-Gita, Ramayana and Mahabharata. A key point to note is that there are usually multiple stories explaining the same fact or occasion or festival. So each version is right in its own merit. This is a result of the natural evolution the stories might have gone in the process of being handed over from generation to generation for centuries. Indian Mythology is one of the richest elements of Indian Culture, which enriches it further and makes it a unique one in the world. Through generations, different stories in Indian mythology have been passed from generation to generation either by word of mouth or through carefully stored scriptures.

It is our endeavour to bring forth the different elements of Indian mythology by a myriad of articles and stories which not only make educational reading but also make a good source of recreational reading. These stories, which form the backbone of Indian mythology, area great medium for people especially parents to inculcate interest in Indian Culture in the younger generation and to impart values of Indian culture to them. The interesting aspect of the stories in Indian Mythology, is that they are usually meant to convey subtle facts, rules and maxims to guide our daily lives. Who doesn't enjoy a well written story? Naturally storytelling is the best medium for conveying even powerful messages.

The mythological literature is intertwined with the ethos of ancient Vedic religion and Vedic civilization, and fundamentally constructed with Hindu systems of philosophy.

Definition and Misconception: Though they are often classified as 'Hindu' or 'Indian mythology', the label does not capture the centrality of religious and spiritual affiliations of the texts that ring true today for most Hindus. They are replete with long philosophical discourses and are often seen as source books for Hindu ethics and practice. It is also to be noted that historical evidence of many acts or places of Hindu narratives have been found, establishing them as historical facts. However, evidence is extremely limited and only allows for the possibility of myths being history.

Vedic Mythology: The roots of mythology that evolved from classical Hinduism come from the times of the Vedic civilization, from the ancient Vedic religion. The characters, theology, philosophy and stories that make up ancient Vedic myths are indelibly linked with Hindu beliefs. The Vedas are said to be four in number, namely Rigveda, Yajurveda, Samaveda, and the Atharva Veda. Some of these texts mention mythological concepts and machines very much similar to modern day scientific theories and machines.

Sources: It is believed that the Hindu mythology dates back to around 7200 BC when the first hymns of the Rigveda were sung praising the elements of nature, namely, the air, the water, the thunder, the sun, the fire, etc. They found expression in early Vedic Gods, namely, Vayu, Varuna, Indra, Surya and Agni. According to modern scholars over a period of time several Vedic Gods were conceptualized. Over next several millennia, in the post-Vedic period, and during the period of the Puranas, the Gods were personified and assumed specific shapes and characteristics, with individual endowments.

This was followed by the period of the epics, when the Ramayana and the Mahabharata were composed. It is believed that they capture and depict, to a large extent, historical events and happenings, and certain modern findings also seem to corroborate this, like the finding of an ancient bridge constructed between India and Sri Lanka. However, more archaelogical evidence is required to further substantiate the actual occurrence of the events around which the two epics are based.

The Puranas deal with stories that are "mythologically" older than the epics and are set in the "Kritha" or "Sathya" yuga, the first of the four great time periods said to compose what is called the Divya yuga lasting over 4,320,000 years. The epics themselves are set in different "yugas" or periods of time in *Hindu mythology*. The Ramayana, written by the poet Valmiki, describes the life and times of Lord Rama (the seventh avatar of Lord Vishnu) and occurs in the Tretha yuga, while the Mahabharata that describes the life and times of the Pandavas, occurs in the Dwapara yuga, a period in which Lord Krishna (the eighth avatar of Lord Vishnu) took birth.

Epics: The most important of these are an 18 voluminous group of works known as the Puranas. The two great Hindu Epics, the Ramayana and the Mahabharata, are other major works of *Hindu mythology*. The epics *Mahabharata* and *Ramayana* are very much religious scriptures. Their stories are deeply embedded in Hindu philosophy and serve as parables and sources of devotion for Hindus.

Cosmology: Hinduism presents a number of accounts pertaining to cosmology, and several explanations have been given as regards the origin of the universe. The most popular belief is that the universe emerged from Hiranyagarbha, meaning the *golden womb*. Hiranyagarbha floated around in water in the emptiness and the darkness of non-existence. Ultimately, this golden egg split and the cosmos was created. Swarga emerged from the golden upper part of the Hiranyagarbha, whereas Prithvi came out from the silver coloured lower half part.

THE WARS

The Weapons: There are several weapons which were believed to be used by the Gods of the Hindu mythology, some of which are Agneyastra, Brahmastra, Chakram, Kaumodaki, Narayanastra, Pashupata, Shiva Dhanush, Sudarshan, Trishul, Vaishnavastra, Vajra, Varunastra, and Vayavastra. A particular weapon was generally associated with a particular God.

The Deluge: The story of a great flood is mentioned in ancient Hindu texts, particularly the Satapatha Brahmana. It is compared to the accounts of the Deluge found in several religions and cultures. Manu was informed of the impending flood and was protected by the Matsya Avatara of Lord Vishnu, who had manifested himself in this form to rid the world of morally depraved human beings and protect the pious, as also all animals and plants. After the flood the Lord inspires the Manusmriti, largely based upon the Vedas, which details the moral code of conduct, of living and the division of society according to the caste system.

The Peoples of the Epics: Hindu mythology is not only about Gods and men, but classifies a host of different kinds of celestial, ethereal and earthly beings.

Sapta Rishis: Lord Brahma, out of his thought, creates seven sages, or Sapta Rishis, to help him in his act of creation. *Sapta Rishis* (*sapta* means seven and *rishis* means sages in Sanskrit). They are Bhrigu, Angira, Atri, Gautama, Kashyapa, Vashishta, and Agastya. The other meaning of Saptarishis is constellation of Great Bear (Ursa Major).

Pitrs: The Pitrs, or fathers, were the first humans.

The Worlds: Hindu mythology defines fourteen worlds (not to be confused with planets)-seven higher worlds (heavens) and seven lower ones (hells). (The earth is considered the lowest of the seven higher worlds.) All the worlds except the earth are used as temporary places of stay as follows: upon one's death on earth, Yama, the god of death (officially called 'Yama Dharma Raajaa'-Yama, the lord of justice) tallies the person's good/bad deeds while on earth and decides if the soul goes to heaven and/or hell, for how long, and in what capacity.

Some versions of the mythology state that good and bad deeds neutralize each other and the soul therefore spends time in either a heaven or a hell, but not both, whereas according to another school of thought, the good and bad deeds don't cancel out each other. In either case, the soul acquires a body as appropriate to the worlds it is entering. At the end of the soul's time in those worlds, it returns to the earth (is reborn as a life form on the earth). It is considered that only from the earth, and only after a human life, can the soul reach supreme salvation Moksha, the state free from the cycle of birth and death and the place beyond the fourteen worlds where the eternal god lives.

The Higher Worlds: Swarga is the third among the seven higher worlds. In common usage, Swarga is used to refer to the 'higher worlds' or heavens in general. The higher worlds (except the earth) are populated with a variety of beings called Suras, consisting of several subdivisions: Deva, Dhanava, Gandharva, Yaksha, Kinnara, and so on. In general, beings of a higher heavenly world can freely visit a lower one. All the posts (kings, etc.) in the heavenly worlds are awarded based on the good deeds one performs while on earth.

The Lower Worlds: The term Naraka indicates the various lower worlds. The lower worlds are filled with Asuras.

Gods and Goddesses: There are many layers of gods in Hinduism. At the top are the trinity: Shiva (the destroyer), Vishnu (the protector), and Brahma (the creator), and their wives (goddesses in their own right): Shakti (also known as Paarvathi, Ambicaa) the goddess of courage and power, Lakshmi the goddess of all forms of wealth, and Saraswati the goddess of learning. The children of the gods are also gods in their own right. Interestingly, Brahma is also considered the ruler of the highest of the heavens (the world called *Sathya*), so in one sense, Brahma is not beyond the fourteen worlds as Shiva and Vishnu are.

The next lower tier of gods are those in charge of the elements: Indra (the god of thunder and lightning; he also rules the world of Swarga), Varuna (the god of the oceans), Agni (the god of fire), Kubera (the treasurer of the gods), Surya (the sun god), Vaayu (the god of wind), and Soma (the moon god). Below these are the 'garden variety' beings, who have superior powers when compared to humans but otherwise serve one of the above gods.

Swarga also has a set of famous heavenly dancers: Urvasi, Menaka, Rambhaa, and Thilottamaa (all female), whose job is to entertain the heavenly court, and upon orders from the heavenly kings, to distract people on the earth from accumulating too much good deeds so as to become a threat to the heavenly kings. Other notable inhabitants of the heavens include the celestial sages, and Naaradha the messenger of the gods. Yama (the god of death and justice) is said to live in Kailash along with his master Shiva. He rules the lower world of Naraka with a band of emissaries called the *Yama duta* (messengers of Yama), who bring the souls of dead persons to Yama for evaluation. Chitragupta is one of those lower level celestial beings who functions as the karmic accountant of all the actions of the human beings on earth.

Incarnations: As the protector of life, one of the duties of Vishu is to appear on the earth whenever a firm hand is required to set things right. The epic Bhagavatham is the chronology of Vishnu's ten major incarnations (there are totally twenty six incarnations): Matsya (fish), Kurma (turtle), Varaaha (boar), Narasimha (lion-faced human)), Vaamana (an ascetic in the form of a midget), Parasuraama (a militant Brahmin), Rama, Balaraama (a shepherd and also the half-brother of Krishna), Krishna, Kalki (a warrior on a white horse) whose appearance also signals the beginning of the end of the epoch.

House of Ikshvaku: Ikshvaku was the son of Manu, the first mortal man, and founder of the Sun Dynasty.

Bharatavarsha: The first king to conquer all of the world was Bharata, son of Dushyanta and Shakuntala. All of this world, Vishwa, is named Bharatavarsha, or *The Land of Bharata*, or *The Cherished Land.*

King Bharata's conquests are described to have stretched over all of modern India, and Pakistan, Bangladesh and Nepal, as well as the ancient Gandhara region of Afghanistan. No account has been known to exceed these geographical boundaries

HINDU COSMOLOGY

The Rig Veda questions the origin of the cosmos in:

> "Neither being (sat) nor non-being was as yet. What was concealed? And where? And in whose protection?... Who really knows? Who can declare it? Whence was it born, and whence came this creation? The devas were born later than this world's creation, so who knows from where it came into existence? None can know from where creation has arisen, and whether He has or has not produced it. He who surveys it in the highest heavens, He alone knows-or perhaps knows not."

But the Rig Veda's view of the cosmos also sees one true divine principle self-projecting as the divine word, Vaak, 'birthing' the cosmos that we know, from the monistic Hiranyagarbha or Golden Womb. The Hiranyagarbha is alternatively viewed as Brahma, the creator who was in turn created by God, or as God (Brahman) himself. The later puranic view asserts that the universe is created, destroyed, and recreated in an eternally repetitive series of cycles. In Hindu cosmology, a universe endures for about 4,320,000,000 years (one day of Brahma, the creator or kalpa) and is then destroyed by fire or water elements.

At this point, Brahma rests for one night, just as long as the day. This process, named pralaya (*Cataclysm*), repeats for 100 Brahma years (311 trillion human years) that represents Brahma's lifespan. It must be noted that Brahma is the creator but not necessarily regarded as God in Hinduism. He is mostly regarded as a creation of God/Brahman. We are currently believed to be in the 51st year of the present Brahma and so about 155 trillion years have elapsed since He was born as Brahma. After Brahma's "death", it is necessary that another 100 Brahma years pass until he is reborn and the whole creation begins anew. This process is repeated again and again, forever.

Brahma's life is divided in one thousand cycles (Maha Yuga, or the Great Year). Maha Yuga, during which life, including the human race appears and then disappears, has 71 divisions, each made of 14 Manvantara (1000) years. Each Maha Yuga lasts for 4,320,000 years. Manvantara is Manu's cycle, the one who gives birth and governs the human race. Each Maha Yuga consists of a series of four shorter yugas, or ages. The yugas get progressively worse from a moral point of view as one proceeds from one yuga to another. As a result each yuga is of shorter duration than the age that preceded it. The current Kali Yuga (Iron Age) began at midnight 17 February/ 18 February in 3102 BC in the proleptic Julian calendar.

Quoted Views on Hindu Cosmology: Professor Arthur Holmes (1895-1965) geologist, professor at the University of

Durham. He writes regarding the age of the earth in his great book, The Age of Earth (1913) as follows:

> "Long before it became a scientific aspiration to estimate the age of the earth, many elaborate systems of the world chronology had been devised by the sages of antiquity. The most remarkable of these occult time-scales is that of the ancient Hindus, whose astonishing concept of the Earth's duration has been traced back to Manusmriti, a sacred book."

When the Hindu calculation of the present age of the earth and the expanding universe could make Professor Holmes so astonished, the precision with which the Hindu calculation regarding the age of the entire Universe was made would make any man spellbound. Alan Watts, a professor, graduate school dean and research fellow of Harvard University, drew heavily on the insights of Vedanta. Watts became well known in the 1960s as a pioneer in bringing Eastern philosophy to the West. He wrote:

> "To the philosophers of India, however, Relativity is no new discovery, just as the concept of light years is no matter for astonishment to people used to thinking of time in millions of kalpas, (A kalpa is about 4,320,000,000 years). The fact that the wise men of India have not been concerned with technological applications of this knowledge arises from the circumstance that technology is but one of innumerable ways of applying it."

It is, indeed, a remarkable circumstance that when Western civilization discovers Relativity it applies it to the manufacture of atom-bombs, whereas Oriental civilization applies it to the development of new states of consciousness." Count Maurice Maeterlinck (1862-1949) was a Belgian writer of poetry, a wide variety of essays. He won the 1911 Nobel Prize for literature. In his book Mountain Paths, says:

> "he falls back upon the earliest and greatest of Revelations, those of the Sacred Books of India with a Cosmogony which no European conception has ever surpassed."

Huston Smith (?) born in China to Methodist missionaries, a philosopher, most eloquent writer, world-famous religion scholar who practices Hatha Yoga. He has said of Hinduism:

"The invisible excludes nothing, the invisible that excludes nothing is the infinite – the soul of India is the infinite."

"Philosophers tell us that the Indians were the first ones to conceive of a true infinite from which nothing is excluded. The West shied away from this notion. The West likes form, boundaries that distinguish and demarcate. The trouble is that boundaries also imprison – they restrict and confine."

"India saw this clearly and turned her face to that which has no boundary or whatever... India anchored her soul in the infinite seeing the things of the world as masks of the infinite assumes – there can be no end to these masks, of course. If they express a true infinity... And It is here that India's mind boggling variety links up to her infinite soul."

"India includes so much because her soul being infinite excludes nothing... It goes without saying that the universe that India saw emerging from the infinite was stupendous."

"While the West was still thinking, perhaps, of 6,000 years old universe – India was already envisioning ages and eons and galaxies as numerous as the sands of the Ganges. The Universe so vast that modern astronomy slips into its folds without a ripple."

Dick Teresi, author and coauthor of several books about science and technology, including "The God Particle".

"Indian cosmologists, the first to estimate the age of the earth at more than 4 billion years. They came closest to modern ideas of atomism, quantum physics, and other current theories. India developed very early, enduring atomist theories of matter. Possibly Greek atomistic thought was influenced by India, via the Persian civilization."

According to Guy Sorman, visiting scholar at Hoover Institution at Stanford and the leader of new liberalism in France:

"Temporal notions in Europe were overturned by an India rooted in eternity. The Bible had been the yardstick for measuring time, but the infinitely vast time cycles of India suggested that the world was much older than anything the Bible spoke of.

It seems as if the Indian mind was better prepared for the chronological mutations of Darwinian evolution and astrophysics."

Carl Sagan on Hindu Cosmology: Carl Sagan was a distinguished Cornell University astronomer and Pulitzer Prize-winning author.

"The main reason that we oriented this episode of Cosmos towards India is because of that wonderful aspect of Hindu cosmology which first of all gives a time-scale for the Earth and the universe—a time-scale which is consonant with that of modern scientific cosmology. We know that the Earth is about 4.6 billion years old, and the cosmos, or at least its present incarnation, is something like 10 or 20 billion years old. The Hindu tradition has a day and night of Brahma in this range, somewhere in the region of 8.4 billion years."

"As far as I know. It is the only ancient religious tradition on the Earth which talks about the right time-scale. We want to get across the concept of the right time-scale, and to show that it is not unnatural. In the West, people have the sense that what is natural is for the universe to be a few thousand years old, and that billions is indwelling, and no one can understand it. The Hindu concept is very clear. Here is a great world culture which has always talked about billions of years."

"Finally, the many billion year time-scale of Hindu cosmology is not the entire history of the universe, but just the day and night of Brahma, and there is the idea of an infinite cycle of births and deaths and an infinite number of universes, each with its own gods."

ROGER BERTSCHAUSEN

"We in the West have long had trouble with time. Early Judaism, Christianity and Islam had no inkling of the long age of the universe. Cosmologies from these religions were based on the notion that the universe started at a finite point in the recent past. St. Augustine set the beginning of the universe at 5000 BCE. For centuries, this figure was embraced by most Westerners. (And some continue to believe it.) Additionally, the early Christians also believed that the end of time as we know it was close at hand."

"This view of time contrasts sharply with other religious perspectives on the age of the universe. In the Hindu tradition, for example, one day in the life of Brahma lasts 4,320,000,000 years. And Brahma lives for the equivalent of 311,040,000,000,000 human years. The historian of religions Huston Smith reports one way of conceiving of the Hindu time-frame."

WARS OF HINDU MYTHOLOGY

The *Wars* of Hindu mythology depict great heroes and demons in battles of celestial proportions, filled with the awesome force of celestial weapons, religious mysticism, magic, celestial and supernatural beings. Overriding the awesome battles and wonderous features is a deep driving purpose of religion and fate.

War in Religion and Myth: While no Hindu epic or scripture fails to describe the horrors of war and its fallout, major wars are fought with a religious purpose: often to eliminate demonic beings, or lords and rulers who pursue war wantonly for ambition and domination.

The most destructive wars in Hindu myth are driven with the mission of good triumphing over evil. Hindu teachings prescribe war as the final option, to be employed only after all peaceful methods are exhausted. But when this time comes, war is taught to be a matter of great personal and religious importance, where every man must do his duty as a warrior, exemplify courage, honour and fearsome prowess even against all the odds, and even at high cost of life. The Bhagavad Gita places duty above all gain and loss, triumph and destruction, no matter how terrible or personal it becomes. Fate is the driving force of all Hindu actions, and the awaiting fate of death and ascent to heaven is the most important object for ordinary human beings, thus making the destructiveness of wars irrelevant so long as honour and courage are exhibited and a righteous purpose is served.

The Avataras of Vishnu: Vishnu, the Inconceivable Supreme, periodically takes birth, an Avatara upon earth to *destroy evil and deliver the pious*. He is also the refuge of the Devas in their battles against Asuras.

The most martial Avataras include Narasimha, Parashurama, Rama and Varaha.

- *Narayanastra:* The personal missile weapon of Vishnu in his Narayana form, this astra lets loose a powerful tirade of millions of deadly missiles simultaneously. The intensity of the shower increases with resistance. The only solution is total submission before the missile, given which it will stop.
- *Vaishnavastra:* The personal missile weapon of Vishnu, once fired it cannot be thwarted by any means, save by the will of Vishnu Himself.
- *Kaumodaki:* The divine mace weapon of Vishnu; invincible and without parallel.
- *Sudarshana Chakra:* The magical *chakra*, a spinning discus with sharp outer spears. The Sudarshan flies at the command of Vishnu, spinning away to tear off the heads of His opponents, or to perform any function desired by Vishnu. It was most famously used by His Avatara Krishna in the Mahabharata.

Shiva: The Lord Destroyer, *Sarvaripati* Shiva is the most fearsome manifestation of the Supreme God. Assigned with destroying all of the universe at the end of time, Shiva is the most fearsome warrior, unconquerable by any and all.

- *Pashupata:* Discharged by the mind, eyes, words or a bow, the Pashupata is the irresistible and most destructive personal weapon of Shiva. Never to be used against lesser enemies and by lesser warriors, the Pashupata is capable of destroying creation and vanquishing all beings.
- *Trishula*: The terrifying trident-staff of Shiva.
- *Tandava:* Is the dance of the Destroyer, which He performs over the body of a demon, and simultaneously destroys all creation, all beings, material and illusion alike: the ultimate martial art.

Shiva employs his power to kill the Asura Tripura, destroying the flying three cities of Tripura. He is restrained and not involved in the wars of the worlds prior to dissolution.

THE KSHATRIYA ORDER

War Sacrifices

- *Ashwamedha:* The famous horse-sacrifice was conducted by allowing a pony to roam freely for a slated period of time, with the king performing the sacrifice laying claim to all the lands it touched. The king whose authority is contested must prove himself in battle or accept the imperial supremacy of the challenging king. When the horse returns safely after the period of time, the main sacrifice is performed, and the king, if successful in obtaining dominance over other kings, is crowned *Emperor of the World*.

  The Ashwamedha allows the opportunity to maintain peace if the kings do not choose to contest the sacrificial horse:
- *Rajasuya:* Considered the ultimate sacrifice, the king performing the sacrifice must openly challenge every king in the world to accept his supremacy or defeat him in battle. If and when the king returns successfully, having beaten all other known rulers, the performance of the sacrifice will send him to the highest abode of

Lord Indra. It was performed by the Pandava hero Yudhisthira in the Mahabharata epic.

- *Vaishnava*: Akin to the conduct of the *Rajasuya*, save only that the entire sacrifice is to please Lord Vishnu, who is the Supreme God.

Levels of Warrior Excellence

- *Atiratha*: A warrior capable of fighting 60,000 warriors simultaneously; circumspect in his mastery of all forms of weapons and combat skills.
- *Maharatha*: A warrior capable of contending with 10,000 warriors simultaneously.

Strategic Formations: the Vyuha

- *Krauncha Vyuha*: The crow-shaped formation of an army; forces are distributed to form spanning wing-sides, with a formidable, penetrating centre depicting the crow's head and break.
- *Padma Vyuha*: A winding, ever-rotating circular formation; considered impenetrable during the *Mahabharata* age by all warriors except Arjuna, Krishna, Dhristadyumna and Abhimanyu. Abhimanyu, had learnt how to break into the formation (in the womb of Subhadra) but not how to break out of it and is trapped inside in the *Mahabharata* war. Some times called as Chakra Vyuha also.
- *Sarpa Vyuha*: Winding snake formation.
- *Padma Vyuha*: Lotus formation; considered impenetrable during the *Mahabharata* age by all warriors save Bhishma, Drona, Arjuna, Pradyumna and Krishna.
- Makara Vyuha.
- Sakata Vyuha.

Devastras: An Astra is a missile-type weapon which is to be hurled at an enemy. Examples include arrows from bows. A Shastra is a personal weapon, like swords and maces, that must be constantly operated by the warrior.

- *Brahmastra*: Imbibed with the mystical force of Creator Brahma, this is considered the most fearsome weapon in mythological works. The releaser of millions of missiles, great fires and a destructive potential capable of extinguishing all creation, if not used by and aimed only at a celestial fighter.

  Modern speculation has equated its destructive potential to a nuclear weapon.
- *Nagastra*: The snake weapon, used by Karna against Arjuna in Kurukshetra war. It is considered as next only to Brahmastra. It has a fame that it never misses it's target.
- *Shakti*: The magical dart weapon of Indra, unfailing at executing its target. Indra granted it to Karna during the Kurukshetra war. The Mahabharata also refers to it as the Amoghastra.
- *Vajra*: The thunderbolt weapon of Indra, who is the God of Thunder and Lightning, akin to Zeus and Jupiter in Greek and Roman mythology.
- *Agneyastra*: The fire weapon, incepted by God Agni, master of the flames.
- *Varunastra*: The water weapon, incepted by God Varuna, master of the oceans, rivers and lakes.
- *Vayavastra*: The wind weapon, incepted by God Vayu, master of wind.

The Devas and Asuras: The perennial battle between the Devas and Asuras is undertaken over the dominion of the three worlds: Swarga, Bhumi and Patala, or *Heaven*, *Earth* and the *Nether worlds*. Both races are technically equal, possessor of great religious and martial powers, but the Devas are committed to the worship of the Supreme Lord and practice of virtue. The Asuras have atheistic and devious tendencies that grow over time. The divide is the greatest in the Kali Yuga, the final age.

- *Sukracharya*: Is the Preceptor of the Asuras, their chief priest and martial guru. Sukracharya is a great worshipper of the Supreme Lord, but remains supportive of the Asuras, who are often identified as atheistic and demonic in nature.

- *Brihaspati*: Is the Guru Preceptor of the Devas. Possessing unparalleled knowledge of the Vedas, scripture, religion and mysticism, Brihaspati's mastery of the military arts is akin to Sukracharya, his counterpart.
- *Indra*: The God of thunder and lightning, he is the King of Swarga, or *Heaven*, and the leader of all the Devas against the demon hordes. The greatest performer of sacrifices, Indra is the most famous and fearsome warrior in the three worlds, but faces opponents often equal or greater to him, and is sometimes unable to vanquish enemies like Indrajit, who was able to humiliate Indra owing to his past sins. When facing opponents like Vritra, Indra seeks the aid of Lord Vishnu.
- *Skanda*: The Vedic God of War, more so the generalissimo.
- *Narakasura*: The great Asura opponent of Vishnu.
- *Vritra*: The brahmin Asura, who was performing a sacrifice to obtain sovereignty of the three worlds.

The Ramayana: The epic story of Ramayana was adopted by several cultures across Asia. Shown here is a Thai historic artwork depicting the battle which took place between Rama and Ravana.

- *Vishvamitra*: Is the preceptor of Rama and Lakshmana, a powerful tapasvin and Brahmarishi. He bestows the knowledge of all divine weaponry to Rama and Lakshmana, leads them to kill powerful demons and instructs them in advanced religion and military arts.
- *Rama*: Is the Seventh Avatara of Vishnu, and the greatest warrior-tapasvin in the three worlds. His knowledge, prowess and tapasya is above all. Rama single-handedly slays the 14,000 demon hordes of Khara (in 14 minutes, according to the Ramayana), the demons

Maricha and Subahu, Ravana's chief commander Prahasta and is responsible for the ultimate killing of Ravana himself.

- *Lakshmana*: Is as powerful and excellent a warrior as his brother, and slays extremely powerful demons, including Atikaya and Indrajit-which is considered to be the turning point of the war.
- *Hanuman*: The Vanara minister of Sugriva is the greatest devotee of Rama, famous for his unerring service, absolute loyalty and great feats of courage. Hanuman is responsible for killing many demons, as well as burning the city of Lanka. His strength is given by his father Vayu, and by virtue of the boons bestowed on him by various Gods, he could increase his size and strength beyond any limit he desired.
- *Prahasta*: The chief commander of Lanka's army, Prahasta defeated the host of the Gods, and subjugated many kings on Ravana's behalf.
- *Ravana*: Is blessed by his fearsome 10,000 year tapasya to be the most powerful being on earth, invulnerable to every God, demon and living being, save man. Although an expert on the Vedas and a great king, and a *numero uno* devotee of Lord Shiva, he is the Emperor of evil by his patronage of demons, desecration of women, the murder of kings and humiliation of the Gods headed by Indra.
- *Indrajit*: As his name suggests, Ravana's first-born son defeated Indra, king of Gods. Master of mystical warfare and celestial weapons, and blessed by boons from Gods, Indrajit was considered the most fearful warrrior, virtually invincible.
- *Kumbhakarna*: The gigantic brother of Ravana is a fearsome monster-demon who sleeps for six months at a stretch, rising for only day and then returning to his slumber. Kumbhakarna is a giant who can slay hundreds of warriors by the sweep of his hand or stomp of his foot.

THE MAHABHARATA

- *Kuru Army:* Of 11 Akshauhinis is formed by the kingdom of Hastinapura in alliance with races like the Samshaptakas, Trigartas, the Narayana army, the Sindhu army and Shalya of Madra.
  - o *Commanders in Chief*: Bhishma, Drona, Karna, Shalya
  - o *Maharathas*: Shalya, Ashwathama, Somadatta, Bhurisrava, Bhagadatta, Jayadratha, Kritavarma
  - o *Atirathas*: Bhishma, Drona, Karna
- *Pandava Army*: Is a coalition of 7 Akshauhinis, primarily comprising of the Panchala and Matsya forces, the Rakshasa forces of Bhima's son, and Vrishni-Yadava heroes.
- *Commanders in Chief*: Dhristadyumna
- *Maharathas*: Yudhisthira, Bhima, Dhristadyumna, Ghatotkacha, Satyaki
- *Atirathas*: Arjuna
- *Bhishma*: The most consummate warrior trained by Parashurama, Bhishma is indestructible by any warrior when he lifts his weapons. Having mastered his preceptor himself and all the kings of the earth, he is the Commander in Chief of the Kuru Army.
- *Drona*: The preceptor of the kshatriyas and kings of the age, Drona is a great master of Vedic military arts, almost every celestial weapon, with great religious knowledge and wisdom. He becomes the second Kuru commander, and is the favourite of Arjuna. Drona's rejection of Karna as a student, owing to his unknown caste lays the foundation for the great Karna-Arjuna rivalry.
- *Arjuna*: Known all over the three worlds as the foremost warrior alive, he is the son of Indra and the most powerful *Atiratha*. He is responsible for vanquishing Bhishma, as well as exterminating an entire *Akshauhini*

of warriors and *Maharathas* in one day, in addition to the armies of Samshaptakas, Trigartas and Narayanas-millions of soldiers and heroic warrios. He is also the protagonist of the most intense personal rivalry of the war, between the two reputed greatest warriors, with Karna, whom he slays. (Pandava's chief army general was Drushtadhymna and not Arjuna as it was mentioned in the earlier editions of this page)

- *Bhima*: The second and most impetuous Pandava, Bhima's personal strength is phenomenal. He is an unsurpassed master of the mace weapon, and a consummate wrestler. He slays all of the one hundred Kuru brothers, and the chief antagonist of the saga, Duryodhana.
- *Abhimanyu*: The son of Arjuna, Abhimanyu is a consummate warrior almost equal to his father. When he enters the unbreakable *Chakra vyuha*, he holds the entire Kuru host, with Drona, Karna and hundreds of other heroic warriors, in addition to hundreds of thousands of foot soldiers at bay single-handedly. He is killed however, by deceit and a merciless and most unlawful slaying while he is unarmed and without a chariot, by all these powerful Kuru heroes.
- *Karna*: The tragic hero of the epic, Karna is the first-born of Kunti, the mother of the five Pandavas, but abandoned as a child owing his mother's maidenhood and fear of destroying her honour. As a result, Karna is raised by charioteers and denied the recognition and benefits of belonging to the Kshatriya order. Karna has to employ deceit to dodge the question of his caste, but obtains training from Parashurama.

  His passion and desire for revenge upon Drona, Arjuna and all of those who denied him opportunity and respect is consummate, and he becomes the most fearsome warrior. The entire rivalry is a question of who is truly

> superior. Karna's prowess meets par with Arjuna's, and Karna devises a fearsome ploy to kill the Pandava prince. Firing off an extremely powerful missile at one instant that dazzles and injures Arjuna, he instantly fires off another powerful arrow to strike down the prince while he is still reeling from the impact. His ploy is thwarted by Krishna, who sinks Arjuna's chariot just so as the arrow passes Arjuna's head by an inch!

It is felt by many contemporary scholars and Hindus that Karna in fact was the superior of Arjuna, and was done in only by the curse of Parashurama owing to his deceit, and Krishna, due to his support of the evil Duryodhana and the horrible slaying of Abhimanyu.

However, as in all other Vedic/Hindu mythological stories, superiority over another was never by means of mere physical prowess; it always meant a superiority in virtue (and hence a combination of both) as well. It is also depicted in the epic that Karna's soul is in fact that of Narakasura, the terrible demon slain by Vishnu in a previous age.

The End of the World: Bronze Chola Statue of Nataraja at the Metropolitan Museum of Art, New York City. The end of the world, all creation and illusion is prophesized to happen at the end of the Kali Yuga. Lord Shiva Nataraja, the Destroyer kills the paramount demon of the time and performs the *Tandava Nritya* (*The Dance of Tandava*) on his back.

The mystical dance is the penultimate martial art, destroying all forms of matter and energy, materials, beings and illusions, which are absorbed within the Supreme Brahman.

Kalki, the final Avatara of Vishnu is also prophesized to appear the end of the Kali yuga, to wage the final battle between good and evil. It is not clear how to reconcile this prophesy with Shiva's role as the Destroyer, but Kalki will appear upon a white horse, amassing an army of the few pious remaining, and incarnations of all of Hindu God-head, to destroy the demons and sin manifest in the world.

THE TWO WORLD

SVARGA

In Hinduism: **Svarga** (or *Swarga*) is set of nether worlds located on Mt. Meru. It is a Heaven where the righteous live in paradise before their next reincarnation. Svarga is seen as a transitory place for righteous souls who performed good deeds but whose conduct is not enough to attain Moksha, or union with God which requires abstinence from both papam(sin) and punyam(good deed). The capital is Amaravati and the entrance is guarded by Airavata. Svarga is presided by Indra, a deva and Lord of Heaven. In Slavic religion *Svarga* is Heaven, the residence of god Svarog.

NARAKA

Naraka is the name of a place of torment, in both Hinduism and Buddhism. The concept is different for each of these.

In Hinduism: Naraka or *Neraka* in Hinduism, is compared to the Abrahamic concept of Hell. However, Naraka in Hinduism is not equivalent to Hell in Christian ideology. Naraka is only a purgatory where the soul gets purified of sin by sufferings, so Naraka and Purgatory are equivalent to Hamistagan of Zoroastrianism, and not Hell. Hell is also a state of consciousness and this suffering need not take place after death, when the soul has vacated the physical body, but during incarnation.

This can be related to the law of karma where our inner and outer actions will sooner or later bear their fruits. In Hindu myth, there are many hells, and Yama, Lord of Justice, sends human beings after death for appropriate punishment. Such punishment can be in boiling oil, etc. Even Mukti-yogyas (souls eligible for mukti or Moksha), and Nitya-samsarins (forever transmigrating ones in Dvaita theology) can experience Naraka for expiation. Cited from *Bhakti Schools of Vedanta*, by Swami Tapasyananda.

In Buddhism: Buddhist texts describe the terrible sufferings of beings in the many subterranean layers of Narakas in intricate if not always consistent detail.

2

HISTORY OF THE JYOTISH, MANTRA AND AYURVEDA

Jyotish has historically been part of a continuous "holistic" approach to living and to spiritual practice within the life of Hindus predominant in India. Jyotish is often discussed as the instructional element of the Rig Veda, and as such is a Vedanga, or "body part" of the Vedas, namely called the *Eye of the Veda*, for its alleged ability to view both phenomenal reality and wisdom itself. Part of a larger Vedic curriculum including mathematics, architecture, medical and military applications. Jyotish has its own sophisticated reference to the noumenal: the planets are "grahas", which are thought to seize or act upon created beings and influence their actions and life. As Hindus believe that humans have fortune and misfortune in life because of karma, many use Jyotish to understand the downs in life due to the influence of planets, *i.e.*, Navagraha and perform religious ceremonies to mitigate bad karma. Jyotish's many lineages or paramparas emphasize that its study is a sadhana or technique of mental and existential development.

In modern times, it is a chief source of reference for many Hindus and other astrologers. Vedic astrologers will frequently prescribe special stones or meditation techniques using mantras to those facing difficult or unclear futures as predicted by means consistent with Jyotish methodology. While in past centuries, Brahmins had been the primary practitioners of Jyotish, since the last century, a renaissance of study of Jyotish and other Vedic sciences emerged in India and the west.

The foundation of jyotish is the notion of bandhu of the Vedas, which is the connection between the microcosm and the macrocosm. Surya, the Sun, is a manifestation of Vishnu, a central aspect of the Supreme, and is also the Atman within man. The term "Vedic astrology" has been recently introduced by American and Western astrologers in the 1980s and 1990s, leading to collaborative organizations such as the now-international. *Jyotisha* (*jyotica*, in Hindi and English usage *Jyotish*) is the Hindu system of astrology, one of the six disciplines of Vedanga, and regarded as one of the oldest schools of ancient astrology to have had an independent origin, affecting all other schools in and around India. The Sanskrit word derives from *jyótis* (disjointed as "Ja"+"Ya"+"O"+"T"+"ish" to get the root meaning as "water or birth"+"in addition to" + "earth" and "stars" + "knowledgeable" equating as one who is knowledgeable, or enlightened with knowledge, of birth, fate, and relationship to water, earth and stars) or which means "light, brightness", but in the plural also "the heavenly bodies, planets and stars".

In India, Jyotish is still commonly used to aid in important decisions in life. In Hindu culture, newborns are traditionally named based on their jyotish charts, and jyotish concepts are pervasive in the organization of the calendar and holidays as well as in many areas of life. Astrolgy is perceived to be vital in Indian culture, in making decisions made about marriage, opening a new business, and moving into a new home.

Branches of Vedic/Hindu Astrology: Vedic astrology (*Aagam Shaastra Jyotisha*—futurity sciences) has three main branches:

- *Siddhanta (Astronomy):* Astronomy and its application to astrology
- *Samhita (Mundane astrology):* Covers Mundane astrology, predicting important events related to countries such as war, earth quakes, political events, astro-meteorology, financial positions, electional astrology; house & construction related matters (Vaastu Shaastra), animals, portents & omens, etc.

- *Hora (Predictive astrology):*

This branch has the following different styles/sub branches:-

- *Jaatak Shastra*/Hora Shastra (Natal Astrology/ horoscopy): Prediction based on individual horoscope.
- *Muhurt or Muhurtha* (Electional astrology): Selection of beneficial time to initiate an activity to get maximum fruition from the life activities.
- *Swar Shastra* (Phonetical astrology): Predictions based on name & sounds.
- *Prashna* (Horary astrology): Predictions based on time when a question is asked by querent/querist.
- *Ankjyotisha / Kabala* (Numerology): A branch of astrology based on numbers.
- *Nadi* Astrology: An ancient treatise having detailed predictions for individuals.
- *Tajik Shastra / Varsha Phal* (Annual Horoscopy): Astrology based on annual solar returns.
- *Jaimini Sutras*: A non-conventional method of timing of events based on Famous Indian astrologer, Acharya Jaimini.
- *Nastjaatakam* (Lost Horoscopy): Art of tracing/ construction of lost horoscopes.
- *Streejaatak* (female astrology): A special branch of astrology dealing with female nativities.

OTHER RELATED BRANCHES

- *Graha Samudriki* (Astro-Palmistry): Palm reading as horoscope.
- *Hasta Rekha / Samudrika Shastra* (Palmistry): Based on palm reading.
- *Padatal Shastra* (Plantarology): Based on reading of lines and signs on the sole.
- *Shakun Shastra* (Omens): Predictions based on omens & portents.

- *Swapna Vidhya* : Interpretation of dreams.
- *Kapal Vidya* (Phrenology)
- *Aakriti Vidya* (Physiognomy): Based on structure & moles on the body.
- *Kerala Jyotisha*: Predictions based on querrist reply regarding name of flower or colour or touching part of body.
- *Remedial Astrology*: Various modes of propitiation of planets based on planetary positions in nativity, transits, elections & for religious functions.

In Vedic literature guidance is given on two other branches viz, Electional astrology and Remedial astrology.

Hindu and Western Astrology: The most easily referred to difference between the two lies in the method of measurement of the Zodiac. Vedic astrology uses primarily the sidereal zodiac (in which stars are considered to be the fixed background against which the motion of the planets is measured), whereas most Western astrology uses the tropical zodiac (the motion of the planets is measured against the position of the Sun on the Spring equinox). This difference becomes only noticeable over time, after the course of several centuries, as a result of the precession of the equinoxes. Synchronically, the two systems are identical, with just a shift of the origin of the ecliptic longitude by about 22 degrees or days, resulting on the placement of planets in the previous sign in Western charts about 80% of the time.

Both Jyotish and Western traditions have existed for millennia. Vedic astrology includes several nuanced sub-systems of interpretation and prediction incorporating unique sacralized elements not found elsewhere, such as its specific system of lunar mansions (called *nakshatras*, encompassing a pantheon of archetypal deities). The nakshatras are used to pick auspicious times of day or month for every human activity as well as to provide insight into the motivations and guiding characteristics of humans and events coming under their influence. Nakshatra cycles, or dashas, are developing a reputation in contemporary culture for the accuracy with which they time events.

A further unique concept in jyotish rarely seen in Western astrology is the concept of Dashas-a mathematical analyses that breaks down human or the subject's lifetime into various sub-periods based on the location of Moon at birth.

Predicctions in jyotish incorporate various elements around the birth chart-influences of transits (similar to Western Astrology though more focused on houses or bhavas) as well as Dashas.

Modern Approaches to Jyotisha: Vedic astrology includes a number of techniques and approaches that have accumulated over the eons with little consensus on what gives consistently accurate results. This collection of techniques and approaches is sometimes referred to as Classical or Traditional Jyotish. However, the march towards new insights and applications continues in the modern epoch, as in earlier times, with the objective as ever to achieve more precise analysis and accurate predictions.

In the 1960s, H.R. Seshadri Iyer, introduced a system including the yoga point, which has become popular in also the West. In the early 1990s, V.K. Choudhry introduced the Systems' Approach for Interpreting Horoscopes, a simplified system of Jyotish.

Fundamentals of Jyotisha: Vedic astrology, *i.e. Jyotish* contains some concepts that are not found in any other school of astrology. Some of the important building blocks are discussed below.

Graha-the Planets: Graha literally means any heavenly body or point that can cast an impact on human affairs. It may be translated as planet for ease. Graha also includes lunar nodes (Rahu and Ketu) and sub-planets (upgrahas) which are not planets but no less effective than planets. The extra-saturnine planets (Uranus, Neptune and Pluto) are not included in the category of Graha.

One's Ascendant, or *lagna*, the rashi which is rising on the eastern horizon at the time of one's birth, is the most influential and important one. Of lesser importance but still some impact is the Janma Rashi, the rashi in which the moon lay while one was born.

There are three different Jyotish chart notations, which are functionally equivalent but quite different in appearance. The following images show the same birth chart in the two main notations-North Indian and South Indian. The third notation is followed in Eastern parts of India.

In the North Indian notation, the house positions are fixed (1st house top middle, with the rest following in counterclockwise order) and the signs of the zodiac are indicated by numbers in the chart (1 for Aries, and so on). Conversely, in the South Indian notation, the signs of the zodiac have fixed positions (Aries always occupies the 2nd box from the left in the top row, with the rest following in clockwise order), and the first house is marked "As" (for ascendant) with the rest following in clockwise order.

The charts are broken into twelve sections, houses or Bhavas, each of which is related to a rashi in an equal house system.

Bhava-the Houses: Two house system is in practice among follower of Jyotish. First one is what Western astrologers call the whole sign house system while the second one is *Sripathi* akin to Porphyry house system. KP also incorporates Placidus house system. The significance of 12 houses are as follow:

- 1st house Native, Appearance, Character, Purpose of Life
- 2nd house Wealth, Family, Meal, Early Education
- 3rd house Younger coborn, Communication (phone, sms, chatting etc)
- 4th house Mother, Education, Home, Property, Vehicle
- 5th house Children, Lover, Recreation, Devotion, Creativity

- 6th house Health, Maternal uncle and aunt, Litigation, Servants
- 7th house Spouse, Business partner, Death, Trade, Agreement
- 8th house Sex, Longevity, Failure, Family of spouse, Dowry
- 9th house Luck, Higher learning, Travelling, Religion, Mentor
- 10th house Profession, Status, Power, Father, Mother-in-law
- 11th house Friends, Hopes, Earnings, Elder coborn, Daughter/Son-in-law
- 12th house Expenses, Sleep, Donation, Foreign stay

Nakshatra-the Lunar Asterism: Like sign or rashi, zodiac may also divided into 27 equal parts (of 13 degree 20 minutes each). This division of zodiac is called Nakshatra. Traditionally nakshatra position of Moon is computed for native's mental make up and calculations of planetary periods (dashas). Each nakshatra is further partitioned into four equal segments known as charan or pad. Nakshatra contains an important place in Astrological match making, *Mahurtha*, *Panchanga* and *Prashana* affairs.

Veshaish Lagna-Special Ascendants: Sage Parasara mentioned a few special lagnas before mentioning the results of various divisional charts and houses. His mention that houses can be counted from special lagnas clearly indicates that he wanted special lagnas to be used instead of lagna for some clear purposes. Some important special lagnas are follows:

- Chandra Lagna (ascendant counted from natal Moon sign-very important langa)
- Surya Lagna (ascendant counted from natal Sun sign)
- Karak Lagna (significator taken as ascendant for all grahas)
- Varnada Lagna (for social company)

- Shri Lagna (for prosperity and marriage)
- Indu Lang (for wealth)
- Hora Lagna (for financial prosperity)
- Gati Lagna (for name and fame)

Varga-the Divisional Charts: The term *Varga* means Division and refers to the various divisions of a sign, based on which Divisional Charts (or simply D-Charts) is constructed. Divisional charts (Vargas or Amsas) are very peculiar to Jyotish, and they are not found in other systems of astrology. Ancient Indian Mentor and Expert, Maharishi Parashara describes 16 divisional charts which are as follows:

- Rasi D-1: Body, Phyiscal Matters and All Generall Maters
- Hora D-2: Wealth, Family
- Drekkana D-3: Siblings, Nature
- Chaturthamsa D-4: Fortune and Property
- Saptamsa D-7: Children/Progeny
- Navamsa D-9: Wife, Dharma and Relationships
- Dasamsa D-10: Actions in Society, Profession
- Dwadasamsa D-12: Parents
- Shodasamsa D-16: Vehicles, Travelling and Comforts
- Vimsamsa D-20: Spiritual Pursuits
- Chatur Vimsamsa D-24: Education, Learning and Knowledge
- Sapta Vimsamsa D-27: Strengths and Weakness
- Trimsamsa: D-30 Evils, Failure, Bad Luck
- Kha Vedamsa D-40: Maternal Legacy
- Aksha Vedamsa D-45: Paternal Legacy
- Shastiamsa D-60: Past birth/Karma

Maharishi Jaimini explaines 4 more divisional charts. They include:

- Panchamsa D-5: Fame & Power
- Shasthamsa D-6: Health

- Ashtamsa D8: Unexpected Troubles
- Eka Dasamsa/Rudramsa D-11: Death and Destruction.

Apart form Rashi (D-1); Navamsha (D-9), Drekkana (D-3), Dasamsa (D-10) and Trimsamsa (D-30) are considered significant divisional charts.

Drishti-the Aspect: Aspect is one of the most important phenomena that not only interlinks the planets with each other but also playing a role of bridge between signs. In Jyotish the word Drishti is tantamount to Aspect, means glance or sight. It is the transfer of influences to another graha or rashi as a result of their situation in relation to each other.

Types of Aspect: The hierarchy of aspect can be categorized into two types as;

- 1-Aspect based on Planet or Sign's Nature
- 2-Aspect based on Relative Distance

1-Aspect based on Planet or Sign's Nature: This is the system of aspect studied in Vedic Astrology. This holds that certain planet or sign sights another planet or sign depends on its nature. This can also be divided into two kinds, namely;

- *Graha Drishti*
- *Rashi Drishti*

Graha Drishti should prefer when analyzing

- Nakshatra Dasha
- Chart with respect to the Moon
- Sahams, *i.e.* Arabic Parts

Rashi Drishti should prefer when analyzing

- Rashi Dasha
- Chart with respect to Special Lagnas (AL GL, HL etc.)
- Vargas, *i.e.* Divisional Charts

2-Aspect based on Relative Distance: This is the same method in vogue in Western Astrology. Tajik Varshphal (Vedic Solar Return Chart) applies this technique to erect 14 different types of aspects also known as varshphala yogas.

Argala-the Intervention: Significations of various houses are interlinked. Support provided by one house to another is called *Argala* and the obstruction offered to supporting houses is called *Virodha argala*.

Graha (planets) in 2nd, 4th and 11th house cause argalas on a given house, whereas the planets in 12th, 10th and 3rd cause virodha argalas to 2nd, 4th and 11th respectively.

Banefic generally give *shubha argalas*, malefic offer *papa argalas*. If however a malefic has an argala on house of which it is a significator, such an aragala can be termed as shubha. For example a malefics in 10th house cast papa argala to 9th house as 10th house is second from 9th. This may make the native non religious and give bad relations with boss/teacher, provided there is no virodh argala from 8th.

Arudha-the Mounted Image: The term Arudha Pada is also known as "Pada". Arudha literally means "mount" and refers to the IMAGE of a sign falling on another due to "reflection of the rays emanating from it and being reflected by its lord.

Keeping the reflection in view, the Karaka (Significator) can be taken to be the Moon. Count from a sign to its lord. Then count as many signs from the lord to arrive at the ARUDHA PADA. For example, if the Lagna Lord is in the fifth house, then count five signs from the Lagna lord to arrive at the ninth house. This ninth house becomes the arudha Pada for the Lagna.

Exception: The Arudha Pada cannot be in the same sign or the seventh from it. In case this happens, then choose the tenth house therefrom. For example, if the Lagna Lord is in the 4th house, then the Arudha lagna should be in the 4th from the 4th house, *i.e.* the 7th house. But since this is not allowed, the tenth therefrom should be chosen. The tenth from the 7th house is the 4th house and the 4th house becomes the Arudha Lagna.

Arudha of 1st house is also called PADA LAGNA or, ARUDHA LAGNA. Arudha lagna stands for "manifestation of self, in this maya (illusory) world". In this manner Arudha Pada can be computed for all the houses. They are called Dhana Pada (2nd), Bhratripada (3rd), Matri Pada (4th), Mantrapada (5th), Satrupada (6th), Dara Pada (7th), Roga pada (8th), Bhagyapada (9th), Rajyapada (10th), Labhapada (11th) and Upapada (12th). Jaimini discussed Arudha lagna (AL) and Upapada (UL) extinsively in his classical treatise.

Yoga-the Planetary Combinations: In Jyotish, *Yoga* means yoka or combination. Yogas are certain planetary combinations. Jyotish classics explaines hundred of thousands of yogas. Chandra (lunar combinations for general luck), Dhana (wealth related) and Raja (power and success related) yogas are often studied.

Shadbala-the Sixfold Strength: Shadbala means six fold strength. Although these strengths are combinedly used for finding the effect of planets on the lives of the natives, there is more use of the strengths and we get the clue of those uses from their names. These strengths need not be used only predicting the results of the dasa, however, can be used for normal horoscopic interpretation.

Shad Bal consists of the following strengths:

- Sthan Bal (Positional strength)
- Dig Bal (Directional strength)
- Kaal Bal (Temporalstrength), inclusive of Ayan Bal (Equinoctial strength)
- Chesht Bal (Motional strength)
- Naisargika Bal (Natural strength)
- Drik Bal (Aspectual strength)

These strengths are computed for the seven Grahas from Sun to Saturn. The lunar nodes (Rahu and Ketu) are not considered.

MANTRA

Mantras have some features in common with spells in general, in that they are a translation of the human will or desire into a form of action. Indeed, Dr. Edward Conze, a scholar of Buddhism, frequently translated "mantra" as "spell". As symbols, sounds are seen to effect what they symbolise. Vocal sounds are frequently thought of as having magical powers, or even of representing the words or speech of a deity. For the authors of the Hindu scriptures of the Upanishads, the syllable Aum, itself constituting a mantra, represents Brahman, the godhead, as well as the whole of creation. A *mantra* is a religious syllable or poem, typically from the Sanskrit language. Their use varies according to the school and philosophy associated with the mantra. They are primarily used as spiritual conduits, words or vibrations that instill one-pointed concentration in the devotee. Other purposes have included religious ceremonies to accumulate wealth, avoid danger, or eliminate enemies. Mantras originated in India with Vedic Hinduism and were later adopted by Buddhists, Sikhs and Jains, now popular in various modern forms of spiritual practice which are loosely based on practices of these Eastern religions. The Sanskrit word *mantra*-consists of the root *man*-"to think" (also in *manas* "mind") and the suffix-*tra* meaning, tool, hence a literal translation would be "instrument of thought". Mantras are interpreted to be effective as sound (vibration), to the effect that great emphasis is put on correct pronunciation (resulting in an early development of a science of phonetics in India). They are intended to deliver the mind from illusion and material inclinations. Chanting is the process of repeating a mantra.

Merely pronouncing this syllable is to experience the divine in a very direct way. Kukai suggests that all sounds are the voice of the Dharmakaya Buddha—*i.e.* as in Hindu Upanishadic and Yogic thought, these sounds are manifestations of ultimate reality. Accepted scholarly etymology links the word with "manas" meaning "mind" and 'trana' for protection.

For many cultures it is the written letters that have power—the Hebrew Kabbalah for instance, or the Anglo-Saxon Runes. Letters can have an oracular function even. But in India special conditions applied that meant that writing was very definitely inferior to the spoken word. The Brahmins were the priestly caste of the Aryan peoples.

It was they that preserved the holy writings—initially the Vedas, but later also the Upanishads. For years, they were the only ones who knew the mantras or sacred formulas that had to be chanted at every important occasion. However, with the advent of egalitarian Hindu schools of Yoga, Vedanta, Tantra and Bhakti, it is now the case that intra-family and community mantras are passed on freely as part of generally practiced Hindu religion. Such was the influence of the more orthodox attitude of the elite nature of mantra knowledge that even the Buddhists, who repudiated the whole idea of caste, and of the efficacy of the old rituals, called themselves the shravakas, that is, "the hearers". A wise person in India was one who had "heard much". *Mantras* then are *sound symbols*. What they symbolise and how they function depends on the context, and the mind of the person repeating them.

Studies in sound symbolism suggest that vocal sounds have meaning whether we are aware of it or not. And indeed that there can be multiple layers of symbolism associated with each sound. So even if we do not understand them, mantras are not simply meaningless mumbo jumbo—no vocal utterance is entirely without meaning. We can look at mantra as a range of different contexts to see what they can mean in those contexts: *Om* may mean something quite different to a Hindu and a Tibetan Buddhist. The analysis of Kukai, a 9th century Japanese Buddhist is revealing.

While Hindu tantras eventually came to see the letters as well as the sounds as representatives of the divine, it was when Buddhism travelled to China that a major shift in emphasis towards writing came about. China lacked a unifying, ecclesiastic language like Sanskrit, and achieved its cultural unity by having a written language that was flexible in pronunciation but more precise in terms of the concepts that each character represented. In fact the Indians had several scripts which were all equally serviceable for writing Sanskrit.

Hence the Chinese prized written language much more highly than did the Indian Buddhist missionaries, and the writing of mantras became a spiritual practice in its own right. So that whereas Brahmins had been very strict on correct pronunciation, the Chinese, and indeed other Far-Eastern Buddhists were less concerned with this than correctly writing something down.

The practice of writing mantras, and copying texts as a spiritual practice, became very refined in Japan, and the writing in the Siddham script in which the Sanskrit of many Buddhist Sutras were written is only really seen in Japan nowadays. However, written mantra-repetition in Hindu practices, with Sanskrit in any number of scripts, is well-known to many sects in India as well.

Om Mani Padme Hum: Probably the most famous mantra of Buddhism is Om mani padme hum, the six syllable mantra of the Bodhisattva of compassion Avalokiteshvara (Tibetan: Chenrezig, Chinese: Guanyin). This mantra is particularly associated with the four-armed Shadakshari form of Avalokiteshvara. The Dalai Lama is said to be an incarnation of Avalokiteshvara, and so the mantra is especially revered by his devotees.

The book *Foundations of Tibetan Mysticism* by Lama Anagarika Govinda, is a classic example of how a mantra like om mani padme hum can contain many levels of symbolic meaning.

Donald Lopez gives a good discussion of this mantra and its various interpretations in his book *Prisoners of Shangri-LA: Tibetan Buddhism and the West*. Lopez is an authoritative writer and challenges the stereotypical analysis of the mantra as meaning "The Jewel in the Lotus", an interpretation that is not supported by either a linguistic analysis, nor by Tibetan tradition, and is symptomatic of the Western Orientalist approach to the 'exotic' East. He suggests that Manipadma is actually the name of a bodhisattva, a form of Avalokiteshvara who has many other names in any case including Padmapani or *lotus flower in hand.*

The Brahminical insistence on absolutely correct pronunciation of Sanskrit broke down as Buddhism was exported to other countries where the inhabitants found it impossible to reproduce the sounds. So in Tibet, for instance, where this mantra is on the lips of many Tibetans all their waking hours, the mantra is pronounced *Om mani peme hung.*

Some Other Mantras used by Tibetan Buddhists: The following list of mantras is from Kailash-Journal of Himalayan Studies, Volume 1, Number 2, 1973. (pp. 168-169) (augmented by other contributors). It also includes renderings of *Om mani padme hum.*

Please note that the word *swaha* is sometimes shown as *svaha*, and is usually pronounced as 'so-ha' by Tibetans. Spellings tend to vary in the transliterations to English, for example, *hum* and *hung* are generally the same word. The mantras used in Tibetan Buddhist practice are in Sanskrit, to preserve the original mantras. Visualizations and other practices are usually done in the Tibetan language.

- *Om wangishwari hum:* This is the mantra of the Mahabodhisattva Manjusri, Tibetan: Jampelyang (Wylie "'jam dpal dbyangs")... The Buddha in his wisdom aspect.
- Om mani padme hum The mantra of Chenrezig, Mahabodhisattva, the Buddha in his compassion aspect.
- *Om vajrapani hum:* The mantra of the Buddha as Protector of the Secret Teachings. *i.e.*: as the Mahabodhisattva Channa Dorje (Vajrapani).
- *Om vajrasattva hum:* The short mantra for Vajrasattva, there is also a full 100-syllable mantra for Vajrasattva.
- *Om ah hum vajra guru padma siddhi hum:* The mantra of the Vajraguru Guru Padma Sambhava who established Mahayana Buddhism and Tantra in Tibet.
- *Om tare tuttare ture swaha:* The mantra of Jetsun Dolma or Tara, the Mother of the Buddhas.

- *Om tare tuttare ture mama ayurjnana punye pushting svaha:* The mantra of Dölkar or White Tara, the emanation of Tara representing long life and health.
- *Om amarani jiwantiye swaha:* The mantra of the Buddha of limitless life: the Buddha Amitayus (Tibetan Tsépagmed) in celestial form.
- *Om dhrum swaha:* The purificatory mantra of the mother Namgyalma.
- *Om ami dhewa hri:* The mantra of the Buddha Amitabha (Hopagmed) of the Western Buddhafield, his skin the colour of the setting sun.
- *Om ah ra pa tsa na dhih:* The mantra of the "sweet-voiced one", Jampelyang (Wylie "'jam dpal dbyangs") or Manjusri, the Bodhisattva of wisdom.
- *Hung vajra phat:* The mantra of the Mahabodhisattva Vajrapani in his angry (Dragpo) form.
- *Om muni muni maha muniye sakyamuni swaha:* The mantra of Buddha Sakyamuni, the historical Buddha.

WISDOM SUTRA

- *Om maitri maitreya maha karuna ye:* The Maitri mantra, bija mantra of Maha Bodhisattva Maitreya.
- *Namo bhagavate Bhaishajya-guru vaidurya-praba-rajaya tathagataya arthate samyak-sambuddhaya tadyata OM bhaishajye bhaishajye bhaishajya-samudgate svaha:* The mantra of the 'Medicine Buddha', from Chinese translations of the Master of Healing Sutra.

Mantra in Sikhism: In the Sikh religion a "Mantar" or "Mantra" is a Shabad (Word or hymn) from Gurbani to concentrate the mind on God and the message of the Ten Gurus.

Mantras have two components of primary importance-Meaning and Sound. First is the actual meaning of the word or words and the second is the effective sound (vibration). For the mantra to be effective, great emphasis is put on correct pronunciation and the level of concentration of the mind on the meaning of the word or words that are recited.

Due to this emphasis, some care has to be taken regarding the place and surrounding in which the mantras are recited; the way in which these are delivered-*i.e.*, a loud; quietly; in a group; with music; without music;, etc. The purpose to mantras is to deliver the mind from illusion and material inclinations and to bring concentration and focus to the mind.

- Chanting is the process of the continuous repeating a mantra.

The main mantras of Sikhism are:

- The Gurmantar, which is Waheguru
- The Mool Mantar which start Ek-onkar, Satnam ....

Mantra in other Traditions or Contexts: Transcendental Meditation, also known simply as 'TM', uses what the group refers to as 'simple mantras'—as a meditative focus. TM was founded by Maharishi Mahesh Yogi. According to the TM website the practice can result in a number of material benefits such as relaxation, reduced stress, better health, better self image; but it can also benefit the world by reducing violence and crime, and generally improve quality of life. The founder was well versed in Hindu tradition, but TM attempts to separate itself from that tradition these days. Simple two-syllable mantras are used.

Mantra practice has also been enthusiastically taken up by various New Age groups and individuals, although this is typically out of context, and from the point of view of a genuine Hindu or Buddhist practitioner lacks depth. The mere repetition of syllables can have a calming effect on the mind, but the traditionalist would argue that mantra can be an effective way of changing the level of one's consciousness when approached in traditional way.

Some forms of Jewish meditation use mantras, although they do not call them by that name. Hasidic Jews sing phrases from the Hebrew Bible over and over, in a form of rhythmic chant, often accompanied by drumming on the table. They also use wordless sacred meditation tunes called niggunim, which are revealed through the higher consciousness of the Rebbes (Hasidic leaders, similar to gurus). Some subgroups of the Breslov Hasidic movement use the mantra Na Nach Nachma, based on the name of their founder, Rabbi Nachman of Breslov. All of these practices are done to achieve deveikut which means "cleaving (holding on) to God." Lubavitch Hasidim of the messianic faith use the mantra of Yechi to draw on the power of their Rebbe.

The spiritual exercises of Surat Shabda Yoga include simran (repetition, particularly silent repetition of a mantra given at initiation), dhyan (concentration, viewing, or contemplation, particularly on the Inner Master), and bhajan (listening to the inner sounds of the Shabda or the Shabda Master).

In the Islamic Sufi tradition, chants of the 99 Names of Allah are popular invocations of attibutes as are the names of the Prophet.

In Neo-Pagan ritual, deities may be invoked by a recitation of their many names or aspects.

In Christianity, repetitive prayer using prayer beads such as a rosary or chotki includes well known mantras such as the Jesus prayer and Hail Mary. A form of Christian meditation was taught by Dom John Main that involves the silent repetition of a mantra.

Also, in the game Guild Wars, mantras are used by the Mesmer profession to protect them from harm and to focus their mental and magical abilities.

Mantra in Hinduism: Mantras were originally conceived in the great Hindu scriptures known as the Vedas. Within practically all Hindu scriptures, the writing is formed in painstakingly crafted two line "shlokas" and most mantras follow this pattern, although mantras are often found in single line or even single word combinations.

The most basic mantra is Aum, which in Hinduism is known as the "pranava mantra," the source of all mantras. The philosophy behind this is the Hindu idea of nama-rupa (name-form), which supposes that all things, ideas or entities in existence, within the phenomenological cosmos, have name and form of some sort. The most basic name and form is the primordial vibration of Aum, as it is the first manifested nama-rupa of Brahman, the unmanifest reality/unreality.

Essentially, before existence and beyond existence is only One reality, Brahman, and the first manifestation of Brahman in existence is Aum. For this reason, Aum is considered to be the most fundamental and powerful mantra, and thus is prefixed and suffixed to all Hindu prayers. While some mantras may invoke individual Gods or principles, the most fundamental mantras, like 'Aum,' the 'Shanti Mantra,' the 'Gayatri Mantra' and others all ultimately focus on the One reality.

In the Hindu tantras the universe is sound. The supreme (para) brings forth existence through the Word (Shabda). Creation consists of vibrations at various frequencies and amplitudes giving rise to the phenomena of the world. The purest vibrations are the var.na, the imperishable letters which are revealed to us, imperfectly as the audible sounds and visible forms.

Var.nas are the atoms of sound. A complex symbolic association was built up between letters and the elements, gods, signs of the zodiac, parts of the body—letters became rich in these associations. For example in the Aitrareya-aranya-Upanishad we find:

> *"The mute consonants represent the earth, the sibilants the sky, the vowels heaven. The mute consonants represent fire, the sibilants air, the vowels the sun? The mute consonants represent the eye, the sibilants the ear, the vowels the mind".*

In effect each letter became a mantra and the language of the Vedas, Sanskrit, corresponds profoundly to the nature of things. Thus the Vedas come to represent reality itself. The seed syllable Om represents the underlying unity of reality, which is Brahman.

Mantra Japa: Mantra japa was a concept of the Vedic sages that incorporates mantras as one of the main forms of puja, or worship, whose ultimate end is seen as Moksha/liberation. Essentially, Mantra Japa means repetition of mantra, and has become an established practice of all Hindu streams, from the various Yoga to Tantra. It involves repetition of a mantra over and over again, usually in cycles of auspicious numbers (in multiples of three), the most popular being 108. For this reason, Hindu malas (bead necklaces) developed, containing 108 beads and a head bead (sometimes referred to as the 'meru', or 'guru' bead). The devotee performing japa using his/her fingers counts each bead as he/she repeats the chosen mantra. Having reached 108 repetitions, if he/she wishes to continue another cycle of mantras, the devotee must turn the mala around without crossing the head bead and repeat.

It is said that through japa the devotee attains one-pointedness, or extreme focus, on the chosen deity or principal idea of the mantra. The vibrations and sounds of the mantra are considered extremely important, and thus reverberations of the sound are supposed to awaken the prana or spiritual life force and even stimulate chakras according to many Hindu schools of thought.

Any shloka from holy Hindu texts like the Vedas, Upanishads, Bhagavad Gita, Yoga Sutra, even the Mahabharata, Ramayana, Durga saptashati or Chandi are considered powerful enough to be repeated to great effect, and have therefore the status of a mantra.

A very common mantra is formed by taking a deity's name. Called Nama japa and saluting it in such a manner: "Aum namah———" or "Aum Jai (Hail!)———" or several such permutations. Common examples are "Aum namah Shivaya" (Aum I bow to Lord Shiva), "Aum Namo Narayanaya"; or "Aum Namo Bhagavate Vasudevaya," (Salutations to the Universal

God Vishnu), "Aum Shri Ganeshaya Namah" (Aum to Shri Ganesha) and "Aum Kalikayai Namah" and "Aum Hrim Chandikayai Namah." (*i.e.*, mantras to Devi.)

Some Hindu Mantras: Arguably the most representative mantra of all the Hindu mantras is the famed Gayatri Mantra:

Om Bhur Bhuvaswa
Tatsavitur Varenyam
Bhargo Devasya Dhimahi
Dhiyo Yo Na Prachodayat.

It is considered one of the most universal of all Hindu mantras, invoking the universal Brahman as the principle of knowledge and the illumination of the primordial Sun.

LEAD ME FROM IGNORANCE TO TRUTH

Asato ma sad gamaya
Tamaso ma jyotir gamaya
Mityorm amatam gamaya
Om anti anti anti
(Bahadragyaka Upanisad I.iii.28)

"from non-being to being lead me, from darkness to light lead me, from death to immortality lead me."

Hare Krishna Maha-mantra: A mantra comprising of the names Hare, Krishna and Rama. It appears originally in the Kali-Sagmraga Upanicad (Kali Santarana Upanisad):

Hare Krishna Hare Krishna
Krishna Krishna Hare Hare
Hare Rama Hare Rama
Rama Rama Hare Hare

In the 16th century, Chaitanya Mahaprabhu, along with his followers, spread this mantra across India through public congregational chanting (sankirtan). Chaitanya and his followers travelled from town to town singing this mantra, claiming that it would awaken love of Krishna (Bhakti) in whoever happened to hear it. It is often referred to as the 'Maha Mantra' by practitioners.

Recently A.C. Bhaktivedanta Swami Prabhupada established ISKCON (the International Society for Krishna Consciousness), a branch of the Brahma-Madhva-Gaudiya Vaishnava sampradaya, he introduced the *Hare Krishna* mantra to the West, describing it as: "an easy yet sublime way of liberation in the Age of Kali."

THE SHANTI MANTRAS

Om sahanaavavatu
Sahanau bhunaktu
Saha viiryan karavaavahai
Tejasvi naavadhiitamastu
Maa vidvishhaavahai
May we be protected together.
May we be nourished together.
May we work together with great vigor.
May our study be enlightening
May no obstacle arise between us.
Om shaantih shaantih shaantih
Om peace, peace, peace.

—Black [krishna] Yajurveda Taittiriya Upanishad 2.2.2

UNIVERSAL PRAYER

Sarvem Svastir Bhavatu
Sarvem Sntir Bhavatu
Sarvem Pkrnam Bhavatu
Sarvem Mangalam Bhavatu.

(May good befall all, May there be peace for all, May all be fit for perfection, and May all experience that which is auspicious.)

Sarve bhavantu Sukhina„Sarve santu nirmaya
Sarve bhadrani pasyantu Ma kaschit dukha bhgbhavet

(Om, May all be happy. May all be healthy. May we all experience what is good and let no one suffer. Om, Peace, Peace, Peace!)

OTHER EXAMPLES

- *Tat Twam Asi* "Thou Art That"
- Tryambakam.
- Surya Namaskara
- Soham "I am He"
- Ram Nam

The Hindu Bija Mantra: The most revered of all Bija mantras is Om/Aum which is the starting point of many other mantras.

Aum Krim Krim Krim Hoom Hum:

Krim Krim Krim Hum Hum Hrim Hrim Swaha

Remarks: The following subsections contain remarks on the nature and use of mantras in their context as Hindu religious practice.

What is Dharma?: A western expert on Hindu philosophy and religion writes:

> *Sanatan (eternal) Dharma as a universal tradition has room for all faiths and all religious and spiritual practices regardless of the time or country of their origin. Yet it places religious and spiritual teachings in their appropriate place relative to the ultimate goal of Self-realization, to which secondary practices are subordinated. Sanatan Dharma also recognizes that the greater portion of human religious aspirations has always been unknown, undefined and outside of any institutionalized belief. Sanatan Dharma thereby gives reverence to individual spiritual experience over any formal religious doctrine. Wherever the Universal Truth is manifest; there is Sanatan Dharma—whether it is in a field of religion, art or science, or in the life of a person or community. Wherever the Universal Truth is not recognized, or is scaled down or limited to a particular group, book or person, even if done so in the name of God, there Sanatan Dharma ceases to function, whatever the activity is called.*

By the laws of Dharma that govern body and mind, you must fear sin and act righteously. Wise men by thinking and behaving in this way become worthy to gain bliss both here and hereafter.
—Natchintanai Scripture

The Significance of the Symbol Om: The symbol Om or Aum (also called Pranava), is the most sacred symbol in Hinduism. Volumes have been written in Sanskrit illustrating the significance of this mystic symbol. Although this symbol is mentioned in all the Upanishads and in all Hindu scriptures, it is especially elaborated upon in the Taittiriya, Chandogya and Mundaka Upanishads.

The goal, which all Vedas declare, which all austerities aim at, and which human desire when they live a life continence, I will tell you briefly it is Om. The syllable Om is indeed Brahman. This syllable Om is the highest. Whosoever knows this symbol obtains all that he desires. This is the best support; this is the highest support. Whosoever knows this support is adored in the world of Brahman.
—Katha Upanishad I, ii, 15-17

The symbol of Om contains of three curves, one semicircle (crescent) and a dot (bindu). The large lower curve symbolizes the waking state; the upper curve denotes deep sleep (or the unconscious) state, and the lower curve (which lies between deep sleep and the waking state) signifies the dream state. These three states of an individual's consciousness, and therefore the entire physical phenomenon, are represented by the three curves. The dot signifies the Absolute (fourth or Turiya state of consciousness), which illuminates the other three states. The semicircle symbolizes maya and separates the dot from the other three curves. The semicircle is open on the top, which means that the absolute is infinite and is not affected by maya. Maya only affects the manifested phenomenon. In this way the form of Om symbolizes the infinite Brahman and the entire Universe.

Uttering the monosyllable Om, the eternal world of Brahman, One who departs leaving the body (at death), he attains the superior goal.

Mantras and Prayers: A mantra is a sacred syllable, word or verse, which has been revealed to a sage in deep meditation. A mantra, when recited with devotion, concentration and understanding, revitalizes the body and mind with mystic power, and harmonizes thought and action.

A mantra, when repeated constantly during meditation, first loudly and then through silent and mental chanting, changes the consciousness.

Kirtan and Bhajan: When a mantra is sung or chanted, whether by oneself or in a group of devoted aspirants, it is termed as kirtan—the glorification of God. Prayers or symbolic stories of God may also be sung in a kirtan.

The singing and chanting of kirtan creates an elevated mental condition for practicing meditation or entering into an intense form of spiritual practice. Kirtan is a powerful and unique method of recharging the subconscious with spiritual vibrations.

Mantra in Zoroastrianism: Manthras are found even in the Zoroastrian religious works. The earliest reference to them is in the Avesta to be used in yasnas (fire ritual-compare with mantras used similarly in Vedic yajnas). Prophet Zoroaster lists down various mantras in the gathas (oldest part of Avesta).

Mantra in Buddhism: Buddhism developed its own system and understanding of mantra, which while similar to the previous practices of Vedic society, also took on its own particularities, especially according to region.

Mantra in Shingon Buddhism: Kkkai advanced a general theory of language based on his analysis of two forms of Buddhist ritual language: *dharani* and *mantra*. Mantra is restricted to esoteric Buddhist practice whereas dharani is found in both esoteric and exoteric ritual. Dharanis for instance are found in the Pali Canon. The term "shingon" (lit true word) is a Japanese translation of the Chinese term for mantra, chen yen.

The word *dharani* derives from a Sanskrit root dhar which means to hold, or maintain. Ryuichi Abe suggests that it is generally understood as a mnemonic device which encapsulates the meaning of a section or chapter of a sutra. This is perhaps related to the use of verse summaries at the end of texts as in the Udana which is generally acknowledged as being in the oldest strata of the Pali Canon. Dharanis are also considered to protect the one who chants them from malign influences and calamities.

The term *mantra* is traditionally said to be derived from two roots: "man", to think; and the action oriented (k.rt) suffix "tra". Thus a mantra can be considered to be a linguistic device for deepening ones thought, or in the Buddhist context for developing the enlightened mind. However it is also true that mantras have been used as magic spells for very mundane purposes such as attaining wealth and long life, and eliminating enemies.

The distinction between dharani and mantra is a difficult one to make. We can say that all mantras are dharanis but that not all dharanis are mantras. Mantras do tend to be shorter. Both tend to contain a number of unintelligible phonic fragments such as Om, or Hum which is perhaps why some people consider them to be essentially meaningless. Kukai made mantra a special class of dharani which showed that every syllable of a dharani was a manifestation of the true nature of reality—in Buddhist terms that all sound is a manifestation of shunyata or emptiness of self-nature. Thus rather than being devoid of meaning, Kukai suggests that dharanis are in fact saturated with meaning—every syllable is symbolic on multiple levels.

One of Kkkai's distinctive contributions was to take this symbolic association even further by saying that there is no essential difference between the syllables of mantras and sacred texts, and those of ordinary language. If one understood the workings of mantra, then any sounds could be a representative of ultimate reality. This emphasis on sounds was one of the drivers for Kkkai's championing of the phonetic writing system, the kana, which was adopted in Japan around the time of Kkkai. He is generally credited with the invention of the kana, but there is apparently some doubt about this story amongst scholars.

This mantra-based theory of language had a powerful effect on Japanese thought and society which up until Kkkai's time had been dominated by imported Chinese culture of thought, particularly in the form of the Classical Chinese language which was used in the court and amongst the literati, and Confucianism which was the dominant political ideology. In particular Kkkai was able to use this new theory of language to create links between indigenous Japanese culture and Buddhism. For instance, he made a link between the Buddha Mahavairocana and the Shinto sun Goddess Amaterasu. Since the emperors were thought to be descended form Amaterasu, Kkkai had found a powerful connection here that linked the emperors with the Buddha, and also in finding a way to integrate Shinto with Buddhism, something that had not happened with Confucianism.

Buddhism then became essentially an indigenous religion in a way that Confucianism had not. And it was through language, and mantra that this connection was made. Kkkai helped to elucidate what mantra is in a way that had not been done before: he addresses the fundamental questions of what a text is, how signs function, and above all, what language is. In this he covers some of the same ground as modern day Structuralists and others scholars of language, although he comes to very different conclusions.

In this system of thought all sounds are said to originate from "a"—which is the short *a* sound in father. For esoteric Buddhism "a" has a special function because it is associated with Shunyata or the idea that no thing exists in its own right, but is contingent upon causes and conditions. In Sanskrit "a" is a prefix which changes the meaning of a word into its opposite, so "vidya" is understanding, and "avidya" is ignorance (the same arrangement is also found in many Greek words, like *e.g.* "atheism" vs. "theism" and "apathy" vs. "pathos"). The letter a is both visualised in the Siddham script, and pronounced in rituals and meditation practices. In the Mahavairocana Sutra which is central to Shingon Buddhism it says: Thanks to the original vows of the Buddhas and Bodhisattvas, a miraculous force resides in the mantras, so that by pronouncing them one acquires merit without limits.

Mantra in Indo-Tibetan Buddhism: Conze distinguishes three periods in the Buddhist use of mantra. Initially, like their fellow Indians, Buddhists used mantra as protective spells to ward of malign influences. Despite a Vinaya rule which forbids monks engaging in the Brahminical practice of chanting mantras for material gain, there are a number of protective for a group of ascetic monks. However, even at this early stage, there is perhaps something more than animistic magic at work. Particularly in the case of the Ratana Sutta the efficacy of the verses seems to be related to the concept of "truth". Each verse of the sutta ends with "by the virtue of this truth may there be happiness.

Later mantras were used more to guard the spiritual life of the chanter, and sections on mantras began to be included in some Mahayana sutras such as the White Lotus Sutra, and the Lankavatara Sutra. The scope of protection also changed in this time. In the Sutra of Golden Light the Four Great Kings promise to exercise sovereignty over the different classes of demigods, to protect the whole of Jambudvipa (the India sub continent), to protect monks who proclaim the sutra, and to protect kings who patronise the monks who proclaim the sutra.

The apotheosis of this type of approach is the Nichiren school of Buddhism that was founded in 13th century Japan, and which distilled many previously complex Buddhist practices down to the veneration of the Lotus Sutra through recitation of the daimoku: "Nam myoho renge kyo" which translates as "Homage to the Lotus Sutra".

Then mantra began, in about the 7th century, to take centre stage and become a vehicle for salvation in their own right. Tantra started to gain momentum in the 6th and 7th century, with specifically Buddhist forms appearing as early as 300CE. *Mantrayana* was an early name for the what is now more commonly known as Vajrayana, which gives us a hint as to the place of mantra in Indo-Tibetan Buddhism.

The aim of Vajrayana practice is to give the practitioner a direct experience of reality, of things as they really are. Mantras function as symbols of that reality, and different mantras are different aspects of that reality—for example wisdom or compassion. Mantras are often associated with a particular deity, one famous exception being the Prajnaparamita mantra associated with the Heart Sutra. One of the key Vajrayana strategies for bringing about a direct experience of reality is to engage the entire psycho-physical organism in the practices.

In one Buddhist analysis the person consists of body, speech and mind. So a typical sadhana or meditation practice might include mudras, or symbolic hand gestures; the recitations of mantras; as well as the visualisation of celestial beings and visualising the letters of the mantra which is being recited. Clearly here mantra is associated with speech. The meditator may visualise the letters in front of themselves, or within their body. They may pronounced out loud, or internally in the mind only.

AYURVEDA

History: In 2001 archaeologists studying the remains of two men from Mehrgarh, India, made the discovery that the people of Indus Valley Civilization, even from the early Harappan periods (c. 3300 BC), had knowledge of medicine and dentistry. The physical anthropologist that carried out the examinations, Professor Andrea Cucina from the University of Missouri-Columbia, made the discovery when he was cleaning the teeth from one of the men. Later research in the same area found evidence of teeth having been drilled, dating back 9,000 years.

Documented references to the origin of Ayurveda are not available. The age of Ayurveda has been established on the basis of correlating the evidence with other disciplines as well as circumstantial evidence. Ayurveda is said to have been first complied as a text by Agnivesha, in his book *Agnivesh tantra*, which was written during Vedic times. The book was later revised by Charaka, and renamed to Charaka Samhit. Other early texts of Ayurveda include the *Charaka Samhit* and the *Sushruta Samhit.* The system was orally transferred via the Gurukul system until a script came into existence.

The earliest scripts would have been written on perishable materials such as Taalpatra and Bhojapatra, which could not be readily preserved. The script was later written on stone and copper sheets. Verses dealing with Ayurveda are included in the Atharvaveda, which implies that some form of Ayurveda is as old as the Vedas. Ayurvedic practices have also evolved over time, and some practices may be considered innovations upon earlier Vedic practices, such as the advances made during the Buddhist period in India.

Hinduism attributes the genesis of Ayurveda to several theories in which the knowledge is believed to have been passed on from being to being, initially, through its realization by the divine sages, and gradually into the human sphere by a complex system of mnemonics. Details of Ayurvedic traditions vary between writers, as is expected when oral traditions are transcribed from multiple sources. The earliest authors of Ayurvedic manuscripts recorded divergent forms of the tradition.

Development: Ayurveda was practiced during the time of Buddha (around 520 BC), and in this period the Ayurvedic practitioners were commonly using Mercuric-sulphur combination based medicines. In this period Mercury, sulphur and other metals were used in conjunction with herbs to prepare the different medications. An important Ayurvedic practitioner of this period was Nagarjuna, a Buddhist herbologist, famous for inventing various new drugs for the treatment of ailments. Nagarjuna was accompanied by Surananda, Nagbodhi, Yashodhana, Nityanatha, Govinda, Anantdev, Vagbhatta, etc. The knowledge of Ayurveda progressed a lot during this period; and is therefore termed as the *Golden Period of Ayurveda*.

After emerging victorious at the Kalinga War, Emperor Ashoka (304 BC-232 BC) influenced by the Buddhist teachings, banned any bloodshed in his kingdom in 250 BC. Therefore many Ayurveda practitioners, who were practicing surgery along with medicine, left the surgical intervention and adopted totally new medicinal treatments. In this period, Ayurveda flourished with the invention of new drugs, new methodology and new innovations. The practice of the accompanying surgery slowly died out.

During the regime of Chandragupta Maurya (375-415 AD), Ayurveda was part of mainstream Indian medical techniques, and continued to be so until the invasion of Alexander, the Mughals and the English.

Chakrapani Dutta (DuttaSharma) was a Vaid Brahman of Bengal who wrote books on Ayurveda such as "Chakradutta" and others. Chakrapani Dutta was the Rajabaidya of King Nayapala (1038-1055). It is believed by some practitioners that Chakradutta is the essence of Ayurveda.

Ayurveda was preserved by the people of India as a traditional "science of life", despite increasing adoption of European medical techniques.

Gurukul System of Ayurveda: In the earlier days of its conception, the system of Ayurvedic medicine was orally transferred via the Gurukul system until a written script came into existence.

In this system, the Guru gave a solemn address where he directed the students to a life of chastity, honesty, and vegetarianism. The student was to strive with all his being to heal the sick. He was not to betray patients for his own advantage. He was required to dress modestly and avoid alcohol or drugs. He was to be collected and self-controlled, measured in speech at all times. He was to constantly improve his knowledge and technical skill. At the patient's home, he was to be courteous and modest, directing all attention to the patient's welfare. He was not to divulge any knowledge about the patient and his family. If the patient was incurable, he was to keep this to himself if it was likely to harm the patient or others.

The normal length of the student's training appears to have been seven years. Before graduation, the student was to pass a test. But the physician was to continue to learn through texts, direct observation (pratyaksha), and through inference (anumna). In addition, the vaidyas attended meetings where knowledge was exchanged. The practitioners also gained knowledge of unusual remedies from laypeople who were outside the Ayurvedic community such as hillsmen, herdsmen, and forest-dwellers.

Traditions of Ayurveda: Three traditions of Ayurveda exist today — two of them based on the compendia of Charka and Sushruta Samhits, and a third tradition known as *Kshyapas*. However, Ayurvedic remedies prior to these traditions also exist, as mentioned in the earlier Vedic literature (2nd millennium BC). Both the Sushruta and the Charaka Samhits are the product of several scholars, having been revised and supplemented over a period of several hundred years. The scholar Vgbhata, who lived in Sindh at the beginning of the 7th century AD, wrote a synthesis of earlier Ayurvedic materials in a collection of verses called the *Ashtnga Hridayam*. Another work associated with the same author, the *Ashtnga Samgraha*, contains much of the same material in a more diffuse form, written in a mixture of prose and verse. The relationship between these two works, and a third intermediate compilation, is still a topic of active research. The works of Charaka, Sushruta, and Vgbhata are considered canonical and reverentially called the *Vriddha Trayi*, "The Triad of Ancients"; or *Brhat Trayi*, "The

Greater Triad." In the early 8th century, Mdhav wrote his *Nidna*, a work on etiology, which soon assumed a position of authority. In the 79 chapters of this book, he lists diseases along with their causes, symptoms, and complications.

Post Brhat Trayi Period: The Brhat Trayi (literally "the three great compositions") is a classic Ayurvedic literary work, which was composed, compiled, and edited by Vagbhatta II, under the title *Ashtnga Samgraha*. At one time, it was believed that those who read and fully understood the contents of *Vriddha Trayi* and the *Brhat Trayi*, were good practitioners of Ayurveda. Legends concerning the origins of the text refer to the Ayurvedic practitioner Vgbhata who lived during the time of the epic Mahabharata and was the chief physician of king Yudhisthira. Most believe that the author of the *Ashtnga Samgraha* was born before 200 AD and is properly known as Vgbhata the 1st. Another man named Vgbhata (who was born about 100 BC) recomposed the text, including the writings of Charaka, Sushruta under a new title *Astang Hridaya*.

Mythology also refers to another Ayurvedic physician known as Vangsen. Myths place him in ancient Bengal where he wrote a classic Ayurvedic book, simply called *Vangsen*. The book is written in easy and understandable language and adds many new chapters to the previous texts.

After Vangsen, a scholar by the name of Madhavacharya composed the book, *Madhav Nidan*. He is thought to have been the prime minister for the Emperor of Vijaynagara. *Madhav Nidan* is widely considered the best Ayurvedic book for the diagnosis of some diseases known during that period.

After *Madhav Nidan*, the next in line of famous Ayurvedic books *Bhav Prakash* was written during the time that the Portuguese first came to India in 1498 by a man named Bhav Mishra of Madras. The period in which he wrote can be pinpointed accurately because in the *Bhav Prakash*, he described the symptoms of a disease called "Firang" (Gonorrhoea and Syphilis), which was introduced to the subcontinent through contact with Europeans. ("Firangi" was a Persian-derived pejorative for Europeans in India, who brought the diseases with them). Bhav Mishra's other contribution to Ayurvedic medicine was the introduction of pulse examination/pulse diagnosis.

Many writers after Bhav Mishra contributed to Ayurvedic literature. Among them Sharangdhar, Chakra Dutta, Vaidya Vinod, Vaidya Vamanotsava, Bhaisajya Ratnawali, and the Lolimb Raj, who wrote the *Vaidya Jeevan* in verse form. The first lines of the verses of the *Vaidya Jeevan* are addressed to the author's "beloved", while the rest of the verse has contains information about curing diseases.

About 200 years ago, Pranacharya Shri Sadanand Sharma wrote the *Ras Tarangini*, which was the "base book" for modernizing Ayurveda practices. In this book, advances in chemistry are included. The book describes the use of many chemical substances as medicine and their successful uses. Upon considering the advice of this book, Ayurvedic practitioners began to process the traditional herbs in sulphate, nitrate, muriate, phosphate and nitromuriate forms. Sarpagandha [Latin: Rauwolfia Serpentina] Muriate, Sarpagandha Sulphate, Sarpagandha Phosphate, Sarpagandha Nitrate, Sarpagandha nitromuriate and many others have been prepared and tested on patients.The *Ras Tarangini* mentiones "Shankhadrav", which is a medicine used internally and externally in many disease conditions. Shankhadrav-based herbal medicine, invented by an Indian physician, is regarded by the National Innovation Foundation, Ahmedabad, India.

Medications: Ayurveda operates on the precept that various materials of vegetable, animal, and mineral origin have some medicinal value. The medicinal properties of these materials have been documented by the practitioners and have been used for centuries to cure illness and/or help maintain good health. Ayurvedic medicaments are made from herbs or mixtures of herbs, either alone or in combination with minerals, metals and other ingredients of animal origin. The metals, animals and minerals are purified by individual processes before being used for medicinal purposes.

Writers and compilers of Ayurvedic literature such as Charaka, Sushruta, Vagabhatta, Bhav Mishra, Shaligram and others have written about the qualities, charecteristics and medicinal uses of the herbs, mineral, metals, chemicals, animal parts, cooked food articles, natural foods, fruits, etc. Among them, the Bhav Prakash Nighantu, written by Bhav Mishra, is known for its detail. The composition of the *Nighantu part* (Ayurvedic Materia Medica) of the Bhav Prakash is part of the classical book. The details of the medicinal herbs are given according to the nature, effects, and curative properties as observed by the Ayurvedic practitioners.

Ayurvedic literature has been written by several authors in languages such as Sanskrit, Hindi, and more recently, in English. The *Shaligram Nighantu* was written in Sanskrit. The *Banaushadhi Chandrodaya* was written in Hindi. The *Indian Materia Medica* was written in English.

Ayurvedic Massage: Ayurvedic massage is a form of treatment for various age related and other common disorders. Some of the advantages which can be cited are pain relief, improved circulation, stress relief, better sleep, flexibilty, athletic performance and emotional benefits. Massage therapy can soothe pain, relax stiff muscles, and reduce the swelling that accompanies arthritis. Advocates claim that, with Ayurvedic massage, deep-seated toxins in the joints and tissues are loosened and released into the system for elimination through natural toxin-release processes.

Current Status: In the early 20th century, Ayurvedic physicians began to organize into professional associations and to promote their case for national recognition and funding. This began to become a reality after Indian independence in 1947.

Use in Personal Care: Ayurveda is also being increasingly used in modern day formats in personal care. For instance, Medimix, a traditionally handmade soap using Ayurvedic principles is one of the leading soap brands in India. In certain states in India, *Charak Samhita* and *Sushruta Samhita* are included in the curriculum of modern medical courses (M.B.B.S).

Modern Scientific Research: The efficacy of certain Ayurvedic regimens, such as the Panchakarma, Kshar Sutra and the Triphala herbs, has been established by medical research. Some of the plants commonly used in Ayurveda have been shown to potentially combat certain ailments in double-blind clinical studies. One such study discovered that some of the plants commonly used in Ayurvedic medicine prevent the breakdown of neurotransmitters, improving memory and concentration in people with Alzheimer's disease.

The traditional methods of teaching Ayurveda, such as undergoing a rigorous study of Sanskrit, are now discarded. Ayurveda is now taught as an integrated course with modern medical sciences and Ayurvedic sciences. These integrated degree-level courses consist of a duration of five and a half years, *i.e.* B.A.M.S. (Bachelor of Ayurvedic Medicine and Surgery), with one additional year of internship in hospital. Standard medical science subjects are taught along with Ayurvedic subjects, *i.e. Maulik Siddhant*, *Materia Medica*, *Kayachikitsa*, etc. in Ayurvedic medical colleges.

Ayurvedic Institutions and Practitioners: Ayurvedic practitioners have been appointed as Honourary Ayurvedic Physician to the President of India. Every year on the occasion of Dhanvantari jayanti, a prestigious Dhanvantari Award is conferred on a famous personality of Medical Sciences including Ayurveda. Today, Kerala is one of the states in India that promotes research and practices of Ayurveda. This has been attributed to its well established Ayurveda centres and Ayurveda pharmaceutical companies, as also the presence of medicinal herbs and plants on the Western Ghats mountain range that runs through the state. There are many Ayurvedic centres (known as *Vaidya shalas*) all over Kerala.

Practice in the West: As a result of strong regulations in medical practice in Europe and America, the most commonly practiced Ayurvedic treatments in the west are massage, dietary and herbal advice. In the United States, the National Institute of Ayurvedic Medicine (established by Scott Gerson) is an example of a research institute that has made modern scientific progress in Ayurvedic practices. Gerson has published part of his work on the antifungal activities of certain Ayurvedic plants in medical journals.

Several Pharmecutical companies and Academic Institutions in the west have come into conflict with Indian academic institutions and traditional Ayurvedic practitioners over the intellectual property rights of herbal products researched by the western agencies. The Ayurvedic practitioners have known about the efficacy of such products for centuries and so contend that they carry precedence with regards to patent rights on such products.

On December 1993, the University of Mississippi Medical Centre had a patent issued to them by U.S patents and trademarks office on the use of turmeric (U.S. patent No. 5,401,504) for healing. The patent was contested by India's "Council for Scientific and Industrial Research" (C.S.I.R) on the grounds that traditional Ayurvedic practitioners were already aware of the healing properties of the substance and have been for centuries, making this patent a case of bio-piracy. After a complex legal battle, the U.S. Patents and Trademarks Office ruled on August 14, 1997 that the patent was invalid because it was not a novel invention, giving the intellectual property rights to the principle back to the traditional practitioners of Ayurveda. R. A. Mashelkar, director-general of the CSIR, was satisfied with the result, saying:

"This success will enhance the confidence of the people and help remove fears about India's helplessness on preventing bio-piracy and appropriation of inventions based on traditional knowledge."

The turmeric patent was just one of the hundreds that the several academic organizations and Pharmecutical companies in the west have claimed by ignoring Ayurvedic knowledge.

Vandana Shiva, a global campaigner for a fair and honest Intellectual Property Rights system, says patents on herbal products derived from Neem, Amla, Jar Amla, Anar, Salai, Dudhi, Gulmendhi, Bagbherenda, Karela, Erand, Rangoon-kibel, Vilayetishisham and Chamkura also need to be revoked.

Seven American and four Japanese firms have filed for grant of patents on formulations containing extracts of the herb Ashwagandha. Fruits, leaves and seeds of the Indian medicinal plant withania somnifera have been traditionally used for the Ayurvedic system as aphrodisiacs, diuretics and for treating memory loss. The Japanese patent applications are related to the use of the herb as a skin ointment and for promoting reproductive fertility. The U.S based company Natreon has also obtained a patent for an Ashwagandha extract. Another US establishment, the New England Deaconess Hospital, has taken a patent on an Ashwagandha formulation claimed to alleviate symptoms associated with arthritis. It is clear that the Ashwagandha plant is catching the attention of scientists and more patents related to Ashwagandha are being filed or granted by different patent offices since 1996.

Scientific Criticism of Ayurveda: Ayurveda claims that illness and disease are a result of imbalance in the doshas, which contradicts modern science's understanding of disease in terms of pathogens, infectious agents and genetic disorders. However, many Ayurvedic schools and institutions, including ones funded by the Government of India, have abandoned the traditional holistic philosophy of Ayurveda and are using modern methods to research the efficacy of traditional Ayurvedic medicines.

Scientific Studies and Standards: Critics object to the lack of rigorous scientific studies and clinical trials of many Ayurvedic products. The National Centre for Complementary and Alternative Medicine states that "most clinical trials of Ayurvedic approaches have been small, had problems with research designs, lacked appropriate control groups, or had other issues that affected how meaningful the results were."

In India, scientific research in Ayurveda is largely undertaken by the statutory body of the Federal Government, the Central Council for Research in Ayurveda and Siddha (CCRAS), through a national network of research institutes. A large number of non-governmental organisations are also conducting research work on different aspects of Ayurveda. However, "even staunch advocates of Ayurveda like cardiologist Dr. M.S. Valiathan...admit that 'clinical studies that would satisfy the liberal criteria of WHO (World Health Organisation) have been alarmingly few from India, in spite of patients crowding in Ayurvedic hospitals'".

Safety Concerns: A research study published in the Journal of the American Medical Association found significant levels of toxic heavy metals such as lead, mercury and arsenic in 20% of Ayurvedic preparations that were made in South Asia for sale in America. The Journal found that, if taken according to the manufacturers' instructions, this 20% of remedies "could result in heavy metal intakes above published regulatory standards" Similar studies have been performed in India, and have confirmed these results. In response to the study, some practitioners of Ayurveda claimed that "heavy metals are integral to some formulations and have been used for centuries. There is no point of doing trials as they have been used safely and have mention in our ancient texts."

Miracle Cures: Some critics also question the safety of those Ayurvedic drugs that are said to provide "miraculous cures". They argue that simply following age-old Ayurvedic formulas is no guarantee of safety and the fundamental processes and concepts on which these ancient processes are based must be exposed to serious scientific scrutiny. However, attacks made against Ayurvedic practitioners such as Swami Ramdev by communist politicians such as Brinda Karat regarding these issues have sometimes been viewed as the politicized spread of misinformation. Such tactics have been condemned by a number of politicians and the practices have had their scientific validity attested to some degree.

3

HINDU'S GRANTH AND VEDAS

INTRODUCTION

Karma is a concept in Hinduism which explains causality through a system where beneficial effects are derived from past beneficial actions and harmful effects from past harmful actions, creating a system of actions and reactions throughout a person's reincarnated lives. Karma in Hinduism explains the problem of evil that persists in spite of an omniscient, omnipotent, benevolent God; it is thus related to theodicy.

Parts of the Mahabharata are sometimes anaylzed as a Karma story (the other parts being related to Moksha), a story where people received the reward of their actions, good and bad. The original Hindu concept of karma was later elaborated on by several other movements within the religion, most notably Vedanta, Yoga, and Tantra. The concept was adopted by other religions such as Buddhism and Jainism, whose views differ from Hinduism as the concept of Karma does not involve a personal supreme God. Karma has had a major influence on worldwide philosophy and spirituality.

Definition: "Karma" literally means "deed" or "act", and more broadly names the universal principle of cause and effect, action and reaction, which Hindus believe governs all life. It is believed that only beings that can distinguish right from wrong, such as adult humans, can accumulate Karma. Animals and young children are not considered to accumulate Karma as they are incapable of discriminating between right and wrong. However, all sentient beings can feel the effects of Karma, which are pleasure and pain. Karma is not fate; humans are believed to act with free will, creating their own destinies. According to the Vedas, if an individual sows goodness, he or she will reap goodness; if one sows evil, he or she will reap evil.

Karma refers to the totality of mankind's actions and their concommitant reactions in current and previous lives, all of which determine the future. However, many karmas do not have an immediate effect; some accumulate and return unexpectedly in an individual's later lives. The conquest of karma is believed to lie in intelligent action and dispassionate reaction.

Unkindness yields spoiled fruits, called *papa*, and good deeds bring forth sweet fruits, called punya. As one acts, so does he become: one becomes virtuous by virtuous action, and evil by evil action.

There are three types of karma in Hinduism:

1. Sanchita karma, the sum total of past karmas yet to be resolved;
2. Prarabdha karma, that portion of sanchita karma that is to be experienced in this life; and
3. Kriyamana karma, the karma that humans are currently creating, which will bear fruit in future.

The Role of God: Although in Buddhism and Jainism, karma is seen as simply a law of nature, several different views exist in Hinduism. In Hinduism, many see God as playing some kind of role, for example, as the dispenser of the fruits of karma. Other Hindus consider the natural laws of causation sufficient to explain the effects of karma. Some interpretations of the Bhagavad Gita suggest an intermediate view, that karma is a law of cause and effect yet God can mitigate karma for His devotees. Another view holds that a Sadguru, acting on God's behalf, can mitigate or work out some of the karma of the disciple.

Thus, according to many Hindus, God does have hand in the process of karma. Unlike Buddhists and Jains who believe that Karma on its own joins the soul when it reincarnates, this Hindu belief describes the role of God in linking Karma to an individual. In fact, Hinduism argues for the existence of an Omniscient God (Sanskrit: *Ishvara*) because the judgment of intelligent actions (*i.e.* Karma) requires intelligence on the part of the judge (*i.e.* God). Unintelligent nature by itself cannot judge the performance of actions of intelligent beings.

Hence the intervention of an Omniscient God is required to dispense the fruits of Karma—which are rewards for good actions (in the form of pleasure) and punishments for evil actions (in the form of pain).

Two Examples from the Puranas: The story of Markandeya, who was saved from death by Shiva, illustrates that God's grace can overcome Karma and death for His beloved devotee.

The story of Ajamila in the Bhagavata Purana also illustrates the same point. Ajamila had committed many evil deeds during his life such as stealing, abandoning his wife and children, and marrying a prostitute. But at the moment of death, he involuntarily chanted the name of Narayana and therefore received Moksha or union with God, and was saved from the messengers of Yama.

Ajamila was actually thinking of his youngest son, whose name was also Narayana. But the name of God has powerful effects, and Ajamila was forgiven for his great sins and attained salvation, despite his bad Karma.

VIEWS OF HINDU TRADITIONS ON KARMA

Advaita Vedanta: Swami Sivananda, an Advaita scholar, reiterates the same views in his commentary synthesising Vedanta views on the Brahma Sutras, a Vedantic text. In his commentary on Chapter 3 of the Brahma Sutras, Sivananda notes that karma is insentient and short-lived, and ceases to exist as soon as a deed is executed. Hence, karma cannot bestow the fruits of actions at a future date according to one's merit. Furthermore, one cannot argue that karma generates apurva or punya, which gives fruit. Since apurva is non-sentient, it cannot act unless moved by an intelligent being such as God. It cannot independently bestow reward or punishment.

There is a passage from Swami Sivananda's translation of the Svetasvatara Upanishad (4:6) illustrating this concept:

> *Two birds of beautiful plumage—inseparable friends—live on the same tree. Of these two one eats the sweet fruit while the other looks on without eating.*

In his commentary, the first bird represents the individual soul, while the second represents Brahman or God. The soul is essentially a reflection of Brahman. The tree represents the body. The soul identifies itself with the body, reaps the fruits of its actions, and undergoes rebirth. The Lord alone stands as an eternal witness, ever contented, and does not eat, for he is the director of both the eater and the eaten.

Swami Sivananda also notes that God is free from charges of partiality and cruelty which are brought against him because of social inequality, fate, and universal suffering in the world. According to the Brahma Sutras, individual souls are responsible for their own fate; God is merely the dispenser and witness with reference to the merit and demerit of souls.

In his commentary on Chapter 2 of the Brahma Sutras, Sivananda further notes that the position of God with respect to karma can be explained through the analogy of rain. Although rain can be said to bring about the growth of rice, barley and other plants, the differences in various species is due to the diverse potentialities lying hidden in the respective seeds. Thus, Sivananda explains that differences between classes of beings are due to different merits belonging to individual souls. He concludes that God metes rewards and punishments only in consideration of the specific actions of beings.

Shaivism: Thirugnana Sambanthar writes about karma in his outline of Shaivism. He explains the concept of karma in Hinduism by distinguishing it from that of Buddhism and Jainism, which do not require the existence of an external being like God. In their beliefs, just as a calf among a large number of cows can find its mother at suckling time, so also does karma find the specific individual it needs to attach to and come to fruition. However Hindus posit that karma, unlike the calf, is an unintelligent entity. Hence, karma cannot locate the appropriate person by itself. Shri Sambantha concludes that an intelligent Supreme Being with perfect wisdom and power (Shiva, for example) is necessary to make karma attach to the appropriate individual. In such sense, God is the Divine Accountant.

Appaya Dikshita, a Saivite theologian and proponent of Shiva Advaita, states that Shiva (God) only awards happiness and misery in accordance with the law of karma. Thus persons themselves perform good or evil actions according to their own inclinations as acquired in past creations, and in accordance with those deeds, a new creation is made for the fulfilment of the law of karma. Shaivas believe that there are cycles of creations in which souls gravitate to specific bodies in accordance with karma, which as an unintelligent object depends on the will of Shiva alone. Thus, many interpret the caste system in accordance with karma, as those with good deeds are born into a highly spiritual family (probably the *brahmana* caste).

Srikantha, another Saivite theologian, believes that individual souls themselves do things which may be regarded as the cause of their particular actions, or desisting from particular actions, in accordance with the nature of the fruition of their past deeds. Srikantha further believes that Shiva only helps a person when he wishes to act in a particular way or to desist from a particular action.

Satguru Sivaya Subramuniyaswami explains in the lexicon section of his book, *Dancing with Shiva*, that karma literally means "deed or act" and more broadly names the universal principle of cause and effect, action and reaction which governs all life. As he explains it, karma is not fate, for man acts with free will creating his own destiny. The Vedas tell us that if we sow goodness, we will reap goodness; if we sow evil, we will reap evil. Satguru Sivaya Subramuniyaswami further notes that karma refers to the totality of our actions and their concomitant reactions in this and previous lives, all of which determine our future. The conquest of karma lies in intelligent action and dispassionate reaction. Not all karmas rebound immediately. Some accumulate and return unexpectedly in this or other births.

Vaishnavism: Ramanuja attempts to fashion a solution to the problem of evil by attributing all evil things in life to the accumulation of evil karma of jivas (human souls), and maintains that God is amala or without any stain of evil.

Madhva, the founder of the Dvaita school, on the other hand, believes that there must be a root cause for variations in karma even if karma is accepted as having no beginning and being the cause of the problem of evil. Since jivas have different kinds of karma, from good to bad, all must not have started with same type of karma from the beginning of time. Thus, Madhva concludes that the jivas are not God's creation as in the Christian doctrine, but are rather entities co-existent with Vishnu, although under His absolute control. Souls are thus dependent on Him in their pristine nature and in all transformations that they may undergo.

According to Madhva, God, although He has control, does not interfere with Man's free will; although He is omnipotent, that does not mean that He engages in extraordinary feats. Rather, God enforces a rule of law and, in accordance with the just deserts of jivas, gives them freedom to follow their own nature. Thus, God functions as the sanctioner or as the divine accountant, and accordingly jivas are free to work according to their innate nature and their accumulated karma, good and bad. Since God acts as the sanctioner, the ultimate power for everything comes from God and the jiva only utilizes that power, according to his/her innate nature.

Swami Tapasyananda further explains the Madhva view by illustrating the doctrine with this analogy: the power in a factory comes from the powerhouse (God), but the various cogs (*jivas*) move in a direction in which they are set. Thus he concludes that no charge of partiality and cruelty can be brought against God. The jiva is the actor and also the enjoyer of the fruits of his/her own actions.

Madhva differed significantly from traditional Hindu beliefs, owing to his concept of eternal damnation. For example, he divides souls into three classes: one class of souls which qualify for liberation (Mukti-yogyas), another subject to eternal rebirth or eternal transmigration (Nitya-samsarins), and a third class that is eventually condemned to eternal hell or Andhatamas (Tamo-yogyas). No other Hindu philosopher or school of Hinduism holds such beliefs. In contrast, most Hindus believe in universal salvation: that all souls will eventually obtain Moksha, even if it is after millions of rebirths.

Gita Interpretations and Role of Guru: Some interpretations of certain verses in the Bhagavad Gita suggests an intermediate view, that karma is a law of cause and effect yet God can mitigate karma for His devotees. Another view holds that a Sadguru, acting on God's behalf, can mitigate or work out some of the karma of the disciple.

Caste and Karma: As stated earlier, there are cycles of creations in which souls gravitate to specific bodies in accordance with karma, which as an unintelligent object depends on the will of God alone. Thus, many interpret the caste system in accordance with karma, as those with good deeds are born into a spiritual family, which is synonymous with the *brahmana* caste. However, Krishna said in the Gita that characteristics of a brahmin are determined by behaviour, not by birth. A verse from the Gita illustrates this point: "The duties of Brahmins, Kshatriyas, Vaishyas as also of Sudras, O scorcher of foes, are distributed according to the gunas (behaviour) born of their own nature." (Chapter 18, verse 41)

Dharma: *Dharma* or *Dhamma* (*Natural Law*) refers to the underlying order in Nature and human behaviour considered to be in accord with that order. Ethically, it means 'right way of living' or 'proper conduct,' especially in a religious sense. With respect to spirituality, dharma might be considered *the Way of the Higher Truths*. Dharma is a central concept in religions and philosophies originating in India. These religions and philosophies are called Dharmic religions. The principal ones are Hinduism (Sanatana Dharma), Buddhism (Buddhadharma), Jainism (Jain Dharma), and Sikhism, all of which emphasize Dharma (the correct understanding of Nature) in their teachings. In these traditions, beings that live in accordance with *Dharma* proceed more quickly toward Dharma Yukam, Moksha or Nirvana (personal liberation). Dharma also refers to the teachings and doctrines of the founders of these traditions, such as those of Gautama Buddha and Mahavira. In traditional Hindu society with its caste structure, Dharma constituted the religious and moral doctrine of the rights and duties of each individual.

Meanings and Origins of the Word Dharma: In the Rigveda, the word appears as an *n*-stem, *dharma*, with a range of meanings encompassing "something established or firm" (in the literal sense of prods or poles), figuratively "sustainer, supporter" (of deities), and in the abstract, similar to the semantics of Greek ethos, "fixed decree, statute, law".

The word is from a root common Indo-Iranian root *dhar* "to fasten, to support, to hold", continuing PIE **dher*, in the IEW connected with Latin *fr–num* "rein, horse tack", Germanic words for "hidden, held back" (OHG *tarni "latens"*), and extended to *dher-gh*, with OCS *drJze, drJzati* "to hold, possess". Etymological identity of *dharma* with Latin *firmus* (whence English *firm*) has been suggested, but remains uncertain.

From the Atharvaveda and in Classical Sanskrit, the stem is thematic, *dharma*, and in Pli, it takes the form *dhamma*. Monier-Williams attempts to gesture at the semantic field of the spiritual and religious meanings of the term with "virtue, morality, religion, religious merit". It being used in most or all philosophies and religions of Indian origin, the "dharmic faiths" including Hinduism (Sanatana Dharma), Buddhism, Jainism and Sikhism, it is difficult to provide a single concise definition for Dharma. The word has a long and varied history and straddles a complex set of meanings and interpretations. Dharma also is practiced in the Surat Shabda Yoga traditions.

Rene Guenon, father of the 20th century school of perennial philosophy, said:

> *It [dharma] is, so to speak, the essential nature of a being, comprising the sum of its particular qualities or characteristics, and determining, by virtue of the tendencies or dispositions it implies, the manner in which this being will conduct itself, either in a general way or in relation to each particular circumstance. The same idea may be applied, not only to a single being, but also to an organized collectivity, to a species, to all the beings included in a cosmic cycle or state of existence, or even to the whole order of the Universe; it then, at one level or another, signifies conformity with the essential nature of beings... (from Guenon's "Introduction to the Study of Hindu Doctrines")*

David Frawley, an expert on Hindu philosophy and religion, comments on Dharma as follows:

> *A universal tradition has room for all faiths and all religious and spiritual practices regardless of the time or country of their origin. Yet it places religious and spiritual teachings in their appropriate place relative to the ultimate goal of Self-realization, to which secondary practices are subordinated. Sanatan Dharma also recognizes that the greater portion of human religious aspirations has always been unknown, undefined and outside of any institutionalized belief. Sanatan Dharma thereby gives reverence to individual spiritual experience over any formal religious doctrine. Wherever the Universal Truth is manifest; there is Sanatan Dharma—whether it is in a field of religion,*

art or science, or in the life of a person or community. Wherever the Universal Truth is not recognized, or is scaled down or limited to a particular group, book or person, even if done so in the name of God, there Sanatan Dharma ceases to function, whatever the activity is called.

According to the Natchintanai Scripture:

By the laws of Dharma that govern body and mind, you must fear sin and act righteously. Wise men by thinking and behaving in this way become worthy to gain bliss both here and hereafter.

Yama, the lord of death, is also known as *Dharma*, since he works within the laws of karma and morality, regulated by divine principles. More familiar is the embodiment of Dharma in Lord Rama, an avatar of Vishnu. The eldest Pandava, Yudhishthira was referred to as *Dharma Raj* (Most pious One) owing to his steadfastness to Truth and Dharma.

In ancient Vedic tradition, the Dharma was decided by the holy Kings or Dharma Raja. Dharma rajas include Manu who by tradition saves the Vedas before the flood, Rama, Yudhisthira, and Buddha.

The teachings, doctrines, philosophies and practices associated with furthering *Dharma* are also referred to as such. Sometimes, specific qualifiers are used-*viz. Buddha-Dharma* and *Jain-Dharma* to distinguish them from Hindu Dharma.

For many Buddhists, the *Dharma* most often means the body of teachings expounded by the Buddha. The word is also used in Buddhist phenomenology as a term roughly equivalent to phenomenon, a basic unit of existence and/or experience.

In scripture translations *dharma* is often best left untranslated, as it has acquired a lively life of its own in English that is more expressive than any simplistic translation. Common translations and glosses include "right way of living," Divine Law, Path of Righteousness, order, faith, "natural harmony," rule, fundamental teachings, and duty. *Dharma* may be used to refer to rules of the operation of the mind or universe in a metaphysical system, or to rules of comportment in an ethical system.

In modern Indian languages, such as Hindi, dharma can also mean simply "religion." In this meaning, for example, a Muslim is a person who follows the dharma of Islam.

Dharma in Hinduism: Within Indian philosophy "dharma" also means "property" and "dharmin" means "property-bearer". In a Sanskrit sentence like "shabdo 'nitya%", "sound is impermanent", "sound" is the bearer of the property "impermanence". Likewise, in the sentence "iha ghata%", "here, there is a pot", "here" is the bearer of the property "pot-existence"-this just goes to show that the categories property and property-bearer are closer to those of a logical predicate and its subject-term, and not to a grammatical predicate and subject.

Origin and Development in Hinduism: A common manner of describing Hinduism among its adherents is as a *way of life*, as "Dharma." It defies dogma and thus seeks to instead align the human body, mind, and soul in harmony with nature.

Our very limitation is guided under and over a universal understanding, that of Dharma. The Atharva Veda, the last of the four books of the Vedas, utilizes symbolism to describe *dharma's* role. Thus we are bound by the laws of time, space and causation according to finite reality, which itself is a limitation imposed by the self-projection of the infinite Brahman as the cosmos. Dharma is the foundation of this causal existence, the one step below the infinite. Indeed, dharma is the projection of divine order from Brahman, and as such marisa

"Prithivim Dharmana Dhritam"

"This world is upheld by Dharma"
—(Atharva Veda)

Proto-dharma: rta in the Vedas: To assess a concept whose explication is bewildering in range, it is useful to trace its nascence and subsequent development in Vedic culture. In the Vedas, which span back to 2000 BCE (and much further in oral tradition), the first concept that is strikingly *dharmic* is that of rta.

Rta literally means the "course of things." At first, the early Hindus (or followers of the "Sanatan Dharma") were notably inquisitive as to the inscrutable order of nature, how the heavenly bodies, the rushing winds and flowing waters, the consistent cycling of the seasons, were regulated. Thenceforth sprang rta, whose all-purpose role it was to signify this order, the path that was always followed. Through all the metamorphoses and permutations of nature, of life in general, there was one unchangeable fact: rta.

Soon it transcended its passive role as a mere signifier and took on a greater one, that of an active imposition of order. Not only the natural principles, but the gods and goddesses themselves, were obliged to abide by rta. Rta became the father, the law of justice and righteousness, unyielding but eminently fair. It grew, as Radhakrishnan states, from "physical" to "divine" in its purvey.

The world's seeming mess of altercating fortune, the caprice of the divinities, was now intelligible. Indeed, there was a single, unchanging harmony working 'behind the scenes.' A right path existed, ready to be taken by the righteous ones. Rta signifies the way life ought to be, shifting from physical to divine, from natural to moral order. Rta was morality, the equitable law of the universe. The conception of this all-transcending, supramental force that is, practically, the same concept as later understandings of dharma, is captured in this early Vedic prayer, pre-empting the liturgical strains of classical Hindu mantras involving *dharma*:

> *"O Indra, lead us on the path of Rta, on the right path over all evils."*
>
> *—(Rig Veda Book X, Chapter CXXXIII, Verse 6)*

Thus we see the logical progression of an early 'course of things' into an all-encompassing moral order, a path and way of righteousness, an all-encompassing harmony of the universe, in the Vedic idea of Rta.

Developing Conceptions: An earlier and insightful demonstration of the continuity of thought from rta to dharma is a brief but "pregnant definition" of dharma given in the Brihadaranyaka Upanishad, a part of the Veda. Founded upon the Hindu ideas of, as R. H. Hume's "intelligent monism," with Brahman the monad, the Upanishads saw dharma as the universal principle of law, order, harmony, all in all truth, that sprang first from Brahman. It acts as the regulatory moral principle of the universe. It is *sat*, truth, a major tenet of Hinduism. This hearkens back to the conception of the Rig Veda that "Ekam Sat," (Truth Is One), of the idea that Brahman is "*Sacchidananda*" (Truth-Consciousness-Bliss). Dharma has imbibed the highest principles of Truth, and as such is the central guiding principle in the Hindu conception of existence. Dharma is not just law, or harmony, it is pure Reality. In the Brihadaranyaka's own words:

> *"Verily, that which is Dharma is truth.*
>
> *Therefore they say of a man who speaks truth, 'He speaks the Dharma,'*
>
> *or of a man who speaks the Dharma, 'He speaks the Truth.'*
>
> *Verily, both these things are the same."*
> *(Brh. Upanishad, 1.4.14)*

Dharma as a Purushartha: In moving through the four stages of life, *viz.* Brahmacharya, Grihastha, Vaanprastha, Sanyaasa, a person also seeks to fulfil the four essentials (*purushaartha*) of Dharma, Artha (worldly gain), Kama (sensual pleasures), and Moksha (liberation from reincarnation or rebirth). Moksha, although the ultimate goal, is emphasized more in the last two stages of life, while Artha and Kama are primary only during Grihasthaashram. Dharma, however is essential in all four stages.

Kane's View: According to Dr.Pandurang Vaman Kane, the word "Dharma" acquired a sense of "the privileges, duties and obligations of a man, his standard of conduct as a member of the Aryan community, as a member of the caste and as a person in a particular state of life."

The God Dharma: Dharma is also the name of a Deva in charge of Dharma. He is born from the right breast of Brahma, is married to ten daughters of Daksha and fathers Shama, kama and Harahsa. He is also the father of the celebrated Rishis Hari, Krishna, Nara and Naryana. In the Epioc Mahabharata Dharma is invoked by Kunti and she begets her eldest son Yudhisthira from him. As such Yudhisthira is know as Dhrmaputra.

Dharma is not to be confused with Yama, the God of the Dead and the God of Death. Yama is a Dhram abididng Deva and is hence called Dharamaraj.

IN BUDDHISM

Buddha's Teachings: For practicing Buddhists, references to "dharma" or *dhamma* in the singular, particularly as "the" Dharma, is used to mean the teachings of the Buddha, and is sometimes referred to as the Buddha-Dharma. This latter signification has nothing to do with the personality of the spiritual teacher Siddhartha Gautama but rather signifies the importance of the attitude of mind that enables an adept or practitioner to re-harmonise his personal nature with the underlying principle (Dharma) behind natural phenomena leading towards the undoing of all egoistic falsehood and ultimately release in nirvana-the peace of liberation (Moksha).

The status of the Dharma is regarded variably by different traditions. Some regard it as an ultimate and transcendent truth utterly beyond worldly things, somewhat like the Christian logos. Others, who regard the Buddha as simply an enlightened human being, see the Dharma as the 84,000 different teachings that the Buddha gave to various types of people based on their needs.

"Dharma" usually refers not only to the sayings of the Buddha but also to the later traditions of interpretation and addition that the various schools of Buddhism have developed to help explain and expand upon the Buddha's teachings. For others still, they see the dharma as referring to the "truth" or ultimate reality or "the way things are" (Tib. Cho).

The Dharma is one of the Three Jewels of Buddhism of which practitioners of Buddhism seek refuge in (what one relies on for his/her lasting happiness). The three jewels of Buddhism are the Buddha (mind's perfection of enlightenment), the Dharma (teachings and methods), and the Sangha (awakened beings who provide guidance and support).

Qualities of Buddha Dharma: The Teaching of the Buddha also has six supreme qualities:

1. (Svakkhato) The Dharma is not a speculative philosophy, but is the Universal Law found through enlightenment and is preached precisely. Therefore it is Excellent in the beginning (S+la... Moral principles), Excellent in the middle (Samadhi... Concentration) and Excellent in the end (PaD na... Wisdom),
2. (Samditthiko) The Dharma can be tested by practice and therefore he who follows it will see the result by himself through his own experience.
3. (Akliko) The Dharma is able to bestow timeless and immediate results here and now, for which there is no need to wait until the future or next existence.
4. (Ehipassiko) The Dharma welcomes all beings to put it to the test and come see for themselves.
5. (Opneyiko) The Dharma is capable of being entered upon and therefore it is worthy to be followed as a part of one's life.
6. (Paccattam veditabbo vinnknhi) The Dharma can be perfectly realized only by the noble disciples (Ariyas) who have matured and enlightened enough in supreme wisdom.

Knowing these attributes, Buddhists believe that they will attain the greatest peace and happiness through the practice of the Dharma. Each person is therefore fully responsible for himself to put it in the real practice.

Here the Buddha is compared to an experienced and skilful doctor, and the Dharma to proper medicine. However efficient the doctor or wonderful the medicine may be, the patients cannot be cured unless they take the medicine properly. So the practice of the Dharma is the only way to attain the final deliverance of Nibbna.

These teachings ranged from understanding karma (cause and effect) and developing good impressions in one's mind, to how to reach full enlightenment by recognizing the nature of mind.

Dharmas in Buddhist Phenomenology: Other uses include *dharma*, normally spelled with a small "d" (to differentiate), which refers to a *phenomenon* or *constituent factor* of human experience. This was gradually expanded into a classification of constituents of the entire material and mental world. Rejecting the substantial existence of permanent entities which are qualified by possibly changing qualities, Buddhist Abhidharma philosophy, which enumerated seventy-five dharmas, came to propound that these "constituent factors" are the only type of entity that truly exists. This notion is of particular importance for the analysis of human experience: Rather than assuming that mental states inhere in a cognizing subject, or a soul-substance, Buddhist philosophers largely propose that mental states alone exist as "momentary elements of consciousness", and that a subjective perceiver is assumed.

One of the central tenets of Buddhism, is the denial of a separate permanent "I", and is outlined in the three marks of existence. The three signs: 1. Dukkha-Suffering (Pali: Dukkha), 2. Anitya-Change/Impermanence (Pali: Anicca), 3. Anatman-No-I (Pali: Annatta). At the heart of Buddhism, is the denial of an "I" (and hence the delusion) as a separate self-existing entity.

Dharma as Righteousness: According to S. N. Goenka, teacher of Vipassana Meditation, the original meaning of dhamma is "dhareti ti dhamma', or "that which is contained". Dharma in the Buddhist scriptures has a variety of meanings, including "phenomenon", and "nature" or "characteristic". Dharma also means 'mental contents', and is paired with citta, which means heart/mind. The pairing is paralleled with the pairing of kaya (body) and vedana (feelings or sensations, that which arise within the body but experienced through the mind), in major sutras such as the Mahasatipatthana sutra. Dharma is also used to refer to the teachings of the Buddha, not in the context of the words of one man, even an enlightened man, but as a reflection of natural law which was re-discovered by this man and shared with the world. A person who lives their life with an understanding of this natural law, is a "dhammic" person, which is often translated as "righteous".

In Sikhism: For Sikhs, the word *"Dharma"* means the "path of righteousness". What is the "righteous path"? That is the question that the Sikh scriptures attempt to answer. The main holy scriptures of the Sikhs is called the Guru Granth Sahib or SGGS for short. It is considered to be more than a holy book of the Sikhs. The Sikhs treat this Granth (*holy book*) as a living Guru. The holy text spans 1430 pages and contains the actual words spoken by the Sikh Gurus and various other Saints from other religions including Hinduism and Islam.

Sikh Dharma is a distinct religion revealed through the teachings of ten Gurus who are accept by the followers as if they were spiritually the same. The Gurus are considered "the divine light" and they conveyed Gurbani (the word of God) in the form of the Guru Granth Sahib to the world. In this faith, God is described as both Nirgun (transcendent) and Sargun (immanent). Further, God pervades in His creation and is omnipresent, but cannot be incarnate. The principal Sikh belief lays stress on one's actions and deeds rather than people's religious labels, rituals or outward appearance or signs.

Background: The primary object of a Sikh's life is to seek union with God and hence, liberation from the cycle of births and deaths (cycle of re-incarnation) which is dictated by a person's thought, deeds and actions in this life. Liberation can be achieved through meditating on God, truthful living and sharing ones wealth in the context of a normal family life and through divine grace. Amrit Pahul – Sikh baptism for both men and women – was instituted in 1699 by Guru Gobind Singh, the tenth Guru. All Sikhs, on taking Amrit, are enjoined to lead a disciplined life by following a code of ethics leading to a "Saint-Soldier" way of life. In 1708, Guru Gobind Singh vested spiritual authority in the Guru Granth Sahib (the Sikh Scriptures) as the eternal Guru and hence Sikh Dharma acknowledges the end of human Guruship. At the same time, the temporal authority was vested in the Khalsa Panth (a community of Sikhs who have taken Amrit).

Other important aspects of a Sikh's life include Sewa (dedication to the service of God's creation) where the emphasis is often upon manual work, undertaking of goodwill towards other faiths and their followers, to defend for justice and assistance of the oppressed. In contract to many other faith, Sikhs believe that when all other means to achieve justice are exhausted, then it is just to wield the sword.

Congregational worship includes the following:

1. Paath-Reading of the Holy scriptures
2. Kirtan-Singing of Shabads (hymns).
3. Langar-A communal vegetarian meal also call free kitchen is an important feature of the Sikh way of life, and food is served to everyone at the end of a Sikh service.
4. Community Centre-Today, in most countries, a Gurdwara, the Sikh place of worship, also serves as a centre to promote Sikh culture and such other needs of the community.
5. Ardas-Sikhs conclude their prayers by doing the Ardas and invoking God's blessings on everyone – not just on Sikhs."

Scriptures and Dharma: The Guru Granth Sahib lays down the foundation of this "righteous path" and various salient points are found.

1. *Sikh is bound by Dharma:* The followers of this faith are bound by Dharma as advocated in their holy scriptures. The committed Sikh is encouraged to follow this path at all times. The first recitation of the SGGS called the Japji Sahib says the following: *"The path of the faithful shall never be blocked. The faithful shall depart with honour and fame. The faithful do not follow empty religious rituals. The faithful are firmly bound to the Dharma. Such is the Name of the Immaculate Lord. Only one who has faith comes to know such a state of mind."* (SGGS Japji page 3.)
2. *Deeds are Recorded:* The persons thoughts and deeds are said to be recorded and the faithful is warned that these will be read out in the presence of the "Lord of Dharma". Two scribes called *"Chitr and Gupt"*, the angels of the conscious and the subconscious mind are busy writing ones thought and deeds. On death the soul of the person he brought before "Lord of Dharma" are these account are read out as recorded in this quote: *"Day and night are the two nurses, in whose lap all the world is at play. Good deeds and bad deeds-the record is read out in the Presence of the Lord of Dharma. According to their own actions, some are drawn closer, and some are driven farther away."*
3. *Dharma Administered by God:* The scriptures further outline how the "Judge of Dharma" administers justice depending on the way that one has conducted life on Earth. The soul is either "cleared" or "subject to God's command" depending on the review of the person history. The holy text says: *"The Righteous Judge of Dharma, by the Hukam of God's Command, sits and administers True Justice".* (SGGS page 38) (4) and those followers who "chant the name of the Lord" are cleared

as outlined thus: *"Her account is cleared by the Righteous Judge of Dharma, when she chants the Name of the Lord, Har, Har."* (SGGS page 78)

Karma and Dharma: Karma and Dharma are intrinsically linked in the Sikh faith. Karma is the baggage of ones thoughts, deeds and action in ones present and past lives. When ones mind is not fixed on the Almighty, one is governed by the Five Evils – Lust, Rage (anger), Ego, Attachment and Greed. The Sikh text tell the faithful that these "Five Evils" have the effect of restricting the person's spiritual development and the person fall in the trap of Maya (worldly affairs) which then begins to control the person daily life and routine. Yogi Harbhanjan Singh Khalsa said the following regarding the influence of the "five evils"-"The folly of man is that all he seeks is self-praise for all that he has no right over – he grooms himself and compliments himself over how he looks like when he sees his reflection in the mirror; expects his wife and children to regard him as good;..."

In Jainism: Dharma is natural. Jain Acharya Samantabhadra writes: "Vatthu sahavo dhammo" the dharma is the nature of an object. It is the nature of the soul to be free, thus for the soul, the dharma ia paralaukika, beyond worldly. However the nature of the body is to seek self-preservation and be engaged in pleasures.

The two Dharmas: Acharya Haribhadra (approx. 6-7th cent.) discusses dharma in Dharma-Bindu. He writes:

soayam-anushhThaatRi-bhedat dvi-vidho

grihastha-dharmo yati-dharmash-cha

Because of the difference in practice, Dharma is of two kinds, for the householders and for the monks.

tatra grihastha-dharmoapi dvi-vidhah

saamanyato visheshhatash-cha

Of the householder's dharma, there are two kinds," ordinary" and "special"

tatra saamnayato grihastha-dharmah kula-krama-agatam-anindyam

vibhavady-apekshayaa nyaato.anushhthaana,

The ordinary grihastha-dharma should be carried out according to tradition, such that it is not objectionable, according to ones abilities such as wealth, in accordance with nyaya (everyone treated fairly and according to laws).

Somadeva suri (10th c.) termss the "ordinary" and "special" dharmas laukika and the paralukika dharmas respectively:

dvau hi dharamau griahasthanam, laukikah, paarlaukikah

lokaashrayo bhavedaadyah, parah syaad-aagama-Ashrayah

A householder follows both laukika and the paralukika dharmas at the same time.

MOKSHA

Moksha or *Mukti* refers, in Indian religions (Hinduism and Buddhism), to liberation from the cycle of death and rebirth and all the suffering and limitation entailed in embodied worldly existence. In higher Hindu philosophy, it is seen as a transcendence of phenomenal being, of any sense of consciousness of time, space, and causation (karma). It is not seen as a soteriological goal in the same sense as in a Christian context, but signifies rather a dissolution of the sense of self as an egoistic personality—the undoing of conditioned mentality-materiality or *nama-roopa* (lit. name-form). Liberation is achieved by (and accompanied with) the complete stilling of all passions—a state of being known as Nirvana. Buddhist thought differs slightly from the Advaita Vedantist reading of liberation. Jainism and Surat Shabda Yoga traditions also believe in Moksha.

Hinduism: In Hinduism, liberation occurs when the individual soul (human mind/spirit) or j+vatman recognizes its identity with the Ground of all being-the Source of all phenomenal existence known as Brahman. It is technically incorrect, nonetheless, to view them-both often spoken of as *Self*-as a monist being of sorts, something possessing substances, qualities or attributes. In actuality, Hindu scripture like the Upanishads and Bhagavad Gita, and especially the works of the non-dualistic Hindu school, Advaita Vedanta, say that the Self or Super-Soul is formless, beyond being and non-being, beyond any sense of tangibility and comprehension. Moksha is seen as a final release from one's worldly conception of self, the loosening of the shackle of experiential duality and a re-establishment in one's own fundamental nature, though the nature is seen as ineffable and beyond sensation. The actual state of salvation is seen differently depending on one's beliefs.

- In Advaita philosophy, the ultimate truth is not a singular Godhead, per se, but rather is oneness without form or being, something that essentially is without manifestation. Moksha is union with this oneness. The concepts of Moksha and Buddhist Nirvana are comparable. Indeed, there is much overlap in their views of consciousness and attainment of enlightenment. For liberal Advaitists, Moksha is seen as complementing, rather than denying, the 'voidness' of Buddhism.
- In dualist and qualified advaitic Hinduism, Moksha means union or close association with God.

In Hinduism also, Moksha is different from Nastik religions such as Jainism and Buddhism although there are many Jains and some Buddhists that believe in the Hindu Moksha. In Hinduism, it is a union with God and to the Nastiks it is a union with all that is, regardless of whether there is a God or not. After Nirvana one obtains Moksha. The Nirvana of Hinduism is Brahma-Nirvana meaning that it will lead to God.

Means to Achieve Moksha: In Hinduism, self-realization (atma siddhi) is the key to obtaining Moksha. The Hindu is one who practices karma and bhakti, known that God exists in many forms for the achievement of Moksha. There are however, other ways in addition to this.

There are believed to be four yogas (disciplines) or margs (paths) for the attainment of Moksha. They are the ways of selfless work (Karma Yoga), of self-dissolving love (Bhakti Yoga), of absolute discernment (Jnana Yoga), and of 'royal' meditative immersion (Raja Yoga). Different schools of Hinduism place varying emphasis on one path or other, some of the most famous being the tantric and yogic practices developed in Hinduism. Today, the two major schools of thought are Advaita Vedanta and Bhakti branches.

1. Bhakti sees the Self as God, most often a personified monotheistic conception of Vishnu, Shiva or Devi (the Mother Goddess). Unlike in Abrahamic traditions, this monotheism does not prevent a Hindu from worship of other aspects of God, beings or teachers, as they are all seen as rays from a single source. However, it is worthy of note that the Bhagavad Gita condemns worship of demigods, as it does not lead to Moksha. The concept is essentially of self-dissolution in love, since the ideal nature of being is seen as that of harmony, euphony, its manifest essence being love. By immersing oneself in the love of God, one's Karmas (good or bad, regardless) slough off, one's illusions about beings decay and 'truth' is soon known and lived.
2. Vedanta finds itself split three-fold, though the dualist and modified non-dualist schools are primarily associated with the foregoing thought of Bhakti. The most famous today is Advaita Vedanta, a non-dual (*i.e.* no separation between the individual and reality/God/ etc.) perspective which often played the role of Hindu foil to contemporary Buddhist philosophy. In general, it focused on intense meditation and moral realignment, its bedrock being the Upanishads, Brahma Sutras and the teachings of its putative founder, Adi Shankara. Through discernment of the real and the unreal, as a peeling of the layers of an onion, the *sadhak* (practitioner) would unravel the maya (illusion) of being

> and the cosmos to find nothing within, a nothingness which was paradoxically being, and transcendentally beyond both such inadequate descriptions. This was *Moksha*, this was atman and Brahman realized as the substance and void of existential duality.

Moksha in the sacred Hindu temple dance, as in the classical Indian dance too, is symbolized by Shiva raising his right leg, as if freeing himself from the gravitation of the material world.

One must achieve Moksha on his or her own. An Arhant or a Siddha may inspire, but does not intervene.

Components of Moksha: Within Moksha or Mukti, there lies the ultimate peace (Shanti), the ultimate knowledge (Videh), the ultimate enlightenment (kaivalya) and the ultimate paradise (Swarga.) One Moksha is beyond the conception of any being other than God but these are some of the known components of the stage of union.

Buddhism: In Buddhism, the concept of liberation, Nirvana, is slightly different from Jainism and Hinduism. It occurs when the self is *extinguished* from the cycle of rebirth. (In Hinduism too, the cycle of rebirth ends on liberation.)

Jainism: In Jainism, Moksha and Nirvana are the same. When a soul (atman) achieves Nirvana, it is released from the cycle of births and deaths, and achieves its pure self. It then becomes a Siddha (literally one who has accomplished his ultimate objective).

In Jainism, attaining Moksha requires annihilation of all karmas, good and bad; because if karma is left, it must bear fruit.

YOGA

Yoga is a family of ancient spiritual practices originating in India. It is one of the six schools of Hindu philosophy, in which it is often paired with Samkhya, and they are referred together as the Samkhya-Yoga school.

Today in India and across the World, Yoga is a vibrant living tradition and is seen as a means to both physical health and spiritual mastery. Karma Yoga (yoga of Action), Jnana Yoga (yoga of Knowledge), Bhakti Yoga (yoga of Devotion), and Raja Yoga (yoga of Meditation) are considered the four main paths of Yoga.

Outside India, Yoga has become primarily associated with the practice of asanas (postures) of Hatha Yoga, a system of Yoga that developed from-and in order to prepare students for the practice of-Raja Yoga.

Yoga as a means of spiritual attainment is central to Hinduism (including Vedanta schools), Buddhism, and Jainism, and has influenced other religious and spiritual practices throughout the world. Hindu texts establishing the basis for yoga include the Upanishads, the Bhagavad Gita, the Yoga Sutras of Patanjali, the Hatha Yoga Pradipika and many others.

ROOTS OF YOGA

Origins: The earliest written accounts of yoga appear in the Rig Veda, which began to be codified between 1500 and 1200 BC. Some historians believe that this 5000-year-old sculpture is of a yogi.

The word "yoga" derives from the Sanskrit root *yuj* ("to yoke"); which is cognate to modern English "yoke", "jugal" and "jugum" in Latin. All derive from the Proto-Indo-European root yeug-meaning "to join" or "unite". It is generally translated as "union of the individual atma (loosely translated to mean soul) with Paramatma, the universal soul." This may be understood as union with the Divine by integration of body, mind, and spirit. A committed practitioner of yoga is referred to as a yogi or yogin (masculine), or *yogini* (feminine). These designations are for serious practitioners, who have already made considerable progress along the path towards yoga.

Images of a meditating yogi from the Indus Valley Civilization are thought to be 6 to 7 thousand years old. The earliest written accounts of yoga appear in the Rig Veda, which began to be codified between 1500 BC and 1200 BC but had been orally transmitted for at least a millennium prior to this. The first quasi-rational, full description of the principles and goals of yoga is to be found in the Upanisads, thought to have been composed between 800 and 300 BC. The Upanisads are also called Vedanta since they constitute the end or conclusion of the Vedas (the traditional body of spiritual wisdom). In the Upanisads, the older practice of offering sacrifices and ceremonies to appease external gods gives way instead to a new understanding that man can, by means of an inner sacrifice, become one with the Supreme Being (referred to as Brahman or Mahtman)—through moral culture, restraint and training of the mind.

BHAGAVAD GITA

The Bhagavad Gita ('Song of the Lord') is thought to have been written some time between 400 and 100 BC. Technically it is not an individual work-it is a section of the epic Mahabharata-but it is frequently published and discussed as if it were. To this day, it remains the single most influential and popular work of Hindu philosophy ever written, and it is also the first work devoted explicitly and wholly to yoga. Its narrative concerns a moral dilemma faced by Prince Arjuna, who is advised by Lord Krishna as to the best course of action regarding how he should regain his lost kingdom.

The first and foremost lesson of the Bhagavad Gita is regarding the importance of action-that we have a moral imperative to act, and that by implication non-action is an immoral choice when faced with a dilemma. But this action should always be conducted without selfish motivation. Thus the principle of Karma Yoga, of selfless action. It distinguishes several types of yoga according to what is most appropriate for the different nature of people, such that a devoted person will be most suited to the duty of Bhakti yoga, an intellectual person to Jnana yoga and so on.

The Bhagavad Gita talks of four branches of yoga:

(1) Karma yoga (sometimes called Kriya yoga), the yoga of action in the world

"With the body, with the mind, with the intellect, even merely with the senses, the yogins perform action toward self-purification, having abandoned attachment. He who is disciplined in yoga, having abandoned the fruit of action, attains steady peace..."
(Ch5:V11-12)

(2) Jnana yoga, the yoga of knowledge and intellectual endeavour

"When he perceives the various states of being as resting in the One, and from That alone spreading out, then he attains Brahman. They who know, through the eye of knowledge, the distinction between the field and the knower of the field, as well as the liberation of beings from material nature, go to the Supreme."
(Ch15:V31/35)

(3) Bhakti yoga, the yoga of devotion to a deity

".... those who, renouncing all actions in Me, and regarding Me as the Supreme, worship me... of those whose thoughts have entered into Me, I am soon the deliverer from the ocean of death and transmigration, Arjuna. Keep your mind on Me alone, your intellect on Me. Thus you shall dwell in me hereafter." (Ch12:V6-8) " And he who serves me with the yoga of unswerving devotion, transcending these qualities [binary opposites, like good and evil, pain and pleasure] is ready for absorption in Brahman."
(Ch14:V26)

(4) Raja yoga, the yoga of meditation

" Establishing a firm seat for himself in a clean place... having directed his mind to a single object, with his thought and the activity of the senses controlled, he should practice yoga for the purpose of self-realization. Holding the body,

head and neck erect, motionless and steady, gazing at the tip of his own nose and not looking in any direction, with quieted mind, banishing fear, established in the brahmacharin vow of celibacy, controlling the mind, with thoughts fixed on Me, he should sit, concentrated, devoted to Me. Thus, continually disciplining himself, the yogin whose mind is subdued goes to nirvana, to supreme peace, to union with Me."
(Ch6:V11-15)

Yoga Sutras of Patanjali: The Yoga Sutras of Patanjali are a book of 196 aphorisms compiled by the sage Patanjali sometime between 100 BC and 200 AD. Patanjali in the Yoga Sutras presents the goal of yoga as 'the cessation of mental fluctuations' (cittavrtti nirodha).

In reference to the Bhagavad Gita classifications, Patanjali's yoga is a form of Raja yoga, as it seeks meditiation as the path towards the ultimate goal. Patanjali himself referred to it as "Ashtanga Yoga" ("Eight-Limbed Yoga"), from the eight steps he set out as the practical path towards attainment of enlightenment. This eight-limbed concept became an authoritative feature of Raja yoga from that point forward, and is a core characteristic of practically every Raja yoga variation (including Hatha yoga) taught today.

Patanjali's Eight Limbs of yoga practice are:

(1) *Yama* (The five "abstentions"): violence, lying, theft, (illicit) sex, and possessions

(2) *Niyama* (The five "observances"): purity, contentment, austerities, study, and surrender to god

(3) *Asana*: Literally means "seat", and in Patanjali's Sutras refers to seated positions used for meditation. Later, with the rise of Hatha yoga, asana came to refer to all the "postures"

(4) *Pranayama* ("Life Force Control"): Control of *prna*, life force, or vital energy

(5) *Pratyahara* ("Abstraction"): Reversal of the sense organs

(6) *Dharana* ("Concentration"): Fixing the attention on a single object

(7) *Dhyana* ("Meditation"): Intense contemplation of the true nature of reality

(8) *Samadhi* ("Liberation"): Super-conscious state of enlightenment

Hatha Yoga Pradipika: Hatha Yoga is a particular system of Yoga introduced by Yogi Swatmarama, a yogic sage of the 15th century in India, and compiler of the Hatha Yoga Pradipika. Hatha Yoga is a development of-but also differs substantially from-the Raja Yoga of Patanjali, in that it focuses on shatkarma, the purification of the physical as leading to the purification of the mind (*ha*) and prana, or vital energy (*tha*). In contrast, the Raja Yoga posited by Patanjali begins with a purification of the mind (*yamas*) and spirit (*niyamas*), then comes to the body via asana (body postures) and pranayama (breath). Hatha yoga contains substantial tantric influence, and marks the first point at which chakras and kundalini were introduced into the yogic canon. Compared to the seated asanas of Patanjali's Raja yoga which were seen largely as a means of preparing for meditation, it also marks the development of asanas as full body 'postures' in the modern sense.

Hatha Yoga in its many modern variations is the style that most people actually associate with the word "Yoga" today. Because its emphasis is on the body through asana and pranayama practice, many western students are satisfied with the physical health and vitality it develops and are not interested in the other six limbs of the complete Hatha yoga teaching, or with the even older Raja Yoga tradition it is based on.

Other Works: The sage Sri Nathamuni supposedly composed the *Yoga-Rahasya* in the 9th or 10th century CE, although no copies of this work are known to exist. Sri Tirumalai Krishnamacharya claimed to have received knowledge of this text in a vision. Krishnamacharya is also responsible for the only known translation of the *Yogayajnavalikya Samhita*, a dialogue between the great sage Yajnavalkya and his learned wife Maithreyi, to whom part of the Rig Veda is attributed. Like the *Gheranda Samhita* and the *Hatha Yoga Pradipika*, the Yogayajnavalikya Samhita is generally considered a tantric yoga work.

Yoga Philosophy: Yoga has been called a science or technology of liberation. This is because, unlike purely theoretical philosophies, yoga seeks to provide the student with a *practical path* (or indeed many possible paths) towards the common goal of liberation. As explained above, Yoga is a diverse tradition, which makes it quite difficult to provide a concise summary of the philosophy. One approach is to consider common elements that are found in all (or nearly all) branches of the tradition.

Within othodox Hindu philosophy there are six schools (astika) that recognise Vedic authority, of which Yoga is one. These schools are traditionally placed into three complimentary pairs-Yoga being paired with Samkhya, which is the oldest of the orthodox philosophical systems in Hinduism. The Samkhya school has deeply influenced the Hindu Yoga school of philosophy. Samkhya philosophy regards the universe as consisting of two eternal realities: Purusha and Prakrti; it is therefore a strongly dualist and enumerationist philosophy. The Purusha is the centre of consciousness, whereas the Prakriti is the source of all material existence. Sage Kapila is traditionally considered to be the founder of the Samkhya school, although no historical verification is possible. The definitive text of classical Samkhya is the extant Samkhya Karika, written by Ishvara Krishna, circa 200 CE.

Returning to the practical side, the first step for any potential student (*shishya* or *chela*) of yoga is to find a suitable teacher. Traditionally, this relationship would be with a guru-who is seen as an embodiment of the Divine-and would involve a relatively full-time committment to study, often involving manual service to the guru as a form of payment for instruction.

A guru may also found an ashram or order of monks. Many gurus write modern translations and elucidations of classical texts, explaining how their particular teachings should be followed. In practice, the modern western student is much more likely to attend a local yoga course and receive instruction from a teacher who are themselves practicing the style of a particular school founded by a guru. It is often a mark of accomplishment and authenticity if a yoga teacher can demonstrate their close link to a guru with a strong lineage.

In all branches of yoga, the ultimate goal is the attainment of *liberation* from worldly suffering and the cycle of birth and death (Samsara). Yoga entails mastery over the body, mind, and emotional self, and transcendence of desire. It is said to lead gradually to knowledge of the true nature of reality. The Yogi reaches the enlightened state (Moksha) where there is a cessation of thought and an experience of blissful union. This union may be of the individual soul (Atman) with the supreme Reality (Brahman), as in Vedanta philosophy; or with a specific god or goddess, as in theistic forms of Hinduism and some forms of Buddhism. Enlightenment may also be described as cessation of mental fluctuations (*citta-nirodha*) accompanied by extinction of the limited ego, and direct and lasting perception of the non-dual nature of the universe.

Common to most forms of yoga is the practice of concentration (*dharana*) and meditation (*dhyana*). *Dharana*, according to Patanjali's definition, is the "binding of consciousness to a single point." The awareness is concentrated on a fine point of sensation (such as that of the breath entering and leaving the nostrils). Sustained single-pointed concentration gradually leads to meditation (*dhyana*), in which the inner faculties are able to expand and merge with something vast. Meditators sometimes report feelings of peace, joy, and oneness.

The focus of *meditation* may differ from school to school, *e.g.* meditation on one of the chakras, such as the heart centre (anahata) or the 'third eye' (ajna); or meditation on a particular deity, such as Krishna; or on a quality like peace. Non-dualist schools such as Advaita Vedanta may stress meditation on the Supreme with no form or qualities (Nirguna Brahman). This resembles Buddhist meditation on the Void.

Yoga and Other Traditions: The goals of yoga are expressed differently in different traditions. In Hinduism, with its variegated viewpoints and sects, Self-Realization and God-Realization are used interchangeably, with the underlying belief that the true nature of self (truth, consciousness, and bliss), revealed through the practice of yoga, has the same nature as the universal self, which may or may not be identified with a 'creator God' depending on the philosophical standpoint of the practitioner. In Buddhism, which does not postulate a creator-type god, yoga may help people deepen their wisdom, compassion, and insight. In Western nations, where there is a strong emphasis on individualism, yoga practice may be an extension of the search for meaning in self, and integration of the different aspects of being.

For the average person still far from enlightenment, yoga can be a way of increasing one's spiritual awareness, or cultivating compassion and insight. While the history of yoga strongly connects it with Hinduism, proponents claim that yoga is not a religion itself, but contains practical steps which can be found in the esoteric spiritual practices of all religions, as well as those who do not consider themselves religious.

Yoga and Buddhism: It is quite likely that Buddha (Siddhartha Gautama), who is estimated to have lived 563 to 483 BC, actually studied what was known of yoga at that time as part of his extensive education in Hindu philosophy. It is also very likely, given the rapid growth of Buddhism after his death and before the Bhagavad Gita and Patanjali's Yoga Sutras were composed, that Buddhism had some influence on those works.

In either case, there is a considerable overlap between the Hindu yoga tradition and Buddhism. Of particular interest is a comparison of the Buddhist eight-fold path and the eight limbs of Patanjali's Yoga. Their moral precepts (the *sila* of

Buddhism, the *yama* and *niyama* of yoga) share the Hindu principle of nonviolence (*ahimsa*); their final steps point towards a common goal. Buddhist *Samma Vayama* (Effort) vs Yogic *Dharana* (Concentration), Buddhist *Samma Sati* (Mindfulness) vs Yogic *Dhyana* (Meditation) and Buddhist *Samma Samadhi* vs Yogic *Samadhi*. In relation to views of the Self, yoga's *asmita-samapatti* is designed to eradicate the wrong views on the Self much in the same way Buddha did it in *Anatta-lakkhana-sutta*.

Yoga is central to Tibetan Buddhism. In the Nyingma tradition, practicioners progress to increasingly profound levels of yoga, starting with Mah yoga, continuing to Anu yoga and ultimately undertaking the highest practice, Ati yoga. In the Sarma traditions, the Annutara yoga class is equivalent. Other tantra yoga practices include a system of 108 bodily postures practiced with breath and heart rhythm timing in movement exercises is known as Trul khor or union of moon and sun (channel) prajna energies, and the body postures of Tibetan ancient yogis are depicted on the walls of the Dalai Lama's summer temple of Lukhang.

Yoga and Tantra: Yoga is often mentioned in company with Tantra, and it is true that these traditions have influenced one another over time. They are both families of spiritual texts, practices, and lineages with origins in the Indian subcontinent and both have been popularized in the West.

Tantra has roots in the first millennium, and incorporates Shiva and Shakti worship. It focuses on the kundalini, a three and a half-coiled 'snake' of spiritual energy at the base of the spine that rises through chakras until union ('samadhi') between Shiva and Shakti is ultimately achieved. These concepts were formally introduced into yoga with the Hatha Yoga Pradipika, and because of the subsequent popularity of Hatha Yoga, many Hindu and western yoga teachers now accept these essentially tantric concepts within the yogic philosophy, and this is the most obvious major intersection between tantra and yoga today. The acceptance of tantric kundalini teachings into modern yoga was reinforced by the New Age movement which accompanied (and fed into) the rise of popularity of yoga in the West.

However, Tantra and Yoga have notable points of difference. Where body consciousness is seen as the root cause of bondage in Yoga, Tantra views the body as a means to understanding, rather than as an obstruction, which bears certain similarities with the Natya Yoga. As a result, in India particularly, one of the two branches of Tantra often carries quite negative connotations involving sexual misbehaviour and black magic, although it must be said most forms actually follow quite mainstream social mores and this is simply an expression of prejudice.

The actual method of Tantra is quite different to traditional Raja Yoga. It emphasises mantra (Sanskrit prayers, often to gods, that are repeated), yantra (complex symbols representing gods in various forms through intricate geometric figures), and rituals that range from simple murti (statue representations of deities) or image worship to meditation on a corpse.

Yogatherapy: It is not clear at this stage to what extent Yoga Therapy can be considered a unique practice, or where it is merely a mixture of traditional Ashtanga yoga with Ayurvedic medicine.

BHAGAVAD GITA

The *Bhagavad Gita* is an ancient Sanskrit text comprising of 700 verses from the Mahabharata (*Bhishma Parva* chapters 25 – 42). Krishna, as the speaker of the Bhagavad Gita is referred to within as Bhagavan (the divine one), and the verses themselves, using the range and style of Sanskrit meter (chandas) with similes and metaphors, are very poetic; hence the title, which translates to "the Song of the Divine One". The Bhagavad Gita is revered as sacred by the majority of Hindu traditions, and especially so by followers of Krishna. In general speech it is commonly referred to as *The Gita*.

The content of the text is a conversation between Krishna and Arjuna taking place on the battlefield of Kurukshetra just prior to the start of a climactic war. Responding to Arjuna's confusion and moral dilemma, Krishna explains to Arjuna his duties as a famous warrior and Prince and elaborates on number of different Yogic and Vedantic philosophies, with examples and analogies. This has led to the Gita often being described as a concise guide to Hindu philosophy. During the discourse, Krishna reveals his identity as the Supreme Being Himself (Bhagavan), blessing Arjuna with an awe-inspiring glimpse of His divine absolute form.

The Bhagavad Gita is also called *G+topanicad*, implying it to be an 'Upanishad'. While technically it is considered a *Sm[ti* text, it has singularly achieved a status comparable to that of *[ruti*, or *revealed knowledge*.

Background: The Bhagavad Gita describes the mind as turbulent and obstinate. 'The Chariot of the Body': The five horses represent the five senses (tongue, eyes, nose, ears and skin). The rein symbolises the mind, the driver is the intelligence, and the passenger is the spirit soul. The discourse on the Bhagavad Gita begins before the start of the climactic battle at Kurukshetra. It begins with the Pandava prince Arjuna, as he becomes filled with doubt on the battlefield. Realising that his enemies are his own relatives, beloved friends, and revered teachers, he turns to his charioteer and guide, Krishna (an avatar Vishnu), for advice.

Krishna counsels Arjuna, beginning with the tenet that the soul is both eternal and immortal. Any 'death' on the battlefield would involve only the shedding of the body, but the soul is permanent. Krishna goes on to expound on the yogic paths of devotion, action, meditation and knowledge. Fundamentally, the Bhagavad Gita proposes that true enlightenment comes from growing beyond identification with the ego, the 'False Self', and that one must identify with the Truth of the immortal Self, (the soul or Atman). Through detachment from the material sense of ego, the Yogi, or follower of a particular path of Yoga, is able to transcend his illusory mortality and attachment to the material world and enter the realm of the Supreme.

To demonstrate his divine nature, Krishna grants Arjuna the boon of cosmic vision (albeit temporary) and allows the prince to see his 'Universal Form'. He reveals that he is fundamentally both the ultimate essence of *Being* in the universe, and also its material body, called the Vishvarupa.

In the Bhagavad-Gita Krishna refers to the war taking place as 'Dharma Yuddha', meaning a righteous war for the purpose of justice. In Chapter 4, Krishna states that he incarnates in each age (yuga) to establish righteousness in the world.

Dating of the Text: Though it is not exactly clear when the Bhagavad Gita was composed, the majority of historians assume a date between 500 and 50 BCE. There is, however, considerable debate on the subject. Based on the differences in the poetic styles and supposed external influences such as Patanjali's *Yoga Sutra*, some scholars have suggested that the Bhagavad Gita was added to the *Mahabharata* at a later date.

Theories based on archaeoastronomical calculations from passages of the Mahabharata place the incidents upon which the Gita is based around 5561 BCE. The traditional date reflecting the beliefs of many devotional Hindus places the text in the 4th millennium BC.

The Scripture of Yoga: The Gita addresses the discord between the senses and the intuition of cosmic order. It speaks of the Yoga of equanimity, a detached outlook. The term Yoga covers a wide range of meanings, but in the context of the Bhagavad Gita, describes a unified outlook, serenity of mind, skill in action, and the ability to stay attuned to the glory of the Self (Atman), and the Supreme Being (Bhagavan). According to Krishna, the root of all suffering and discord is the agitation of the mind caused by selfish desire. The only way to douse the flame of desire is by simultaneously stilling the mind through self discipline and engaging oneself in a higher form of activity.

However, abstinence from action is regarded as being just as detrimental as extreme indulgence. According to the

Bhagavad Gita, the goal of life is to free the mind and intellect from their complexities, and to focus them on the glory of the Self, by dedicating one's actions to the divine. This goal can be achieved through the Yogas of meditation, action, devotion and knowledge. The Gita describes the best Yogi as one who constantly contemplates God.

Krishna summarizes the Yogas through eighteen chapters. There are four kinds of Yoga-Raja Yoga or *Psycho-Physical Meditation*, Bhakti Yoga or *Devotion*, Karma Yoga or *Selfless Action*, and Jnana Yoga or *Self Transcending Knowledge*.

While each path differs, their fundamental goal is the same-to realize Brahman (the *Divine Essence*) as being the ultimate truth upon which our material universe rests, that the body is temporal, and that the *Supreme Soul* (Paramatman) is infinite. Yoga's aim (Moksha) is to escape from the cycle of reincarnation through realization of the ultimate reality. There are three stages to self-realisation enunciated from the Bhagavad Gita:

1. *Brahman:* The impersonal universal energy
2. *Paramatma:* The Supreme Soul sitting in the heart of every living entity.
3. *Bhagavan:* God as a personality, with a transcendental form.

The below are quotations from Krishna concerning the four principal yogas of the Bhagavad Gita:

On the Goal of Yoga: " And whoever, at the time of death, quits his body, remembering Me (Krishna) alone, at once attains My (Krishna's-Transcendental) nature. Of this there is no doubt."

On Bhakti Yoga: Put simply, Bhakti Yoga is *Service in Love and Devotion to God* (Krishna in the context of the Bhagavad Gita).

"I consider the Yogi-devotee-who lovingly contemplates on Me with supreme faith, and whose mind is ever absorbed in Me-to be the best of all the Yogis". "After attaining Me, the great souls do not incur rebirth in this miserable transitory world, because they have attained the highest perfection." "... those who, renouncing all actions in Me, and regarding Me as the Supreme, worship Me... For those whose thoughts have entered into Me, I am soon the deliverer from the ocean of death and transmigration, Arjuna. Keep your mind on Me alone, your intellect on Me. Thus you shall dwell in Me hereafter." "And he who serves Me with the yoga of unswerving devotion, transcending these qualities [binary opposites, like good and evil, pain and pleasure] is ready for liberation in Brahman." "Fix your mind on Me, be devoted to Me, offer service to Me, bow down to Me, and you shall certainly reach Me. I promise you because you are My very dear friend." "Setting aside all meritorious deeds (Dharma), just surrender completely to My will (with firm faith and loving contemplation). I shall liberate you from all sins. Do not fear."

On Karma Yoga: Karma Yoga is essentially *Acting, or doing one's duties in life as per his / her* dharma, *or duty, without concern of results*-a sort of constant sacrifice of action to the Supreme. It is action done without thought of gain. In a more modern interpretation, it can be viewed as duty bound deeds done without letting the nature of the result affecting ones actions. It is said that the results can be of 3 types-as aimed for, opposite of what is aimed for, or a mixture of these. If one can perform his duties (as prescribed in the Vedas) without any anticipation of the result of his actions, he is bound to succeed. It includes, but is not limited to, dedication of one's chosen profession and its perfection to God. It is also visible in community and social service, since they are inherently done without thought of personal gain.

Krishna advocates 'Nishkam Karma Yoga' (the Yoga of Selfless Action) as the ideal path to realize the Truth. Allocated work done without expectations, motives, or thinking about its outcomes tends to purify one's mind and gradually makes an individual fit to see the value of reason and the benefits of renouncing the work itself. These concepts are vividly described in the following verses:

"To action alone hast thou a right and never at all to its fruits; let not the fruits of action be thy motive; neither let there be in thee any attachment to inaction."

"Fixed in yoga, do thy work, O Winner of wealth (Arjuna), abandoning attachment, with an even mind in success and failure, for evenness of mind is called yoga."

"With the body, with the mind, with the intellect, even merely with the senses, the Yogis perform action toward self-purification, having abandoned attachment. He who is disciplined in Yoga, having abandoned the fruit of action, attains steady peace..."

In order to achieve true liberation, it is important to control all mental desires and tendencies to enjoy and sense pleasures. The following verses illustrate this:

"When a man dwells in his mind on the object of sense, attachment to them is produced. From attachment springs desire and from desire comes anger."

"From anger arises bewilderment, from bewilderment loss of memory; and from loss of memory, the destruction of intelligence and from the destruction of intelligence he perishes."

On Jnana Yoga: Jnana Yoga is a process of learning to discriminate between what is real and what is not, what is eternal and what is not. Through a steady advancement in realization of the distinction between Real and the Unreal, the Eternal and the Temporal, one develops into a *Jnana Yogi*. This is essentially a path of knowledge and discrimination in regards to the difference between the immortal soul (atman) and the body.

In the second chapter, Krishna's counsel begins with a succinct exposition of Jnana Yoga. Krishna argues that there is no reason to lament for those who are about to be killed in battle, because never was there a time when they were not, nor will there be a time when they will cease to be. Krishna explains that the self (atman) of all these warriors is indestructible. Fire cannot burn it, water cannot wet it, and wind cannot dry it. It is this Self that passes from body to another body like a person taking worn out clothing and putting on new ones. Krishna's counsel is intended to alleviate the anxiety that Arjuna feels seeing a battle between two great armies about to commence. However, Arjuna is not an intellectual. He is a warrior, a man of action, for whom the path of action, Karma Yoga, is more appropriate.

> *"When a sensible man ceases to see different identities due to different material bodies and he sees how beings are expanded everywhere, he attains to the Brahman conception."*

> *"Those who see with eyes of knowledge the difference between the body and the knower of the body, and can also understand the process of liberation from bondage in material nature, attain to the supreme goal."*

On Raja Yoga: Raja Yoga is the stilling of the mind and body through meditating techniques, geared at realizing one's true nature. This practice was later described by Patanjali in his Yoga Sutras.

> *"To practice yoga, one should go to a secluded place and should lay kusa grass on the ground and then cover it with a deerskin and a soft cloth. The seat should be neither too high nor too low and should be situated in a sacred place. The yogi should then sit on it very firmly and practice yoga to purify the heart by controlling his mind, senses and activities and fixing the mind on one point. One should hold one's body, neck and head erect in a straight line and stare steadily at the tip of the nose. Thus, with an unagitated, subdued mind, devoid of fear, completely free from sex life, one should meditate upon Me within the heart and make Me the ultimate goal of life. Thus practicing constant control of the body, mind and activities, the mystic transcendentalist, his mind regulated, attains to the kingdom of God [or the abode of Krishna] by cessation of material existence."*

Note: Alternative versions of the above verse state that the top of the nose (between the eyebrows) should be meditated upon, rather than the tip.

Influence of the Bhagavad Gita: In many ways seemingly a heterogeneous text, the Gita reconciles many facets and schools of Hindu philosophy, including those of Brahmanical (*i.e.*, orthodox Vedic) origin and the parallel ascetic and Yogic traditions. It comprises primarily Vedic (as in the four Vedas, as opposed to the Upanishads/Vedanta), Upanishadic, Sankhya and Yogic philosophies. For its religious depth, quintessential Upanishadic and Yogic philosophy and beauty of verse, the Bhagavad Gita is one of the most compelling and important texts of the Hindu tradition. It is considered by many as one of the world's greatest religious and spiritual scriptures.

It had always been a creative text for Hindu priests and Yogis. Although it is not strictly part of the 'canon' of Vedic writings, almost all Hindu traditions draw upon the Gita as authoritative. Some claim that it may have been inserted into the Mahabharata at a later date, but this is only natural as it sounds more like an Upanishad (which are commentaries that followed the Vedas) in thought than a Purana (histories), of which tradition the Mahabharata is a part.

For the Vedantic schools of Hindu philosophy, it belongs to one of the three foundational texts (Sanskrit: Prasthana Trayi, literally three points of departure)(the other two being the Upanishads and Brahma Sutras). Every such school is required to have a commentary on the three. The oldest available commentary is from Adi Shankara but he mentions older commentators. He is followed by classical commentators like Anandagiri, Shridhara Swami, Madhuskdana Sarasvat+, Ramanuja, Madhvacharya, Nimbarka, Vallabha and Dnyaneshwar. While the traditional text commented upon by many scholars, including Adi Shankara and Ramanuja, consists of 700 verses, a recension of the text from Kashmir has an additional 15. The renowned philosopher Abhinavagupta (10-11th century CE) has written a commentary on this recension called Gitartha-Samgraha. Other ancient and medieval scholars (like Vedanta Desika in the Tatparya-Chandrika) seem to be aware of such additional verses but prefer not to comment on them.

Among the great sages and philosophers who have drawn inspiration from the Bhagavad Gita is Sri Chaitanya Mahaprabhu, who initiated public singing of the "Hare Krishna" mantra.

Mahatma Gandhi derived great moral strength from Bhagavad gita, which is evident in his words:

"The Geeta is the universal mother. I find a solace in the Bhagavadgeeta that I miss even in the Sermon on the Mount. When disappointment stares me in the face and all alone I see not one ray of light, I go back to the Bhagavad Gita. I find a verse here and a verse there, and I immediately begin to smile in the midst of overwhelming tragedies-and my life has been full of external tragedies-and if they have left no visible or indelible scar on me, I owe it all to the teaching of Bhagavad Gita."

Swami Vivekananda, the follower of Sri Ramakrishna, was known for his commentaries on the four Yogas-Bhakti, Jnana, Karma and Raja Yoga. He drew from his knowledge of the Gita to expound on these Yogas. Swami Sivananda advises the aspiring Yogi to read verses from the Bhagavad Gita every day. Paramahamsa Yogananda, writer of the famous "Autobiography of a Yogi", viewed the Bhagavad Gita as one of the world's most divine scriptures.

A minority of Hindus, belonging to some Saivite sects, reject the Gita's authority.

Upon witnessing the world's first atomic blast in 1945, J. Robert Oppenheimer, American physicist and director of the Manhattan Project, quoted "Now I am become Death, the destroyer of worlds" based on verse 32 from Chapter 11 of the Bhagavad Gita. In Stanley Kubrick's Vietnam War film Full Metal Jacket, the US Marine Animal Mother has "I am become Death" written on his helmet, possibly in reference to

Oppenheimer. Coincidentally, in Kubrick's next film, Eyes Wide Shut, a shloka from the Bhagavad Gita is used during an explicit sex scene, and was removed from the British version of the film as a result of protests from the Hindu community.

Translations: Numerous readings and adaptations of the Bhagavad Gita's 700 verses are published in many languages. Traditionally the commentators belong to spiritual traditions or schools (sampradaya) and Guru lineages (parampara), which claim to preserve teaching stemming directly from Krishna himself and thus to be most faithful to the original message.

It should be kept in mind that different translators and commentators have widely differing views on what multi-layered Sanskrit words and passages truly signify, and their best possible presentation in English depending on the sampradaya they are affiliated to. Especially in Western philology, interpretations of particular passages often do not agree with traditional views.

MAHABHARATA

The *Mahabharata* (Devanagari), is one of the two major Sanskrit epics of ancient India, the other being the *Rmyaga*. With more than 74,000 verses, plus long prose passages, or some 1.8 million words in total, it is one of the longest epic poems in the world. Taken together with the Harivamsa, the *Mahabharata* has a total length of more than 90,000 verses.

It is also of immense religious and philosophical importance in India, in particular for including the Bhagavad Gita, an important text of Hinduism.

The title may be translated as "Great India", or "the great tale of the Bharata Dynasty", according to the *Mahabharata*'s own testimony extended from a shorter version simply called *Bhrata* of 24,000 verses The epic is part of the Hindu *itihsas*, literally "that which happened", along with the *Ramayana* and the *Purgas*.

Traditionally, the *Mahabharata* is ascribed to Vyasa. Due to its immense length, its philological study has a long history of attempting to unravel its historical growth and composition layers. In its final form, it was completed by the first century, with its central core *Bharata* (consisting of 24,000 verses) dating back to the 6th century BCE, and some parts possibly dating back as far as the 8th century BCE. The events depicted in the *Mahabharata* are thought to have taken place around the 12th century BCE.

Influence: With its philosophical depth and sheer magnitude, a consummate embodiment of the ethos of not only India but of Hinduism and Vedic tradition, the *Mahabharata*'s scope and grandeur is best summarized by one quotation from the beginning of its first *parva* (section): "What is found here, may be found elsewhere. What is not found here, will not be found elsewhere." This quotation rightly sums up Mahabharata, within which one finds myriads of relationships, stories and events.

In its scope, the *Mahabharata* is more than simply a story of kings and princes, sages and wisemen, demons and gods; its author, Vyasa, says that one of its aims is elucidating the four goals of life: kama (pleasure), artha (wealth), dharma (duty) and Moksha (liberation). The story culminates in Moksha, believed by Hindus to be the ultimate goal of human beings. Karma and dharma play an integral role in the *Mahabharata*.

The *Mahabharata* includes large amounts of Hindu mythology, cosmological stories of the gods and goddesses, and philosophical parables aimed at students of Hindu philosophy. Among the principal works and stories that are a part of the *Mahabharata* are the following (often considered isolated as works in their own right):

- Bhagavad Gita (Krishna instructs and teaches Arjuna. Anusasanaparva.)
- Damayanti (or Nala and Damayanti, a love story. Aranyakaparva.)
- Krishnavatara (the story of Krishna, the *Krishna Lila*, which is woven through many chapters of the story)

- Rama (an abbreviated version of the Ramayana. Aranyakaparva.)
- Rishyasringa (also written as Rshyashrnga, the horned boy and rishi. Aranyakaparva.)
- Vishnu sahasranama (the most famous hymn to Vishnu, which describes His 1000 names; Anushasanaparva.)

Textual History and Organization: It is undisputed that the full length of the *Mahabharata* has accreted over a long period. The *Mahabharata* itself (1.1.61) distinguishes a core portion of 24,000 verses, the *Bharata* proper, as opposed to additional "secondary" material, while the Ashvalayana Grhyasutra (3.4.4) makes a similar distinction. According to the *Adi-parva* of the *Mahabharata* (shlokas 81, 101-102), the text was originally 8,800 verses when it was composed by Krishna Dwaipayana Vyasa and was known as the *Jaya* ("*Victory*"), which later became 24,000 verses in the *Bharata* recited by Vaisampayana, and finally over 90,000 verses in the *Mahabharata* recited by Ugrasravas.

Not unlike the field of Homeric studies, research on the *Mahabharata* has put an enormous effort into recognizing and dating various layers within the text. Oldenberg (1922) stipulated that the supposed original poem once carried an immense "tragic force", but dismissed the full text as a "horrible chaos".

The earliest known references to the *Mahabharata* and its core *Bharata* date back to the 6th-5th century BCE, in the Ashtadhyayi (sutra 6.2.38) of Pgini (c. 520-460 BCE), and in the *Ashvalayana Grhyasutra* (3.4.4), while various characters from the epic are also mentioned in earlier Vedic literature. This indicates that the core 24,000 verses, known as the *Bharata*, as well as an early version of the extended *Mahabharata*, were composed by the 6th-5th century BCE, with parts of *Jaya*'s original 8,800 verses possibly dating back as far as the 9th-8th century BC.

However, the earliest testimony of the existence of the full text of the *Mahabharata* is by the Greek Sophist Dion

Chrysostom (c. 40-105), who mentions that "the Indians possess an Iliad of 100,000 verses". The later copper-plate inscription of the Maharaja Sharvanatha (533-534) from Khoh (Satna District, Madhya Pradesh) also describes the *Mahabharata* as a "collection of 100,000 verses" (*shatasahasri samhita*). The redaction of this large body of text was carried out after formal principles, emphasizing the numbers 18 and 12.

The addition of the latest parts may be dated by the absence of the *Anushasana-parva* from *MS Spitzer*, the oldest surviving Sanskrit philosophical manuscript dated to the first century, that contains among other things a list of the books in the *Mahabharata*. From this evidence, it is likely that the redaction into 18 books took place in the first century. An alternative division into 20 parvas appears to have co-existed for some time. The division into 100 sub-parvas (mentioned in Mbh. 1.2.70) is older, and most parvas are named after one of their constituent sub-parvas. The Harivamsa consists of the final two of the 100 sub-parvas, and was considered an appendix (*khila*) to the *Mahabharata* proper by the redactors of the 18 parvas.

The Adi-parva is dedicated to the snake sacrifice (*sarpasattra*) of Jayamejaya, explaining its motivation, detailing why all snakes in existence were intended to be destroyed, and why in spite of this, there are still snakes in existence. This sarpasattra material was often considered an independent tale added to a version of the *Mahabharata* by "thematic attraction" (Minkowski 1991), and considered to have particularly close connection to Vedic (Brahmana literature), in particular the Panchavimsha Brahmana which describes the Sarpasattra as originally performed by snakes, among which are snakes named Dhrtarashtra and Janamejaya, two main characters of the *Mahabharata*'s sarpasattra, and Takshaka, the name of a snake also in the *Mahabharata*. The Shatapatha Brahmana gives an account of an Ashvamedha performed by Janamejaya Parikshita.

According to Mbh. 1.1.50, there were three versions of the epic, beginning with *Manu* (1.1.27), *Astika* (1.3, sub-parva 5) or *Vasu* (1.57), respectively. These versions probably correspond to the addition of one and then another 'frame' settings of dialogues. The *Vasu* version corresponds to the oldest, without frame settings, beginning with the account of the birth of Vyasa. The Astika version adds the Sarpasattra and Ashvamedha material from Brahmanical literature, and introduces the name *Mahabharata* and identifies Vyasa as the work's author. The redactors of these additions were probably Pancharatrin scholars who according to Oberlies (1998) likely retained control over the text until its final redaction. Mention of the Hunas in the *Bhishma-parva* however appears to imply that this parva may have been edited around the 4th century.

Historicity: The historicity of the Mahabharata war is unclear. The epic's setting certainly has a historical precedent in Vedic India, where the Kuru kingdom was the centre of political power in the late 2nd and early 1st millennia BCE.

Ancient Indian scholars have calculated chronologies for the *Mahabharata* war, the 5th century mathematician Aryabhatta arriving at an approximate date for the Kurukshetra battle of 3137 BCE. The Aihole inscription of Pulakesin II (7th century CE) dates the Kurukshetra War to 3102 BCE. Vriddha-Garga, Varahamihira and Kalhana dated the War to 653 years after 3102 BCE.

Contentious and disputable attempts to date the events of the *Mahabharata* with the help of archaeoastronomy have claimed dates in the 6th millennium BCE..

According to Varahamihira, Yudhisthira lived 2526 years before the beginning of the Saka era (Brhatsamhita 13.3).

According to the Puranas, there is a time gap of 1015 or 1500 years between Parikshit's birth during the *Mahabharata* war and the coronation of king Mahapadma Nanda (ca. 364-382 BCE). Between Mahapadma Nanda and the last Andhra king Pulomavi, the Puranas count 836 or 829 years. Vayu Purana has the Saptarsi in Magha when Yudhisthira lived, in Purvasadha when Nanda lived and in Satabhisaj at the end of

Andhra rule. This could correspond to a difference of 1000 (or more) years between Pariksit (seven generations after Pratipa) and Nanda, and 400 (or more) years between Nanda and the end of Andhra rule.

The Brhadaranyaka Upanisad has eight generations between Pariksit and Yaska. Pargiter remarked that the Great Bear (the rksas or the Saptarsi) "was situated equally with regard to the lunar constellation Pusya while Pratipa was king." The Puranas list a number of kings between the Mahabharata War and Mahapadma Nanda which indicates that 1451 or 1503 years could have passed between them. Pargiter has argued that there were 26 kings between Adhisimakrishna and Mahapadma Nanda.

Synopsis: The epic employs the story within a story structure popular in many Indian religious and secular works. It is recited to the King Janamejaya by Vaisampayana, a disciple of Vyasa.

The core story of the work is that of a dynastic struggle for the throne of Hastinapura, the kingdom ruled by the Kuru clan. The two collateral branches of the family that participate in the struggle are the Kauravas, the elder branch of the family, and the Pandavas, the younger branch.

The struggle culminates leading to the Great battle of Kurukshetra, and the Pandavas are ultimately victorious. The *Mahabharata* itself ends with the death of Krishna, and the subsequent end of his dynasty, and ascent of the Pandava brothers to Heaven. It also marks the beginning of the Hindu age of Kali (Kali Yuga), the fourth and final age of mankind, where the great values and noble ideas have crumbled, and man is speedily heading toward the complete dissolution of right action, morality and virtue. Some of the most noble and revered figures in the *Mahabharata* end up fighting on the side of the Kauravas, due to conflicts of their dharma, or duty. For example, Bhishma had vowed to always protect the king of Hastinapura, whoever he may be. Thus, he was required to fight on the side of evil knowing that his Pandavas would end up victorious only with his death.

Authorship: The epic is traditionally ascribed to Maha Rishi Veda Vyasa, who is one of the major dynastic characters within the epic. The first section of the *Mahabharata* states that it was Ganesha who, at the behest of Vyasa, fixed the text in manuscript form. Lord Ganesha is said to have agreed, but only on condition that Vyasa never pause in his recitation. Vyasa then put a counter-condition that Ganesha understand whatever he recited, before writing it down. In this way Vyasa could get some respite from continuously speaking by saying a verse which was difficult to understand. This situation also serves as a popular variation on the stories of how Ganesha's right tusk was broken (a traditional part of Ganesha imagery). This version attributes it to the fact that, in the rush of writing, the great elephant-headed divinity's pen failed, and he snapped off his tusk as a replacement in order that the transcription not be interrupted.

Bhishma: Janamejaya's ancestor Shantanu, the king of Hastinapura has a short-lived marriage with the goddess Ganga and has a heroic son, Devavrata (later to be called Bhishma). Devavrata, a young man already with a reputation as a fearsome warrior, is the heir apparent to the throne.

Many years later, when the king goes hunting, he spots Satyavati, the daughter of a fisherman, and wants to marry her. Eager to secure his daughter's and her children's future happiness, the fisherman refuses to consent to the marriage unless Shantanu promises to make the future son of Satyavati the king upon his death, instead of Devavrata. To solve the king's dilemma, Devavrata agrees to that. Finding that the fisherman, though convinced of Devavrata's commitment, is not sure about the prince's children honouring the promise, Devavrata makes a severe vow of lifelong celibacy to guarantee his father's promise. Hearing such a vow, unheard of amongst warriors, the heavens bestow Devavrata with the name Bhishma, 'the person of the terrible oath'.

When King Shantanu is on his deathbed, his concern for his children and the stability of the kingdom delays his death. To ease the king's pains Bhishma promises to stay alive until the kingdom is safe and secure. Again, an awesome promise as all kingdoms are under constant threat. This promise was to cost him dearly, giving him a long life with constant tribulations and battles. Later, though seriously wounded, Bhishma could not give up his soul until the final battle resulted in the rule of the righteous Pandavas.

The Pandavas: Unfortunately Satyavati's sons die young and her grandson Pandu ascends the throne as his elder brother Dhrtarashtra is blind. Pandu whilst out hunting deer, is however cursed by a sage (whom he accidentally kills while he is having sex with his wife, mistaking their moans of pleasure to be the sounds of a deer) that he can never engage in sexual act with any woman. He retires to the forest along with his two wives. Kunti, using a boon granted by another sage whom Kunti, tended and cared for with great dilligence to summon the gods Dharma, Vayu, and Indra, his elder queen Kunti gives birth to three sons Yudhishthira, Bhima, and Arjuna through their respective "fathers".

The sons of course inherit the primary character of their respective father. Kunti shares her boon with her "sister" queen Madri, who bears the twins Nakula and Sahadeva through the Ashwini twins. However Pandu and Madri cannot resist temptation, indulge in sex and die in the forest and Kunti returns to Hastinapura with her sons. The rivalry between the Pandavas and the Kauravas starts from childhood itself. Dhrtarashtra's sons, the Kauravas, led by the eldest Duryodhana, detest their cousins the Pandavas. However, they were the favourite of their teacher Drona and (the Pandavas) grow up to be exceptional. Each one of the Pandavas is said to have one exceptional strength or virtue-Yudhisthira is the most virtuous, Arjuna the bravest warrior, Bhima the strongest, Nakula the most handsome and Sahadeva wise and able to predict the future.

When the princes of Hastinapura come of age, a tournament is held to display their strength and skill. When Arjuna was hailed as a master of archery, a young man challenges him for a duel. He declares his name is Karna, and he is the son of a charioteer. When asked to prove that he is of royal birth, which is the criterion for joining the tournament, Duryodhana, spotting a potential ally, jumps over to his side and gives his kingdom of Anga. Karna is forever grateful for this act. Because of this, he becomes Duryodhana's closest friend and plays a crucial role in the war.

The House of Wax: Meanwhile Duryodhana plots to get rid of the Pandavas and tries to kill the Pandavas secretly by burning their palace which is made of lac. However, the Pandavas are warned by their uncle, Vidura who sends them a miner to dig a tunnel. Therefore, when Duryodhana's servants set the house on flames, they will be able to escape in safety. After escaping from the tragedy, the Pandavas arrive in a forest and rest. Bhima and Arjuna want to confront the Kauravas, but Kunti and Yudhisthira decide against it. Bheeshma goes to the river Ganga to perform the last rites of the Pandavas. Vidura then informs him that the Pandavas are alive and to keep the secret to himself.

City of Ekchakra: The Pandavas stay in the city of Ekchara in the guise of Brahmans. Kunti and Bhima then learn of a cruel and terrible rakshasa named Bakasura who has made a deal with the villagers that if he receives 1 villager a month to eat, he will not harm the villagers. Bhima sets out to eliminate this rakshasa. A great fight arises and Bhima with his might kills him. In order to avoid being caught by the villagers, the Pandavas leave the City of Ekchakra and move on.

Draupadi: In course of this exile the Pandavas are informed of a "competition" called a swayamvar taking place with the prize being the hand of the Panchal princess and the daughter of King Drupad, Draupadi. The Pandavas enter the competition in disguise as Brahmans, the task being to string a mighty steel bow and shoot with a steel arrow the eye of a rotating fish on the ceiling while concentrating on the reflection underneath. No king manages to come close to do so. They fail to even pick up the bow! Karna, the only one who picks up the bow, is about to try is halted by Draupadi by the excuse that he is the son of a charioteer and may not participate.

Arjuna becomes successful and manages to complete the task. When he returns with his bride, Arjuna goes to his mother to show her his prize, exclaiming, "Mother, I have brought you a present!". Kunti, not noticing the princess, tells Arjuna that whatever he has won must be shared with his brothers. To ensure that their mother never utters a falsehood even by mistake, the brothers take her as a common wife. All of the Pandavas love Draupadi dearly. In some interpretations, Draupadi alternates months or years with each brother. At this juncture they also meet Krishna who would become their lifelong ally and guide.

Indraprasth: Duryodhana and Shakuni are furious when they learn that the Pandava brothers are alive and that King Dhritrashtra has sent Vidur to call them back to Hastinapura. Karna, as usual, is ready to fight them, but Shakuni realizes that with King Drupad and Krishna on the side of the Pandavas it would be difficult to defeat them. Dhritrashtra consoles Duryodhana and assures him that his rights as the Heir Apparent to the throne of Hastinapura will be fully protected.

In Kampilya, King Drupad and Shri Krishna advise Yudhisthira to fight for his right to the throne of Hastinapura. Just then Vidur arrives and tells the Pandava brothers that they have been invited back to Hastinapura along with their bride. The Pandavas and Draupadi return to Hastinapura. Dhritrashtra conceals his disappointment and orders everyone to welcome them. Determined to establish peace between the Kauravas and the Pandavas, Bhishma suggests giving half the Kingdom to Yudhisthira.

Dhritrashtra agrees to this suggestion. Krishna and Balram, also give their consent and it is decided that Yudhisthira's coronation as King of Indraprasth be held in Hastinapura. This land given to them again becomes another unjustice to the Pandavas as it neither has any agricultural soil neither any buildings nor people. Krishna consolidates the Pandavas saying that Indraprasth is not a waste but instead a Land of Action. Taking the advice of Krishna, the Pandavas make Indraprasth a beautiful town where justice is always met and the inhabitants are happy.

The Rajsuya Yagna: Shortly after this, Arjuna and Subhadra (Krishna's sister) get married and return to Indraprastha to be welcomed by Draupadi. Here, Yudhisthira seeks Sri Krishna's advice on performing the Rajsuya Yagna which will make him the emperor of India. Krishna advises him that Jarasandha who has imprisoned 86 kings must be killed as he may interfere in the ceremony. Hence Yuddhisthira decides to send Krishna, Bhima and Arjuna to challenge Jarasandh for combat. Jarasandh chooses to fight with Bhima. Bhima and Jarasandh were so equally matched in strength that they fought for nearly fourteen days without rest. When Jarasandha finally showed signs of exhaustion, Krishna prompted Bhima to make an end of him. After Jarasandha had been destroyed, Jarasandha's son was crowned King of Magadha. The Rajsuya Yagna is celebrated and Yudhisthira is recognized as an Emperor.

The House of Illusion: Duryodhana is unhappy about the prosperity of the Pandavas, Shakuni consoles him and later loses in a game of dice to Yudhisthira. Duryodhana walks around Yudhisthira's 'Maya Mahal" ("The House of Illusion") and falls into one of the pools. Draupadi calls him the "blind son of a blind father." Duryodhana, Karna and Shakuni plan to avenge Draupadi for her taunting remarks.

Duryodhana's Game: Duryodhana, who now has a friend in the peerless warrior Karna becomes aware of Yudhisthira becoming the emperor. This proves too much for Duryodhana who feels death would be better than watching one's foes prosper. His maternal uncle Shakuni, convinced that however brave his nephew may be, he was no match for his cousins, decides to use a ruse to destroy the Pandavas. He forces Dhrtarashtra to invite the Pandavas for a game of dice in which he wins everything from Yudhisthira, including himself, his brothers and Draupadi through the use of a trick. The jubilant Kauravas insult them in their helpless state and even try to disrobe Draupadi in front of the entire court. Her honour is saved by the grace of Krishna. When the elders intervene and Dhrtarashtra has to restore everything to the Pandavas, Shakuni forces another game of dice which he again wins. The Pandavas are required to go into exile for 13 years, and on the 13th year they must remain hidden. If discovered by the Kauravas, they will be forced into exile for another 12 years.

The Years in Exile: The Pandavas having lost the game of dice go on exile for 12 years and a year of hiding. During the period of exile, they visit many religious places and are often visited by Krishna. Draupadi who has been insulted by Dushasana (Duryodhana's brother), takes a vow never to tie up her hair until she had blood from Dushasana's thigh to wash her hair with. This constantly reminds her husbands of how war was inevitable. Krishna advises Arjuna that since war was inevitable, he should enter heaven to seek the divine weapons held by Gods and that he who is favoured by Lord Indra would be able to do so.

Through the prayer of Lord Indra, Arjuna gains access to heaven from where he obtains the divine weapons and also learns how to use them. Finally, Lord Indra advises Arjuna to learn the art of dance as it would come to his aid in the 13th year of hiding. It is during this time that the Pandavas get to face a demon called Hidumba. Bhima kills him and marries his sister, Hidumbi. With her, he begets a son called Ghatothkacha.

The Battle at Kurukshetra: When the Pandavas return from their exile after many hardships, they request for a peace treaty with the Kauravas to gain Indraprastha back. However, Duryodhana disagrees and argues that since the Pandavas where "caught" in their year of hiding, they must go into another 13 years of exile before they can have Indraprastha. The Pandavas on Krishna's advice again ask for a peace treaty asking for at least five villages for the five brothers, from the Kauravas' vast kingdom. Duryodhana refuses to give in. Krishna intervenes to mediate peace but is unsuccessful. War becomes inevitable.

The two sides summon vast armies to their help and line up at Kurukshetra for a war. The Kingdoms of Dwaraka, Kasi, Kekaya, Magadha, Matsya, Chedi, Pandya and the Yadus of Mathura and some other clans like the Parama Kambojas from Transoxiana were allied with the Pandavas; the allies of the Kauravas comprised the kings of Pragjyotisha, Anga, Kekaya (Kekaya brothers who were enemies of the Kekeya brothers on the Pandava side), Sindhudesa (including Sindhus, Sauviras and Sivis), Mahishmati, Avanti in Madhyadesa, Madras, Gandharas, Bahlikas, Kambojas (with Yavanas, Sakas, Tusharas etc.) and many others. Prior to war being declared, Krishna's brother, Balarama, had left to go on pilgrimage, thus he does not take part in the battle itself.

Arjuna, seeing himself facing grandsire Bhishma and his teacher Drona on Duryodhana's side due to their vow to serve the state of Hastinapura is heartbroken and at the idea of killing them he fails to lift his Gandiva bow. Krishna who has chosen to drive Arjuna's chariot wakes him up to his call of duty in the famous Bhagavad Gita section of the epic. Though initially sticking to chivalrous notions of warfare, the Kauravas and Pandavas soon descended into dishonourable warfare. At the end of the 14 days slaughter only the Pandavas and Krishna survive with a few old warriors from the Kaurava side.

The end of the Pandavas: Beholding the carnage, the noble mother of the Kauravas, Gandhari who had lost all her sons, curses Krishna to be a witness to a similar annihilation of his family, for though divine and capable of stopping the war, he had not done so. Krishna who had incarnated precisely to destroy the wicked kings accepts the curse, which bears fruit

36 years later. He then departs from the world and the Pandavas who had ruled righteously all along, now tired, decide to renounce everything. Clad in skins and rags they retire to the Himalayas and ascend the peaks towards heaven in their bodily form. Legend reveals that a mangy, stray dog travels along with them. One by one the Pandavas and Draupadi fall on their way.

As each one stumbles, Yudhishtra gives the rest the reason for their fall (Draupadi was partial to Arjuna, Nakula and Sahadeva were vain and proud of their looks, Bhima and Arjuna were proud of their strength and archery skills, respectively). Only the virtuous Yudhisthra who had tried everything to prevent the carnage and the dog remain. The dog reveals himself to be the god Dharma, who reveals the nature of the test and assures Yudhishtra that his fallen siblings and wife are in heaven. Yudhistra alone transcends to heaven in his bodily form for being just and humble.

Arjuna's grandson Parikshita rules after them and dies bitten by a snake. His furious son, Janamejaya, decides to perform a snake sacrifice (sarpasattra) in order to destroy the snakes. It is at this sacrifice that the tale of his ancestors is narrated to him.

RAMAYANA

The *Rmyaga* is an ancient Sanskrit epic attributed to the poet Valmiki and is an important part of the Hindu canon (*smrti*). The name *Rmyaga* is a tatpurusha compound of *Rma* and *ayana* "going, advancing", translating to "the travels of *Rma*". The *Rmyaga* consists of 24,000 verses in seven cantos (*kgas*) and tells the story of a prince, Rama of Ayodhya, whose wife Sita is abducted by the demon (*Rkshasa*) king of Lanka, Rvana. In its current form, the Valmiki Ramayana is dated variously from 500 BC to 100 BC, or about co-eval to early versions of the *Mahabhrata*. As with most traditional epics, since it has gone through a long process of interpolations and redactions, it is impossible to date it accurately.

The Ramayana had an important influence on later Sanskrit poetry, primarily through its establishment of the Sloka meter. But, like its epic cousin Mahabharata, the Ramayana is not just an ordinary story. It contains the teachings of ancient Hindu sages and presents them through allegory in narrative and the interspersion of the philosophical and the devotional. The characters of Rama, Sita, Lakshmana, Bharata, Hanumn and Ravana (the villain of the piece) are all fundamental to the cultural consciousness of India.

One of the most important literary works on ancient India, the Ramayana has had a profound impact on art and culture in the Indian Subcontinent and Southeast Asia. The story of Rama also inspired a large amount of later-day literature in various languages, notable among which are the works of the sixteenth century Hindi poet Tulsidas and the Tamil poet Kambar of the 13th century.

The Ramayana is not just a Hindu religious tale. Starting from the 8th century, the colonisation of Southeast Asia by Indians began. Several large empires like the Khmers, the Majapahits, the Sailendras, the Champas and Sri Vijaya were established. Because of this, the Ramayana became popular in Southeast Asia and manifested itself in text, temple architecture and performance, particularly in Indonesia (Java, Sumatra, Bali and Borneo), Thailand, Cambodia, Laos, Malaysia, Myanmar, Philippines and Vietnam.

Structure of Valmiki Ramayana: Valmiki's *Ramayana*, the oldest version of Ramayana is the basis of all the various version of Ramayana that are prevalent in the various cultures. The text survives in numerous complete and partial manuscripts, the oldest surviving of which is dated from the eleventh century AD. The current text of Valmiki Ramayana has come down to us in two regional versions from the north and the south of India. Valmiki Ramayana has been traditionally divided into seven books, dealing with the life of Rama from his birth to his death.

1. *Bala Kanda* – Book of the young Rama which details the miraculous birth of Rama, his early life in Ayodhya, his slaying of the demons of the forest at the request of Vishvamitra and his wedding with Sita.
2. *Ayodhya Kanda* – Book of Ayodhya in which Dasharatha comes to grief over his promise to Kaikeyi and the start of Rama's exile.
3. *Aranya Kanda* – Book of the Forest which describes Rama's life in the forest and the abduction of Sita by Ravana.
4. *Kishkindya Kanda* – Book of Kishkinda, the Vanara kingdom in which Rama befriends Sugriva and the Vanara army and begins the search for Sita.
5. *Sundara Kanda* – Book of Sundara (Hanuman) in which Hanuman travels to Lanka and finds Sita imprisoned there and brings back the good news to Rama.
6. *Yuddha Kanda* – Book of the War, which narrates the Rama-Ravana war and the return of the successful Rama to Ayodhya and his coronation.
7. *Uttara Kanda* – Epilogue, which details the life of Rama and Sita after their return to Ayodhya, Sita's banishment and how Sita and Rama pass on to the next world.

There have been speculations on whether the first and the last chapters of Valmiki's *Ramayana* were indeed written by the original author. Many experts are of the opinion that they are integral part of the book in spite of the many differences in style and some contradictions in content between these two chapters and the rest of the book. These two chapters contain most of the mythological interpolations found in the Ramayana, such as the miraculous birth of Rama and his divine nature as well as the numerous legends surrounding Ravana.

'MAIN CHARACTERS'

- Rama is the hero of this epic tale. He is portrayed as an incarnation of the god Vishnu. He is the eldest and the favourite son of the King of Ayodhya, Dasharatha. He is a popular prince loved by one and all. He is the epitome of virtue. Dasharatha, forced by one of his wives Kaikeyi commands Rama to relinquish his right to the throne for fourteen years and go into exileand by his father. While in exile, Rama kills the demon king Ravana.

- Sita is the wife of Rama and the daughter of king Janaka. Sita is the epitome of womanly purity and virtue. She follows her husband into exile and there gets abducted by Ravana. She is imprisoned in the island of Lanka by Ravana. Rama rescues her by defeating the demon king Ravana.
- Hanuman is a vanara belonging to the kingdom of Kishkinda. He worships Rama and helps find Sita by going to the kingdom of Lanka crossing the great ocean.
- Lakshmana, the younger brother of Rama, chose to go into exile with him. He spends his time protecting Sita and Rama. He is deceived by Ravana and Maricha into believing that Rama was in trouble while Sita gets abducted.
- Ravana, a rakshasa, is the king of Lanka. He received a boon from Brahma that he will not be killed by either gods, demons or by spirits, after performing a severe penance for ten thousand years. He was also the most intelligent and erudite living being of his time. He has ten heads and twenty arms. After getting his reward from Brahma, Ravana begins to lay waste the earth and disturbs the deeds of good Brahmins. Rama is born a human to defeat him, thus overcoming the boon given by Brahma.
- Dasharatha is the king of Ayodhya and the father of Rama. He has three queens, Kousalya, Sumitra and Kaikeyi, and three other sons, Bharata, Lakshmana and Shatrughna. Kaikeyi, Dasharatha's favourite queen forces him to make his son Bharata heir apparent and

send Rama into exile. Dashatara dies heartbroken after Rama goes into exile.

- Bharata is the second son of Dasharata. When he learns that his mother Kaikeyi had forced Rama into exile and caused Dasharata to die broken hearted, he storms out of the palace and goes in search of Rama. When Rama refuses to break his exile to return to the capital to assume the throne, he requests and gets Rama's sandals and places them on the throne. Bharata then rules Ayodhya as a representative of Rama.
- Vishvamitra is the sage who takes Rama into the forest at the behest of defeating the demons destroying his Vedic sacrifices. On the way back he takes Rama into Mithila where Rama sees and falls in love with Sita.

Synopsis: Rama, the hero of *Ramayana*, is a popular deity worshipped by Hindus, the route of his wanderings being, each year, trodden by devout pilgrims. The poem is not a mere literary monument, it is a part of Hinduism, and is held in such reverence that the mere reading or hearing of it, or certain passages of it, is believed by the Hindus to free them from sin and grant every desire to the reader or hearer. According to Hindu tradition, Rama is an incarnation (Avatar), of the god Vishnu, who is part of the Hindu Trinity. The main purpose of this incarnation is to demonstrate the righteous path (dharma) for the life on earth.

Rama's Youth: Brahma, creator of the universe, could not revoke a boon he gave the demon king Ravana, as a reward for his severe penances, that he should not be slain by gods, demons, or spirits. Having been then rewarded, Ravana began with the help of his evil supporters, the *Rakshasas*, to lay waste the earth and to do violence to the good, especially the Brahmin priests, disturbing their sacrifices. All the gods, watching this devastation, went to Brahma to find a way to deliver themselves and the earth of this evil. Brahma went to Vishnu and conveyed the anguish of the gods and requested that Vishnu incarnate on earth as a human to destroy Ravana, as Ravana had not asked for protection against humans or beasts in his wishes to Brahma.

Meanwhile, the good king Dasharatha of Ayodhya, who had ruled over his kingdom of Kosala for a long time, was beginning to become anxious about his successor, for he had no sons to take over the kingdom after him. Taking advice from his ministers and priests Dasharatha organised a *Putrakameshti Yagna*, a sacrifice for progeny. Vishnu decided to be born as the eldest to Dasharatha and caused a divine being to emerge from the sacrificial fire. The divine being gave Dasharatha a golden vessel filled with nectar and asked him to give it to his queens. Dasharatha divided it amongst his three queens, Kausalya, Sumitra and Kaikeyi. In due course they became pregnant and gave birth to four sons: Queen Kausalya gives birth to the eldest son, Rama. Bharata is born to Queen Kaikeyi, and twins, Lakshmana and Shatrughna, are born to Queen Sumitra.

The boys grew up learning the scriptures and the art of bowmanship from the sage Vasishta. One day, the sage Vishvamitra visited the kingdom and asked King Dasharatha to send Rama to protect him from demons who had been disturbing his sacrifices. Although very reluctant, Dasharatha agreed to send Rama and Lakshmana with Vishvamitra. As the brothers fulfilled their duties, Vishvamitra was pleased with them and bestowed upon them various celestial weapons.

Towards the end of their stay with Vishvamitra, Rama chanced to pass near the kingdom of Mithila and heard that its king, Janaka, had offered his peerless daughter, Sita, in marriage to the man who could bend the mighty bow of god Shiva, which had been kept at Janaka's court. Rama at once determined to accomplish the feat, which had been tried in vain by so many suitors. When he presented himself at court Janaka was at once won by his youth and beauty. Five thousand men drew in the mighty bow, resting upon an eight-wheeled chariot. Rama, without any apparent effort, bent it until it broke and Janaka gladly gave him his beautiful daughter. After the splendid wedding ceremonies were over, the happy pair travelled back to Ayodhya.

Rama's Exile: King Dasharatha, began to feel weary of reigning, and decided to make Rama, his eldest son and heir-apparent, the co-regent (*Yuvaraja*). His happy people received the announcement of his intention with delight and the whole city was in the midst of the most splendid preparations for the ceremony. Dasharatha went to discuss the celebrations with his favourite wife Kaikeyi. However, Kaikeyi's jealousy was aroused by her evil maid Manthara, because the son of Kausalya and not her own son Bharata, at that time absent from the city, was to be made king. She fled to an ante-chamber where Dasharatha found her in tears..

To Dasharatha's concerned queries, Kaikeyi recalled that, ages ago, the old king had granted her two boons. She now demanded the fulfilment of these before she would consent to smile upon him. Dasharatha agreed and Kaikeyi revealed her demands. She required him, first, to appoint her son Bharata as co-regent and, second, to exile Rama for fourteen years to the terrible forest of Dandaka. Dasharatha was heart-broken, but had to abide by his promise. Rama, the obedient son, immediately agreed to relinquish his claim to the throne and started to leave for his exile. His faithful wife Sita and his loving brother Lakshmana also decided to go along with Rama. With Dasharatha lying grief-stricken, Rama left for the forest, followed by the lamenting people of Ayodhya. Soon after, king Dasharatha died, overcome by grief.

Sita's Abduction: Rama, Sita and Lakshmana left behind Ayodhya and its people, crossed the river Ganges and went into the forest. They found an idyllic place called Chitrakuta to establish their hermitage. No more beautiful place could be imagined. Flowers of every kind, delicious fruits, and on every side the most pleasing prospects, together with perfect love, is stated to have made their hermitage a paradise on earth. In the forest, Rama befriended the old vulture-king, Jatayu.

Meanwhile, Bharata returned to Ayodhya and, being also devoted to Rama, became furious with Kaikeyi for her role in exiling Rama and for the death of his father. Determined to bring back Rama, he headed for the forest. When he found Rama and pleaded with him to return and assume the throne, Rama politely refused, saying that he was duty-bound to see that his father's promise was fulfilled. Reluctantly Bharata agreed to return to the kingdom, requesting that Rama give to him his sandals. Back in Ayodhya, Baratha placed Rama's sandals on the throne of Ayodhya, and ruled as Rama's proxy from a village called Nandigrama near Ayodhya, awaiting his return. He also vowed to end his own life if Rama failed to return after fourteen years.

One day, the rakshasi Surpanakha, a sister of the demon king Ravana, chanced upon Rama's hermitage and saw the handsome Rama and became enamoured. Taking the form of a beautiful young girl, she tried to seduce Rama. Rama, ever faithful to his wife Sita, did not respond and asked her to approach Lakshmana. Lakshmana too refused, stating his duty towards his brother and his sister-in-law while in exile. An infuriated Surpanakha blamed Sita for the men scorning her charged at her in her original demonic form. However, Lakshmana saved Sita by severing Surpanakha's nose and ears. Surpanakha flew back to Ravana complaining about the young exiles.

Ravana, after hearing of the beautiful Sita from Surpanakha, resolved to kill Rama in revenge and take Sita for himself. He enlisted the aid of the demon Maricha. Maricha turned himself into a golden deer that Sita wanted for herself. She asked Rama to get it for her, but after Rama left to find it, Maricha began screaming to trick Lakshmana. Lakshmana, convinced Rama was in danger, resolved to go out and find his brother. Before leaving Sita alone in the hut, Lakshmana drew a circle in the dirt saying that Sita would be safe as long as she stayed in the circle. Ravana approached the hermitage in the guise of an old man and asked Sita to give him some food. Initially hesitant to step out of Lakshmana's circle, Sita finally stepped out to give the old man some food. At this moment Ravana grabbed Sita and fled in his airborne vehicle, (Pushpaka Vimana). Jatayu, seeing them fly, attempted to save Sita, but Ravana engaged Jatayu in combat and chopped off the vulture's wings. On returning to the hermitage, Rama and Lakshmana found it empty and anxiously began a search. Through Jatayu, whom they found lying mortally wounded, Rama and Lakshmana learnt of Sita's fate.

Vanara Kingdom: Continuing their search, they encountered the vanara king of Kishkindha, Sugriva, and Hanuman, one of his generals, among whom Sita had dropped from the chariot her scarf and some ornaments. Sugriva had been deposed from his kingdom by his brother, Vali, who had also taken his wife Roma from him. Rama agreed to defeat Vali if Sugriva would assist in the search for Sita. The agreement made, Sugriva challenged Vali to a duel. While the duel was progressing, Rama shot from his bow and killed Vali. Sugriva regained his kingdom and his wife.

Sugriva and Rama sent the vanara soldiers in various directions in search of Sita. However, their efforts didn't bear fruit until they met another ancient vulture, Sampati, who was the brother of the slain Jatayu. Sampati was earthbound and deformed-his wings were burnt when he flew too close to the Sun (a story that can be considered to be similar to that of Icarus's). His brother, being hardier, had saved him from falling to his death. While Jatayu was the physically stronger of the two, Sampati possessed a compensating gift of vision. Sampati's vision was incredibly powerful, spanning several hundred yojanas and enabling him to see farther than anyone else. On hearing of Ravana's killing his brother, he readily agreed to help the vanaras. He was soon able to spot Sita in the southern direction. He could see her imprisoned in a garden of Ashoka trees on the island of Lanka, beyond the southern ocean.

Hanuman in Lanka: Sugriva dispatched his army to the south with his nephew Angada at the head. Hanuman went with Angada as his general. When they reached deep south, they found a great ocean stretching between them and land of Lanka. They could find no means by which to cross the ocean. Commanding his soldiers to remain where they were, Hanuman expanded his body to enormous proportions, leaped the vast expanse of water, and alighted upon a mountain *Trikuta* from which he could look down upon Lanka. Perceiving the city to be closely guarded, he assumed the form of a cat, and thus, unsuspected, crept through the barriers and examined the city.

He found Ravana in his apartments, surrounded by beautiful women, but Sita was not among them. Continuing his search, he at last discovered her, her beauty dimmed by grief, seated under a tree in a beautiful asoka grove, guarded by hideous rakshasas with the faces of buffaloes, dogs, and swine. Assuming the form of a tiny monkey, Hanuman crept down the tree, and giving her the ring of Rama, took one from her. He offered to carry her away with him, but Sita declared that Rama must himself come to her rescue, and as proof of finding her Sita gave Hanuman a priceless jewel to take back to Rama. While they were talking together, Ravana appeared, and, after fruitless wooing, announced that if Sita did not yield herself to him in two months he would have her guards "mince her limbs with steel" for his morning repast.

In his rage, Hanuman destroyed a mango grove and was captured by the rakshasa guards, and brought before Ravana. Hanuman proclaimed that he was a messenger of Rama, and demanded that Ravana restore Sita to Rama or fall victim to Rama's wrath. Furious at hearing Hanuman's words, Ravana ordered Hanuman's death.

Vibhishana, Ravana's righteous brother, intervened and counselled Ravana to follow the scriptures, reminding that it was improper to execute a messenger, and instead told him to exact the appropriate punishment for Hanuman's crime. Ravana accepted and ordered his rakshasas to set fire to Hanuman's tail. As soon as this was done, Hanuman made himself very small, slipped from his bonds, and, jumping upon the roofs, spread a conflagration through the city of Lanka. He leaped back to the mainland, conveyed the news of Sita's captivity to Rama and Sugriva, and was soon engaged in active preparations for the campaign.

Battle of Lanka: Rama decided that as long as the ocean was not bridged, it was impossible for any one but Hanuman to cross it. Rama meditated for three days without food or water, but in vain. In his anger at being so ignored, Rama turned his weapons against the ocean, until from the terrified waves arose Varuna, the god of the ocean, who promised him that if Nila and Nala from his army built a bridge, the waves should support the materials as firmly as though it were built on land.

Terror reigned in Lanka at the news of the approach of Rama. Vibishana, Ravana's brother, deserted to Rama, because of the demon's rage when he advised him to make peace with Rama. Fiercely fought battles ensued, in which even the gods took part—Vishnu and Indra taking sides with Rama, and the evil spirits fighting with Ravana.

After the war had been fought for some time, with varying results, and a great number of troops on both sides were killed, it was decided to determine the victor by single combat between Ravana and Rama. Even the gods were terrified at the fierceness of the conflict. At each shot Rama's mighty bow cut off a head of Ravana, which at once grew back, and the hero was in despair until Vibhishana told him to aim at Ravana's belly-button. Rama took careful aim.

As Ravana fell by this weapon, flowers rained from heaven upon the happy victor, and his ears were ravished with celestial music. Touched by the grief of Ravana's widow, Mandodari, Rama ordered a splendid funeral for his foe, and then sought the conquered city.

Sita was led forth, beaming with happiness at finding herself re-united to her husband; but her happiness was destined to be of short duration. Rama received her with coldness and with downcast eyes, saying that she could no longer be his wife, after having dwelt in the house of Ravana. Sita assured him of her innocence; but on his continuing to revile her, she ordered her funeral pyre to be built, since she would rather die by fire than live despised by Rama. The sympathy of all the bystanders was with Sita, but Rama saw her enter the flames without a tremor. Soon Agni, the god of fire, appeared, bearing the uninjured Sita in his arms. Her innocence thus publicly proved by the trial by fire, she was welcomed by Rama, whose treatment she tenderly forgave.

The conquest won, Ravana defeated, and Sita restored, Rama returned in triumph to Ayodhya, and assumed the governance to the great delight of Bharata and the people of Ayodhya.

Sita Banished: Ayodhya was prosperous, the people were happy, and for a time all went well. It was not long, however, before whispers concerning Sita's long stay in Lanka spread through the city, and Rama came to hear the whisperings that a famine in the country was due to the guilt of Sita, who had suffered the caresses of Ravana while in captivity. Under the pressure from the citizens of Ayodhya, Rama banished her to the forest in which they had spent together the happy years of their exile.

Without a murmur the unhappy Sita dragged herself to the forest, and, torn with grief of body and spirit, found the hermitage of Valmiki, where she gave birth to twin sons, Lava and Kush. Here she reared them, with the assistance of the hermit, who was their teacher, and under whose care they grew to manhood, handsome and strong.

It chanced that about the time the youths were twenty years old, Rama began to think the gods were angered with him because he had killed Ravana, who was the son of a Brahman. Rama became determined to propitiate them by means of Ashvamedha, the great sacrifice, in which he caused a horse to be turned loose in the forest. When his men went to retake it, at the end of the year, they found it caught by two strong and beautiful youths who resisted all efforts to capture them. When his men couldn't retake the horse, Rama went to the forest in person, only to learn that the youths were his twin sons, Lava and Kush. Struck with remorse, Rama recalled the sufferings of his wife Sita, and on learning that she was at the hermitage of Valmiki, requested her to come with him.

Sita had time to recover from the love of her youth, and the prospect of life with Rama, she felt, was not altogether pleasant. She appealed to the earth, if she had never loved any man but Rama, if her truth and purity were known to the earth, let it open its bosom and take her to it. While the people stood trembling with horror, the earth opened, a gorgeous throne appeared, and the goddess of earth, seated upon it, took Sita beside her and conveyed her to the realms of eternal happiness, leaving the too late repentant people to wear out the remaining years in penitence.

Morals in Ramayana: In his *Ramayana,* Valmiki expresses his view of human code of conduct through Rama: life is evanescent and the hedonistic approach to it is meaningless. However, that should not allow one to be indifferent to one's own rights and duties laid down in the ancient texts. He thus adopts the view that Dharma is what is proclaimed in the Veda and it should be followed for its own sake, not for what it brings you in pain or pleasure. Doing this will ensure one's welfare in this and the next world. In addition, Ramayana also reinforces the need for thinking about the consequences before making promises, for if you make them you must keep them, no matter how hard it may be.

Sankshepa Ramayana, the brief narration of the entire Ramayana story by the sage Narada to Valmiki, forms the first *sarga* of Valmiki Ramayana. Narada lists the sixteen qualities of the ideal man and says that Rama was the complete man possessing all sixteen of these qualities. Although Rama himself declares "he is but a man, and never once claims to be divine, Rama is regarded by Hindus as one of the most important Avatar of the god Vishnu and as an ideal man.

Valmiki portrays Rama not as a supernatural being, but as a human with all the attendant shortcomings, who encounters moral dilemmas but who overcomes these by simply adhering to the *dharma*—the righteous way. There are several instances narrated in Valmiki Ramayana which cast shadows on the pristine character of the hero and reinforce the theme of Ram struggling with mortal flaws and prejudices whilst struggling to follow the path of dharma. When Rama killed Vali to aid Sugriva regain his throne, it was not in fair combat, but while hiding behind a tree. When Sita was freed from Ravana's prison, Rama forced Sita to undergo an ordeal by fire to prove her purity and later as the king, Rama killed the Shudra Shambuka for performing a yogic penance not in keeping with his perceived low station in the society, though this latter incident is contested and may have crept in because of reinterpretation later on.

Concept of Dharma-Artha-Kama as per Ramayana: The concepts of Dharma, Artha, Kama (and Moksha) are very old Hindu concepts. They are also known as Purusharthas. There are two prominent instances of it being defined in *Ramayana*. The first was when Bharat came to forest (Chitrakoot) to meet Rama. Rama asked him whether he followed the rules of Dharma, Artha and Kaama properly. As per Rama it is defined as: Artha should not interfere with Dharma and vice versa. Similarly Kaama should not interfere with either Dharma or with Artha. Since Bharat was already knowledgeable he was to be reminded in very short words.

But Dharma here means the duties and welfare one does for the society. Making wells, for example, is part of the dharma of a king. Arth means earnings. As it is further asked by Rama: The king has to see that there is enough income from taxes, the salaries of the employees are given at proper time and the tax should not be more than 1/6th (16.6%) of a person's income. Kaama means pleasure here. One is allowed to have pleasure but without affecting the duties and earnings.

The other instance of this concept comes in Yudha Kanda. Here Kumbhakarna, Ravana's brother, advises Ravana that one should use dharma in the morning, artha in the daytime and Kaama at night. He further says to Ravana that he (Ravana) is busy with Kaama all the time and this will take him to destruction. Interestingly one of Ravana's ministers Mahodara scolds Kubhakarna and to please his master says that a King can enjoy Kaama at any time.

Textual History: Traditionally the epic belongs to the Treta Yuga, one of the four eons of Hindu chronology and is attributed to Valmiki, is an active participant in the story.

It is composed in Epic Sanskrit, an early variant of Classical Sanskrit, so that in principle the core of the work may date to as early as the 5th century BCE. Since in its current form, after hundreds of years of transmission through recitations and in manuscript form, the epic has gone thorough numerous variations, it cannot be dated by linguistic analysis as a whole, and should be considered to have emerged over a long process, spanning from the 5th to 1st centuries BC.

The core events told in the epic may well be of even greater age, the names of the characters, Rama, Sita, Dasharata, Janaka, Vasishta and Vishvamitra are all known in the Vedic literature such as the Brahmanas which are older than the Valmiki Ramayana. However, nowhere in the surviving Vedic poetry is a story similar to the Ramayana of Valmiki. Brahma, one of the main characters of *Ramayana*, and Vishnu, who according to *Bala Kanda* was incarnated as Rama are not Vedic deities, and come first into prominence with the epics themselves (and further during the 'Puranic' period of the later 1st millennium AD).

There is general consensus that books two to six form the oldest portion of the epic while the first book *Bala Kanda* and the last the *Uttara Kanda* are later additions. The author or authors of *Bala Kanda* and *Ayodhya Kanda* appear to be familiar with the eastern Gangetic basin region of northern India and the Kosala and Magadha region during the period of the sixteen janapadas as the geographical and geopolitical data is in keeping with what is known about the region. However, when the story moves to the *Aranya Kanda* and beyond, it seems to turn abruptly into fantasy with its demon-slaying hero and fantastic creatures. The geography of central and south India is increasingly vaguely described. The knowledge of the location of the island of Sri Lanka also lacks detail. Basing his assumption on these features, the historian H.D. Sankalia has proposed a date of the 4th century BC for the composition of the text. A. L. Basham, however, is of the opinion that Rama may have been a minor chief who lived in the 8th or the 7th century BC.

The events of the epic have also been dated to as early as 6000 BC by adherents of archaeoastronomy.

Variant Versions: The epic story of Ramayana was adopted by several cultures across Asia. Shown here is a Thai historic artwork depicting the battle which took place between Rama and Ravana.

As in many oral epics, multiple versions of the Ramayana survive. In particular, the Ramayana related in north India differs in important respects from that preserved in South India and the rest of South-East Asia. There is an extensive tradition of oral storytelling based on the Ramayana in Thailand, Cambodia, Malaysia, Laos, Vietnam, and Indonesia.

In many Malay versions, Lakshmana is given greater importance than Rama, whose character is considered somewhat weak.

Within India: There are diverse regional versions of the Ramayana written by various authors in India. Some of them differ significantly from each other. During the twelfth century AD, Kamban wrote *Ramavatharam*, known popularly as Kambaramayanam in Tamil. Although based on Valmiki Ramayana, Kambaramayanam is a true classic and unique in that Kamban has modified and reinterpreted many anecdotes in Valmiki Ramayana to suit the Tamil culture and his own ideas. Valmiki's Ramayana inspired the Sri Ramacharit Manas by Tulasidas in 1576, an epic Awadhi (a dialect of Hindi) version with a slant more grounded in a different realm of Hindu literature, that of Bhakti.

It is an acknowledged masterpiece of India. It is popularly known as *Tulsi-krita Ramayana*. Gujarati poet Premanand wrote a version of *Ramayana* in the 17th century. Other versions include, a Bengali version by Krittivas in the 14th century, in Oriya by Balarama Das in the 16th century, in Marathi by Sridhara in the 18th century, a Telugu version by Ranganatha in the 15th century, a Kannada Ramayana by the 16th century poet Narahari, Kotha Ramayana in Assamese by the 14th century poet Madhava Kandali and Adhyathma Ramayanam Kilippattu, a Malayalam version by Thunchaththu Ezhuthachan in the 16th century.

There is a sub-plot to Ramayana, prevalent in some parts of India relates to the adventures of Ahi Ravana and Mahi Ravana, the evil brother of Ravana, which enhances the role of Hanuman in the story. Hanuman rescues Rama and Lakshmana after they are kidnapped by the Ahi-mahi Ravana at the behest of Ravana and held prisoner in a subterranean cave, ready to be sacrificed to the goddess Kali.

There have been reports of a version of the Ramayana story prevalent amongst the Mappilas of Kerala. This version, known as *Mappila Ramayana*, forms a part of the Mappillapattu. *Mappillapattu* is a genre of folk singing popular amonst the musims of Kerala and Lakshadweep. Being of Muslim origin, the hero of this story is a sultan. There are no major changes in the names of characters except for that of Rama's which is changed to 'Laman'. The language and the imagery projected in the Mappilapattu are in accordance with the social fabric of the earlier Muslim community.

Southeast Asian Versions: Many other Asian cultures have adapted the Ramayana, resulting in other national epics. Aspects of the Chinese epic Journey to the West were inspired by the Ramayana, particularly the character Sun Wukong, who is believed to have been based on Hanuman. Kakawin Rmayaga is an old Javanese rendering of the Sanskrit Ramayana from the ninth century Indonesia. It is a faithful rendering of the Hindu epic with very little variation. Phra Lak Phra Lam is a Lao language version, whose title comes from Lakshmana and Rama. The story of Lakshmana and Rama is told as the previous life of the Buddha. In Hikayat Seri Rama of Malaysia, Dasharatha is the great-grandson of the Prophet Adam. Ravana receives boons from Allah instead of Brahma.

Thailand's popular national epic Ramakien is derived from the Hindu epic. In *Ramakien*, Sita is the daughter of Ravana and Mandodari (*T'os'akanth* (=Dasakand) and *Mont'o*). Vibhisana (*P'ip'ek*), the astrologer brother of Ravana, predicts calamity from the horoscope of Sita. So Ravana has her thrown into the waters, who, later, is picked by Janaka (*Janok*). While the main story is identical to that of the *Ramayana*, many other aspects were transposed into a Thai context, such as the clothes, weapons, topography, and elements of nature, which are described as being Thai in style. It has an expanded role for Hanuman and he is portrayed as a lascivious character. Ramakien can be seen in an elaborate illustration at the Wat Phra Kaew temple in Bangkok.

Other Southeast Asian adaptations include Ramakavaca of Bali, Maradia Lawana of the Philippines, the Reamker of Cambodia and the Yama Zatdaw of Myanmar.

Contemporary Versions: Contemporary versions of the Ramayana include Sri Ramayana Darshanam by Dr. K. V. Puttappa (Kuvempu) in Kannada and Ramayana Kalpavrikshamu by Viswanatha Satyanarayana in Telugu, both of which have been awarded the Jnanpith Award. The modern Indian author Ashok Banker has so far written a series of six English language novels based on the Ramayana. In September 2006, the first issue of Ramayana 3392 A.D. was published by Virgin Comics, featuring the Ramayana as reinvisioned by author Deepak Chopra and filmmaker Shekhar Kapur.

Ramayana Landmarks: Amongst the ruins of the Vijayanagara empire near Hampi, is a cave known as Sugriva's Cave. The cave is marked by coloured markings. The place holds its similarity to the descriptions of 'kishkinda' in Sundarakanda. Rama is said to have met Hanuman here. The place is also home to the famous Hazararama temple (Temple of a thousand Ramas).

VEDAS

Vedas: The *Vedas* are the main scriptural texts of Hinduism, also known as the Sanatana Dharma, and are a large corpus of texts originating in Ancient India. The Vedas, regarded as *[ruti* ("that which is heard"), form part of an oral tradition in the form of an ancient teacher-disciple tradition. As per Hindu tradition the Vedas were 'revealed' to the Rishis referred to in the texts, not composed or written by them. Even though many historians have tried to affix dates to the Vedas there is as yet no common consensus as there is for the scriptures of other religions. The Vedas are arguably the oldest surviving scriptures in the world. The Vedanta and Mimamsa schools of Hindu philosophy assert that the Vedas are apaurusheya ("unauthored"), that is, they have neither human nor divine origin, and are eternal in nature. As per Hindu tradition, the sage Vedavyasa divided the Vedas into Rig-Veda, Yajur-Veda, Sama-Veda and Atharva-Veda at the beginning of the Kali Yuga.

Etymology: The word "veda" means "knowledge", and is derived from the root "vid", Sanskrit for "know", reconstructed as being derived from the Proto-Indo-European root "weid-", meaning "see" or "know". "Weid-" is also the source of the English word "wit", as well as "vision" through Latin. The Czech and Slovak words for "science" are "vda" resp. "veda", derived from western Slavic "vdet" resp. "vediee" for "know".

Overview: The Sanskrit word veda means "knowledge", more particularly "sacred book". In its widest sense the term designates not only the sacred texts, but also the voluminous theological and philosophical literature attached thereto, the Brahmanas, Aranyakas, Upanishads, and Sutras. But usually the term veda applies only to the four collections (Samhitas) of hymns and prayers composed for different ritualistic purposes: the Rig-Veda, Sama-Veda, Yajur-Veda, and Atharva-Veda. Of these only the first three were originally regarded as canonical; the fourth attained to this position after a long struggle. Though differences exist in the language of the four Vedas, still there is such agreement on cardinal points as against later Sanskrit that the term Vedic, which is in common use for the oldest form of the language of India, is amply justified.

The Rig-Veda: The Rig-Veda ("Veda of verses"; from ric, or before sonants rig, "laudatory stanza") is the oldest and most important of these collections. In its present form it contains 1028 hymns (including eleven supplementary ones in the eighth book), arranged in ten mandalas (cycles), or books, which vary in extent, only the first and tenth being approximately equal. The poems themselves are of different authorship and date from widely different periods.

The actual date of these ancient scriptures is a nebulous topic. Yet, the description of an extremely cold climate leads some to believe that the Vedas are close to 20,000 years old, but there are some modern scholars who think that the number is exaggerated and should be about 5000. No matter what the age, it is the belief by many these texts were and are the oldest in the world. They express philosophies, realities and truths about life. The texts themselves show that the collection is the result of the work of generations of poets, extending over many centuries. Books II to VII inclusive are each the work of a single poet, or rishi (seer), and his descendants; hence they are aptly called "family books". Book III is attributed to the family of Vishvamitra, IV to that of Vamadeva, V to that of Vasishtha. The hymns in books I and X are all composed by different families. The ninth consists exclusively of hymns addressed to Soma, the deified plant, the juice of which was used for the

Soma sacrifice. Books II to VII are the oldest, and book X the most recent, in point of origin.

Hymns to the same deity are usually grouped together. Thus, approximately 500 hymns are addressed to two gods alone: Indra, the god of lightning and storms, and Agni, the god of fire. The term god is actually false, the "gods" (devas) being only highly elevated prophets, angels, or phenomenons. The Vedas clearly state that there is only one God, the same as Jews, Muslims, Christians belief alike. One Vedic missionary is the Arya Samaj, its churches are located all over the world, especially in India, the USA, and can teach those who search the Vedas.

The element of nature-worship is a marked feature in most of the hymns, with are invocations of different deities. The value of the great collection as presenting the earliest record of the mythology of an Indo-European people is apparent. Several of the gods go back to the time of Indo-Iranian unity, *e.g.* Yama (the Avestan Yima), Soma (haoma), Mitra (the later Persian Mithra). Some of the divinities, especially the higher ones, still exhibit the attributes which enable us to trace their origin to the personification of natural phenomena. Thus Indra personified thunder, Agni fire, Varuna the sea, Surya the sun, Ushas the dawn, the Maruts the storm, and others were of a somewhat similar character. Indra was the favourite god of the Vedic Aryans; almost one fourth of all the hymns in the Rig-Veda are addressed to him and they are among the best in the collection.

Next to Indra stands Agni. Many hymns are in honour of Soma. Other gods invoked are the two Ashins, somewhat resembling the Diocsuri of ancient Greece, the terrible Rudra, Parjanya the rain-god, Vayu the wind-god, Surya the sun-god, Pushan the protector of roads and stray kine. Prayers are also addressed to groups of divinities like the Adityas and the Vishve Devas (all the gods). Only a few hymns sing the praise of Vishnu and of shiva in his earlier form as Rudra, though these two deities became later the chief gods of the Hindu pantheon. Goddesses play a small part, only Ushas, the goddess of dawn, has some twenty hymns in her honour; these poems are of exceptional literary merit.

The number of secular hymns are small, but many of them are of particular interest. They are of various content. In one (book X, 34) a gambler laments his ill luck at dice and deplores the evil passion that holds him in his grasp. In the same book (X, 18) there occurs a funeral hymn, from which important information may be gained concerning the funeral rites of the Vedic age. Evidently cremation was most in vogue, though burial was also resorted to. There are also some riddles and incantations or prayers exactly like those in the Atharva-Veda. Historical references are occasionally found in the so-called danastutis (praises of gifts), which in most cases are not independent poems, but laudatory stanzas appended to some ordinary hymn, and in which the poet gives thanks for generosity shown to him by some prince.

Some six or seven hymns deal with cosmogonic speculations. It is significant that some of the hymns, chiefly in book X, are cast in the form of a dialogue. Here we may possibly discern the beginnings of the Sanskrit drama. The poetry of the Rig-Veda is neither popular nor primitive, as it has been erroneously considered, but is the production of a refined sacerdotal class and the result of a long period of cultural development. It was intended primarily for use in connection with the Soma sacrifice, and to accompany a ritual, which, though not so complicated as at the time of the Brahmanas, was far from simple.

The Rig-Veda has come down to us in only one recension, that of the Shakala school. Originally there were several schools: The "Mahabhashya" (great commentary), about the second century B.C., knows of twenty-one, while some later writings know of two only. In these schools the transmission of the hymns was most carefully attended to; a most elaborate mnemonic system was devised to guard against any changes in the sacred text, which has thus come down to us practically without variants.

Editions of the Rig-Veda were published by Max Muller, "Rig-Veda-Samhita with the Commentary of Sayancharya" (6 vols., London, 1849-74; 2nd ed., 4 vols., 1890-95); "The Hymns of the Rig-Veda in the Samhita and Pada Texts" (2nd ed., 2 vols., London, 1877); Aufrecht, "Samhita Text", in Roman characters (2nd ed., Bonn, 1877); selections in Lanman's "Sanskrit Reader" (Boston, 1884); Bothlingk, "Sanskrit-Chrestomathie" (3rd ed., Leipzig, 1897); Windisch, "Zwolf Hymnen des Rig-Veda", with Sayana's commentary (Leipzig, 1883). Translations were made into: English verse by Griffith (2 vols., Benares, 1896-97); selections in prose by Max Muller in "Sacred Books of the East", XXXII (Oxford, 1891); continued by Oldenburg, ibidem, XLVI (1897); German verse by Grassmann (2 vols., Leipzig, 1876-77); German prose by Ludwig (6 vols., Prague, 1876-88). On the Rig-Veda in general see: Kaegi, "The Rig-Veda", tr. Arrowsmith (Boston, 1886); Odenberg, "Rig-Veda", books I-VI in "Göttinger Gesellschaft der Wissenschaften", new series, XI (Berlin, 1909).

***Righteousness (Dharma) in the Rugveda*:** The Vedic sages created the institution of sacrificial fires (yadnya) as the point of union of God and man, on the earth. Later that very institution became the central focus of the spread of Vedic culture (sanskruti). A sacrificial fire is the very core of social life and the formation of social organisations. According to the Vedic sages The Supreme God exists in the form of a sacrificial fire. Performing sacrificial fires was Their sole code of Righteousness. Somyag is a sacrifice which is accorded the central focus in the Rugveda. Som represents vision and fire symbolises light. It is because of the sun and the rain that all living beings survive. Food too is generated from them. This being the attitude of Vedic sages towards sacrificial fires They linked every important action of life to them.'

The Sama-Veda: The Sama-Veda ("Veda of chants") consists of 1549 stanzas, taken entirely (except 75) from the

Rig-Veda, chiefly from books VIII and IX. Its purpose was purely practical, to serve as a text-book for the udgatar or priest who attended the Soma sacrifice. The arrangement of the verses is determined solely by their relation to the rites attending this function. The hymns were to be sung according to certain fixed melodies; hence the name of the collection. Though only two recensions are known, the number of schools for the veda is known to have been very large. The Sama-Veda was edited: (with German tr.) by Benfey (Leipzig, 1848); by Satyavrata Samashrami in Bibl. Ind. (Calcutta, 1873); Engl. tr. by Griffith (Benares, 1893).

The Yajur-Veda: The Yajur-Veda ("Veda of sacrificial prayers") consists also largely of verses borrowed from the Rig-Veda. Its purpose was also practical, but, unlike the Sama-Veda, it was compiled to apply to the entire sacrificial rite, not merely the Soma offering. There are two recensions of this Veda known as the "Black" and "White" Yajur-Veda. The origin and meaning of these designations are not clear. The White Yajur-Veda contains only the verses and sayings necessary for the sacrifice, while explanations exist in a separate work; the Black incorporates explanations and directions in the work itself, often immediately following the verses. Of the black there are again four recensions, all showing the same arrangement, but differing in many other respects, notably in matters of phonology and accent. By the Hindus the Yajur-Veda was regarded as the most important of all the Vedas for the practice of the sacrificial rites. The four recensions of the Yajur-Veda have been separately edited: (1) "Vajasaneyi Samhita" by Weber (London and Berlin, 1852), tr. Griffith (Benares, 1899); (2) "Taittiriya S." by Weber in "Indische Studien", XI, XII (Berlin, 1871-72); (3) "Maitrayani S." by von Schroeder (Leipzig, 1881-86); (4) "Kathaka S." by von Schroeder (Leipzig, 1900-09).

The Artharvana-Veda: The Artharva-Veda ("Veda of the atharvans or fire priests") differs widely from the other Vedas in that it is not essentially religious in character and not connected with the ritual of the Soma sacrifice. It consists chiefly of a variety of spells and incantations, intended to curse as well as to bless. There are charms against enemies, demons, wizards, harmful animals like snakes, against sickness of man or beast, against the oppressors of Brahmans.

But there are also charms of a positive character to obtain benefits, to insure love, happy family-life, health and longevity, protection on journeys, even luck in gambling. Superstitions from primitive ages were evidently current among the masses. To some of the spells remarkably close parallels can be adduced from Germanic and Slavic antiquity. The Atharvana-Veda is preserved in two recensions, which, though differing in content and arrangement, are of equal extent, comprising 730 hymns and about 6000 stanzas, distributed in twenty books. Many of the verses are taken from the Rig-Veda without change; a considerable part of the sayings is in prose.

The books are of different age; the first thirteen are the oldest, the last two are late additions. Book XX, consisting entirely of hymns in praise of Indra, all taken from the Rig-Veda, was undoubtedly added to give the Atharvana's connection with the sacrificial ceremonial and thus to insure its recognition as a canonical book. But this recognition was attained only after a considerable lapse of time, and after the period of the Rig-Veda. In the "Mahabharata" the canonical character of the Atharvana is distinctly recognized, references to the four Vedas being frequent.

Though as a whole this collection must have come into existence later than the Rig-Veda, much of its material is fully as old and perhaps older. For the history of religion and civilization it is a document of priceless value. The Atharvana-Veda has been edited by Roth and Whitney (berlin, 1856); Engl. tr. in verse by Griffith (2 vols., Benares, 1897); prose by Bloomfield in "Sacred Books of the East", XLII; by Whitney, revised by Lanman (2 vols., Cambridge, Mass, 1905). Consult Bloomfield, "The Atharaveda" in "Grundriss der Indoarischen Philologie", II (Strasburg, 1899).

Organization: The Mantras are collected into anthologies called Samhitas. There are four Samhitas: the *Rk* (poetry), *Sman* (song), *Yajus* (prayer), and *Atharvan* (a kind of priest). They are commonly referred to as the Rig-Veda, Sama-Veda, Yajur-Veda, and Atharva-Veda respectively. Each Samhita is preserved in a number of versions or recensions (shakhas), the differences among them being minor, except in the case of the Yajur Veda, where two "White" (*shukla*) recensions contain the Mantras only, while four "Black" (*krishna*) recensions interspersed the Brahmana parts among the Mantras.

The Rig-Veda contains the oldest part of the corpus, and consists of 1028 hymns. The Sama-Veda is mostly a rearrangement of the Rig-Veda for musical rendering. The Yajur-Veda gives sacrificial prayers and the Atharva-Veda gives charms, incantations and magical formulae. In addition to these there are some stray secular material, such as legends.

The next category of texts are the Brahmanas. These are ritual texts that describe in detail the sacrifices in which the Mantras were to be used, as well as comment on the meaning of the sacrificial ritual. Each of the Brahmanas is associated with one of the Samhitas. The Brahmanas may either form separate texts, or in the case of the Black Yajur Veda, can be partly integrated into the text of the Samhita. The most important of the Brahmanas is the Shatapatha Brahmana of the White Yajur Veda.

The Aranyakas and Upanishads are theological and philosophical works. They are mystic or spiritual interpretations of the Vedas, and are considered their putative end and essence, and thus known as Vednta ("the end of the Vedas"). They often form part of the Brahmanas (*e.g.* the Brhadaranyaka Upanishad). They are the basis of the Vedanta school of Darsana.

Position and Compilation: Hindu tradition regards the Vedas as shruti: uncreated, eternal and being revealed to sages (rishis). The rishi Krishna Dwaipayana, better known as Veda Vyasa – "Vyasa" meaning "editor" or "compiler" – reputedly distributed this mass of hymns into the four books of the Vedas, each book being supervised by one of his disciples. Paila arranged the hymns of the *Rig Veda*. Those that were chanted during religious and social ceremonies were compiled by Vaishampayana under the title *Yajus mantra Samhita*. Jaimini is said to have collected hymns that were set to music and melody—"Saman". The fourth collection of hymns and chants known as the *Atharva Samhita* was collated by Sumanta.

Philosophies and sects that developed in the Indian subcontinent have taken differing positions on the Vedas. In Buddhism and Jainism, the authority of the Veda is repudiated, and both evolved into separate religions. The sects which did not explicitly reject the Vedas remained followers of the Sanatana Dharma, which is known in modern times as Hinduism.

Study: Elaborate methods for preserving the text (memorizing by heart instead of writing), subsidiary disciplines (Vedanga), exegetical literature, etc., were developed in the Vedic schools. Sayana, from the 14th century, is known for his elaborate commentaries on the Vedic texts. While much evidence suggests that everyone was equally allowed to study the Vedas and many Vedic "authors" were women, the later dharmashastras, from the Sutra age, dictate that women and Shudras were neither required nor allowed to study the Veda. These dharmashastras regard the study of the Vedas a religious duty of the three upper varnas (Brahmins, Kshatriyas and Vaishyas). In modern times, Vedic studies are crucial in the understanding of Indo-European linguistics, as well as ancient Indian history.

Many forms of Hinduism encourage the Vedic mantras to be interpreted as liberally and as philosophically as possible, unlike the texts of the three Abrahamic religions. In fact, over-literal interpretation of the mantras is actually discouraged, and even the three layers of commentaries (Brahmanas, Aranyakas, and Upanishads), which form an integral part of the [ruti literature, interpret the seemingly polytheistic, ritualistic, and highly complex Samhitas in a philosophical and metaphorical way to explain the "hidden" concepts of God (Ishwara), the Supreme Being (Brahman) and the soul or the self (Atman). Many Hindus believe that the very sound of the Vedic mantras is purifying for the environment and the human mind. Each may contain a thousand layers of meaning.

Cosmogony: The Vedic view of the world and cosmogony sees one true divine principle self-projecting as the divine word, *Vaak*, 'birthing' the cosmos that we know from 'Hiranyagarbha' or Golden Womb, a primordial sun figure that is equivalent to Surya. The varied gods like Vayu, Indra, Rudra (the Destroyer), Agni (Fire, the sacrifical medium) and the goddess Saraswati (the Divine Word, or Vaak) are just some examples of the myriad aspects of the one underlying nature of the universe.

The word Veda is often derived from 5 roots these days:

- Vid jnaane: To know
- Vid sattaayaam: To be, to endure
- Vid labhe: To obtain
- Vid vichaarane: To consider
- Vid chetanaakhyaananiveseshu: To feel, to tell, to dwell

To these roots is added the suffix 'ghaw' according to Ashtadhyayi 3.3.19, the celebrated text of Sanskrit grammar of Panini. Accordingly, the word Veda means 'the means by which, or in which all persons know, acquire mastery in, deliberate over the various lores or live or subsist upon them.'

Traditionally, the Vedic literature as such signifies a vast body of sacred and esoteric knowledge concerning eternal spiritual truths revealed to sages (Rishis) during intense meditation. They have been accorded the position of revealed scriptures and are revered in Hindu religious tradition. Over the millennia the Vedas have been handed over generation to generation by oral tradition and hence the name "shruti" or "that which is heard". According to tradition they are un-authored (apaurusheya) and eternal.

The Vedic literature is also called by several other names:

- *Nigama:* Traditional wisdom transmitted from generation to generation
- *Amnaaya:* The root texts or primordial texts of (Hindu) tradition
- *Trayi:* The Vedic texts comprising of Versified mantras, prose mantras, and melodies.

Dating: The Hindus fundamental belief is that the Vedas are sanatan-eternal-and apaurusheya-not composed by human entity. At the beginning of every cosmic cycle of brahma, Paramatma utters the divine words. Later, at various periods great rishis perceive these divine words and imparted this knowledge orally through generations. It is believed that this Vedic knowledge totally disappeared at the end of Brahmas cosmic cycle and reappeared again in Brahma's next cycle of creation. Later a part of vedic knowledge was written. Maha Rishi Veda Vyas simplified this one Veda by dividing it into four: Rig, Sam, Yajur, Atharva. In Bharatvarshas true tradition the vedas are eternal. In the light of these beliefs, the historical dating of these texts is a concept foreign to Hinduism and the province of secular (academic) philology.

Many historians regard the samhitas as one of the oldest oral traditions. The newest parts of the Vedas are estimated to date to around 500 C.E; the oldest text (RigVeda) may be assumed to have been completed orally by 1500 BCE after being composed over hundreds of years, but most Indologists agree that a long oral tradition possibly existed before it was written down by the second century B.C. Some parts of the Rig Veda as well as the other Vedas are written in Sanskrit.

Some writers have used astronomical references in the Rigveda to date it to as early as the 4th millennium BC. This astronomical evidence has often been claimed to support the Out of India theory in relation to origins of the Indo-European languages.

Upavedas: The Upavedas are derived from the Vedas and are specific applications of the teachings of the Vedas. The main Upavedas are:

1. Ayurveda-Indian healing system, it lays more stress on living with nature instead of fighting it, hence preventive instead of corrective medicine.
2. Dhanur Veda-Martial arts.

Ayurveda and Dhanurveda have points in common. They both work with Marma, or natural Pran(Life Energy) that flows in the body. Ayruveda heals the body, while Dhanurveda is used for defending the body. This concept is also known to Chinese as Acupuncture and related Chinese Martial Arts.

3. Stahapatya Veda-Architecture, sculpture and geomancy. Used especially for Temple design.
4. Gandharv Veda-Music, poetry and dance.

Some other fields like Jyotish (Indian Astrology), Tantra (based on the Puranas, which are in turn based on Vedas), Shiksha and Vyakara (Grammar and pronunciation) are also based on the Vedas.

VIEWS OF MODERN WRITERS

Sri Aurobindo: One of the best commentaries to the Vedas in the modern times is written by Sri Aurobindo. Rig Veda is considered by many to be a book written by barbaric culture worshipping violent Gods. Sri Aurobindo realised that this was due to the biased view of Westerners who had some preconceived views on Hindu culture.

Taking the cue from Swami Dayananda Saraswati, founder of the Arya Samaj, Sri Aurobindo decided to look for hidden meanings in the Vedas. He looked at the Rig Veda as a psychological book, inspiring the people to move towards God, but in a hidden language. So Indra is the God of Indriya, or the senses (sight, touch, hear, taste etc.). Vayu means air, but in esoteric terms means Prana, or the Life force. So when the Rig Vedas says "Call Indra and Vayu to drink Soma Rasa" they mean use the Mind senses and Prana to receive Divine Bliss (Soma means wine of Gods, but in several texts also means Divine Bliss, as in Right-handed Tantra).

Agni, or God of Fire, is the hidden Divine Spark in us, which we have to fan, so it grows and engulfs our whole body. So the sacrifice of the Vedas actually means sacrificing ones ego to the internal Agni, or Divine spark.

These essays by Sri Aurobindo originally appeared in the Arya, and have been published by Sri Aurobindo Ashram under the titles, *The Secret of the Veda,* and *Hymns to the Mystic Fire.*

VEDIC CHANT

The oral tradition of the Vedas (Zrauta) consists of several pathas, "recitations" or ways of chanting the Vedic mantras. Such a Vedic chant is often considered the oldest unbroken oral tradition in existence. The various pathas are designed to allow the complete and perfect memorization of the text and its pronunciation, including the Vedic pitch accent.

Pathas: Mainly the students are first taught the Samhita patha. Other pathas include "vakya", "pada", "krama", "jata", "mala", "sikha", "rekha", "dhvaja", "danda", "ratha", "ghana".

A *pathin* is a scholar who has mastered the patha. Thus, a *ghanapaathin* (or *ghanapaati* in Telugu) has learnt the chanting of the scripture up to the advanced stage called *ghana*. Ghanapathins chant the ghana by intoning a few words of a mantra in different ways, back and forth. The sonority natural to Vedic chanting is enhanced in ghana.

The padapatha consists of dividing the sentence (vakya) into individual pada or words. The kramapatha consists of pairing two words at a time. In Jatapatha, the words are braided together, so to speak, and recited back and forth. The Ghanapatha or the "Bell" mode of chanting is so called because the words are repeated back and forth in a bell shape. The samhita, vakya and krama pathas can be described as the natural or prakrutipathas. The remaining 8 modes of chanting are classified as Vikrutipathas as they involve reversing of the word order. The backward chanting of words does not alter the meanings in the Vedic (sanskrit) language.

The chief purpose of such methods is to ensure that even not even a syllable of a mantra is altered to the slightest extent, which has resulted in the most stable oral tradition of texts worldwide.

Divine Sound: The insistence on preserving pronunciation and accent as accurately as possible is related to the belief that the potency of the mantras lies in their sound when pronounced. The shakhas thus have the purpose of preserving knowledge of uttering divine sound originally heard by the rshis.

Portions of the Vedantic literature elucidate the use of sound as a spiritual tool. They assert that the entire cosmic creation began with sound: "By His utterance came the universe." (Brihad-aranyaka Upanishad 1.2.4). The Vedanta-sutras add that ultimate liberation comes from sound as well (anavrittih shabdat).

Primal sound is referred to as *Shabda Brahman*-"God as word". Closely related to this is the concept of *Nada* Brahman-"God as sound". *Nada*, a Sanskrit word meaning "sound, noise", is related to the term *nad+*, "river", figuratively denoting the stream of consciousness-a concept that goes back to the Rig Veda, the most ancient of the Vedas. Thus, the relationship between sound and consciousness has long been recorded in India's ancient literature. Vedic texts, in fact, describe sound as the pre-eminent means for attaining higher, spiritual consciousness.

Mantras, or sacred sounds, are used to pierce through sensual, mental and intellectual levels of existence (all lower strata of consciousness) for the purpose of purification and spiritual enlightenment.

Modern practitioners claim that the sounds of Sanskrit phonemes (aksharas) have been shown to affect the mind, intellect, and auditory nerves of those who chant and hear them, claiming that they affect the seven chakras of the spinal column, as well as the three pranic channels of the subtle body.

In Puranic Hinduism: The chanting of popular Hindu mantras like Om (found throughout the Vedas) or the Hare Krishna mantra (found in the Kalisantarana Upanisad) is also sometimes referred to as "Vedic chant" even if the chanting is not done according to a patha. The Gayatri Mantra is Rigvedic, but due to its popularity in Hinduism it is often chanted freely, and thus would also sometimes not strictly qualify.

The *Upanishads* also known as *Vednta* and *Zruti(ira)* are part of the Vedas and form the Hindu scriptures which primarily discuss philosophy, meditation and nature of God; they form the core spiritual thought of Vedantic Hinduism. The Upanishads are mystic or spiritual contemplations of the Vedas, their putative end and essence, and thus known as *Vednta* ("the end/culmination of the Vedas"). The Upanishads were composed over several centuries. The oldest, such as the Brhadaranyaka and Chandogya Upanishads, have been dated to around the eighth century BCE. The roots of many Indian religions are built upon the foundation of the Upanishads.

Etymology: The Sanskrit term *upanicad* derives from *upa-* (near), *ni-*(down) and *sad* (to sit), *i.e.* referring to the "sitting down near" a spiritual teacher (guru) in order to receive instruction in the Guru-shishya tradition or parampara. The teachers and students appear in a variety of settings (husband answering questions about immortality, a teenage boy being taught by Yama, etc.).

TRADITIONAL ETYMOLOGY

Upa + ni + cad (sad)

Upa = an *upasarga* (prefix) meaning *Sm+pyam*-Nearest, *i.e. tm* (Oneself); *ni* = an *upasarga* (prefix) meaning *Ni[caya*-definitely ascertained knowledge;*cad* = a *dhtu* (verbal root) which was originally *sad*. It becomes *cad* due to the affix *kvip*, which forms a noun in the sense of the verbal action. *Sad* has three meanings: (1) *Viaragam*-dissolves, disintegrates, destroys, (2) *Gati* or *Prpti*-go, lead, attain, know, (3) *Avasdana*-puts an end to.

Thus, *Upanicad* means: (1) Definitely ascertained knowledge of *tm* (Oneself) which dissolves, disintegrates, destroys ignorance. (2) Definitely ascertained knowledge of *tm* (Oneself) which leads one to *Brahman*; makes one gain, know *Brahman*. (3) Definitely ascertained knowledge of *tm* (Oneself) which puts an end to *sacsra* (a life of becoming, characterized by birth, death, suffering, etc.)

Definition of *Upanicad* based on the Introductory *Zagkarabhcyam* on *Kamha Upanicad* and *Bhadragyaka Upanicad*. The word *Upanicad* ultimately means Self-knowledge = *tmavidy*, Knowledge of *Brahman* = *Brahmavidy*. The *Mgkkya Upanicad Mahvkya* (verse 2) *Ayam tm Brahma* "This *tm* is *Brahman*," confirms the view of the *Upanicad*, that in truth, you (the individual self, free from incidental attributes) are *Brahman* (the infinite and the ultimate basis of all reality).

Major Upanishads: Different Upanishads are affiliated with the four Vedas (Rigveda, Yajurveda, Samaveda and Atharvaveda). The Upanishads were transmitted orally by the Vedic schools sakhas. The longest and oldest Upanishad are the Bhadragyaka and the Chndogya respectively.

The language of the Upanishads is Sanskrit, the oldest among them still classifying as late Vedic Sanskrit. The oldest Upanishads, the Bhadragyaka and the Chndogya are composed in prose. These early texts may date back to the 8th-7th centuries BCE. Later followed a series of Upanishads composed in verse, such as the ca, Mgdukya, Katha, and bvetcvatara Upanishads.

According to tradition, there were over two hundred *Upanishads*, but the philosopher and commentator Shankara only composed commentaries to eleven of them. The Upanishads commented on by Shankara are generally regarded as the oldest ones. The Muktika Upanishad lists 108 Upanishads. In 1656, at the order of Dara Shikoh, the Upanishads were translated from Sanskrit into Persian.

These philosophical and meditative tracts form the backbone of Hindu thought. Of the early Upanishads, the Aitareya and

Kauo+tki belong to the Rig Veda, Kena and Chndogya to the Samaveda, *oa and Taittir+ya and B'hadra yaka to the Yajurveda, and Pracna and Mu'd.aka to the Atharvaveda. In addition, the Mdukya, Katho, 'vet'vatara are very important. Others also include Mahnrya'a and Maitreyi Upanishads as key.

Place in the Hindu Canon: Scholars of the Vedic books consider the four Vedas as poetic liturgy, collectively called mantra or samhit-, adoration and supplication to the deities of Vedic religion, in parts already melded with monist and henotheist notions, and an overarching order (Rta) that transcended even the Gods.

The Brhmana were a collection of ritual instructions, books detailing the priestly functions (which first were available to all men, and so concretized into strictly Brahmin privilege). These came after the Mantra.

Vedanta, is chiefly composed of *ranyakas* and Upanishads. The Aranyakas ("of the forest") detail meditative yogic practices, contemplations of the mystic one and the manifold manifested principles. The Upanishad basically realized all the monist and universal mystical ideas that started in earlier Vedic hymns, and have exerted an influence unprecedented on the rest of Hindu and Indian philosophy. However, by adherents they are not considered philosophy alone, and form meditations and practical teachings for those advanced enough to benefit from their wisdom.

Contents: The Upanishads hold information on basic Hindu beliefs, including belief in a world soul, a universal spirit, Brahman, and an individual soul, Atman (Smith 10). A variety of lesser gods are seen as aspects of this one divine ground, Brahman (different from Brahma). Brahman is the ultimate, both transcendent and immanent, the absolute infinite existence, the sum total of all that ever is, was, or ever shall be. For Advaita (non-dual) philosophers Brahman is not a God in the monotheistic sense, as they do not ascribe to it any limiting characteristics, not even those of being and non-being, and this is reflected in the fact that in Sanskrit, the word Brahman has no gender (masculine or feminine or neuter). Dvaita philosophy holds that Brahman is ultimately a personal God, Vishnu, or Krishna (*brahmano hi pratisthaham*, Bhagavad Gita 14.27).

"Who is the Knower?" "What makes my mind think?" "Does life have a purpose, or is it governed by chance?" "What is the cause of the Cosmos?"

UPANISHADS

The sages of the Upanishad try to solve these mysteries and seek knowledge of a Reality beyond ordinary knowing. They also show a preoccupation with states of consciousness, and observed and analysed dreams as well as dreamless sleep.

Philosophy: Due to their mystical nature and intense philosophical bent that does away with all ritual and completely embraces principals of One Brahman and the inner Atman (Self), the Upanishads have a universal feel that has led to their explication in numerous manners, giving birth to the three schools of Vedanta.

The Vedantin philosopher Adi Shankara summed up all the Upanishad in one phrase "Tat Tvam Asi" (Thou Art That) and said that in the end, the ultimate, formless, inconceivable Brahman is the same as our soul, Atman. We only have to realize it through discrimination and piercing through Maya.

A distinctive quotation that is indicative of the call to self-realization, one that inspired Somerset Maugham in titling a book he wrote on Christopher Isherwood, is as follows:

Get up! Wake up! Seek the guidance of an Illumined teacher and realize the Self. Sharp like a razor's edge is the path, The sages say, difficult to traverse.

Death Instructing Nachiketa in the Katho (Word) Upanishad: The Upanishads also contain the first and most definitive explications of aum as the divine word, the cosmic vibration that underlies all existence and contains multiple trinities of being and principles subsumed into its One Self. The *Isha* says of the Self (Verses 6, 7 & 8 of Isha Upanishad):

Whoever sees all beings in the soul and the soul in all beingsdoes not shrink away from this. In whom all beings have become one with the knowing soulwhat delusion or sorrow is there for the one who sees unity? It has filled all. It is radiant, incorporeal, invulnerable, without tendons, pure, untouched by evil. Wise, intelligent, encompassing, self-existent, it organizes objects throughout eternity.

ISHA UPANISHAD VERSES 6, 7, & 8

"*Aum Shanti Shanti Shanti*" This, too, is found first in the Upanishads, the call for tranquility, for divine stillness, for Peace everlasting.

Dara Shikoh, the Muslim sufi, and son of Mughal emperor Shah Jahan, translated the Upanishads in Persian in order to find in it elements of monotheism that might pave the way for a common mystical bond between Islam and Hinduism. The Kau+tki and Maitryagi Upanishads are sometimes added to extend the canon to 13. They are also the oldest Upanishads, likely all of them dating to before the Common Era. From linguistic evidence, the oldest among them are likely the Bhadragyaka and Chndogya Upanishads, belonging to the late Vedic Sanskrit period; the remaining ones are at the transition from Vedic to Classical Sanskrit.

Canon by Vedic Shakha: The older Upanishads are associated with Vedic Charanas (Shakhas or schools). The Aitareya Upanishad with the Shakala shakha, the Kau+tki Upanishad with the Bashakala shakha; the Chndogya Upanishad with the Kauthuma shakha, the Kena Upanishad, and the Jaiminiya Upanishad Brahmana, with the Jaiminiya shakha; the Kamha Upanishad with the Caraka-Katha shakha, the Taittir+ya and Zvetvatara with the Taittiriya shakha; the Maitryagi Upanishad with the Maitrayani shakha; the Bhadragyaka and *ca Upanishads with the Vajasaneyi Madhyandina shakha, and the MG

Kkya and Mug: aka Upanishads with the Shaunaka shakha. Additionally, parts of earlier texts, of Brahmanas or passages of the Vedas themselves, are sometimes considered Upanishads.

The Muktika Canon: The following is a list of the 108 canonical Upanishads of the Advaita school, according to the Muktika Upanishad (number 108), 1:30-39 (which does not list the associated Veda). In this canon:

- 10 Upanishads are associated with the Rigveda and have the Shnti beginning *vagme-manasi*.
- 16 Upanishads are associated with the Samaveda and have the Shnti beginning *pyyantu*.
- 19 Upanishads are associated with the White Yajurveda and have the Shnti beginning *pkrgamada*.
- 32 Upanishads are associated with the Black Yajurveda and have the Shnti beginning *sahanvavatu*.
- 31 Upanishads are associated with the Atharvaveda and have the Shnti beginning *bhadram-kargebhi*.

PURANAS

Purana is the name of a genre (or a group of related genres) of Indian written literature (as distinct from oral literature). Its general themes are history, tradition and religion. It is usually written in the form of stories related by one person to another.

There are many texts designated as 'Purana.' The most important are:

Mahpurgas and *Upapurgas*—Written in Sanskrit. They usually adhere to the 'Panca-laksana' typology. They tell of the creation of the universe and the human race, narrate the genealogies of kings and saints, and contain assorted narratives, stories, and philosophical and religious topics.

Included among the texts of distinctly lesser importance that also bear the name Puranas are:

Sthala Purgas—Scriptures usually extolling the virtues of a certain Hindu temple. They narrate stories of the temple's creation and spiritual history.

Kula Purgas—Scriptures that deal with the origin and legends of a particular caste.

The designation 'Purana' implicitly confers on a text a kind of factual aura, somewhat similar to the designation 'History' in Western discourse.

MAHAPURANAS AND UPAPURANAS

Structure and Content: Mah-(Sanskrit 'great', 'mighty') and Upa-(Sanskrit 'lower', 'additional') Puranas are written in Sanskrit. Traditionally they are said to narrate five subjects, called Panca-laksana (Sanskrit 'five distinguishing marks'), which are:

1. Sarga—The creation of the universe.
2. Pratisarga—Secondary creations, mostly re-creations after dissolution.
3. Vama—Genealogy of gods and sages.
4. Manvantara—The creation of the human race and the first human beings.
5. Vamnucaritam—Dynastic histories.

Most Mahapuranas and Upapuranas deal with these subject matters, although the bulk of their text consists of historical and religious narratives. Some scholars have suggested that these 'distinguishing marks' are shared by other traditional religious scriptures of the world (*e.g.* the Bible). A Purana usually gives prominence to a certain deity—(Shiva, Vishnu or Krishna, Durga)—and depicts the other gods as subservient. Most use an abundance of religious and philosophical concepts in their narration, from Bhakti to Samkhya.

Classification: Traditionally it is said that there are eighteen Mahapuranas and eighteen Upapuranas. Of the Mahapuranas it is said that six belong to the quality (*guna*) of goodness, six to passion, and six to ignorance.

According to the *Padma Purana,* these are the Mahapuranas and their corresponding qualities:

- *Goodness (Sattva):* Vishnu Purana, Bhagavata Purana, Naradeya Purana, Garuda Purana, Padma Purana, Varaha Purana
- *Passion (Rajas):* Brahmanda Purana, Brahma Vaivarta Purana, Markandeya Purana, Bhavishya Purana, Vamana Purana, Brahma Purana
- *Ignorance (Tamas):* Matsya Purana, Kurma purana, Linga Purana, Shiva Purana, Skanda Purana, Agni Purana

Some Upapuranas are: Sanat-kumara, Narasimha, Brihannaradiya, Shiva-rahasya, Durvasa, Kapila, Vamana, Bhargava, Varuna, Kalika, Samba, Nandi, Surya, Parasara, Vasishtha, Devi-Bhagavata, Ganesha, and Hamsa. Most of these have not been critically edited yet, and are available mostly through devotional publications, in multiple versions and recensions.

Special Purana :Adhata Purana: Apart from the system of classification above mentioned, the Puranas are enumerated and classified in multiple ways. The canonical lists of Puranas vary from place to place and from time to time.

Author and Disemmination: Traditionally, the Puranas are said to have been composed by the sage Vyasa, the narrator of the Mahabharata epic. Vyasa in Sanskrit means 'Divider,' and some scholars therefore take this simply as a term meaning 'Editor'. The texts, these scholars say, were probably written all over India and are being rewritten and re-edited to the present day all over the world.

The Puranas, being in Sanskrit, are usually not directly accessible to the common man as read texts. They are, however, available in vernacular translations and are disseminated by Brahmin scholars, who read from them and tell their stories, usually in Katha sessions (in which a travelling brahmin settles for a few weeks in a temple and narrates parts of a Purana, usually with a Bhakti perspective).

Chronology: The Itihasa-Purana is mentioned in the Chandogya Upanishad. There are also references to the Puranas in the Atharvaveda 11.7.24 and the Satapatha Brahmana 11.5.6.8. and 13.4.3.13. There are probably also references to the Itihasa in the Nirukta. The Itihasa-Purana was considered to be almost as sacred and ancient as the Vedas, *i.e.* the "fifth Veda" according to the Brihad-aranyaka Upanishad. However, the ancient Itihasa-Purana was probably not exactly the same as the text of the Puranas that we know today. Scholars argue that some contents of the Puranas may date to an earlier period. According to Pargiter, the original Purana may date to the time of the final redaction of the Vedas.

Pargiter has argued that in the Puranas, the Puranic Krta Yuga "ended with the destruction of the Haihayas [by Rama Jamadagnya]; the Treta began approximately with Sagara and ended with Rama Dasarathi's destruction of the Raksasas; and the Dvapara began with his reinstatement at Ayodhya and ended with the Bharata battle".

Vedic and Puranic Genealogies: The Puranas also lay emphasis on keeping a record of genealogies, thus Vayu Purana says: "As seen by good people in the ancient times the suta's duty was to preserve the genealogies of gods, rsis and glorious kings and the traditions of great men." (Vayu P. 1. 31-2)

The Vedic and Puranic genealogies indicate a greater antiquity of the Vedic culture. The Puranas themselves state that these lists are incomplete. But the accuracy of these lists is disputed. In Arrian's Indica, Megasthenes is quoted as stating that the Indians counted from Shiva (Dionysos) to Chandragupta Maurya (Sandracottus) "a hundred and fifty-three kings over six thousand and forty-three years." The Brhadaranyaka Upanishad (4.6.), ca. 8th century BCE, mentions 57 links in the Guru-Parampara ("succession of teachers"). This would mean that this Guru-Parampara would go back about 1400 years, although the accuracy of this list is disputed. The list of kings in Kalhana's Rajatarangini goes back to the 19th century BCE.

The Puranic genealogies indicate that Manu Vaivasvata lived 95 generations before the Bharata War.

NOTABLE PURANAS

- *The Bhagavata Purana*-It is concerned with Vishnu Bhakti, telling of the exploits and deeds of Vishnu's Avataras. Its tenth canto (its longest) narrates the deeds of Krishna and, probably for the first time in Sanskrit, tells of his exploits as a child, a theme later elaborated by many Bhakti movements.
- *The Devi-bhagavata Purana*-an Upapurana extolling the virtues of the goddess Durga as the supreme being. It has become (along with the Devi Mahatmya of the Mrkandeya Purana) a basic text for Devi worshipers.
- *The Skanda Purana*-probably the longest of all. A vast storehouse of parables, legends and stories, with multiple versions and recensions. Many untraced quotes from a Purana are conveniently attributed to this Purana.

Sthala Puranas: This corpus of texts narrates the virtues and stories connected with a certain temple or shrine (the word 'Sthala' means 'Place' in Sanskrit). There are numerous Sthala Puranas, most written in vernaculars, some with Sanskrit versions as well. Most claim to have a Sanskrit origin, and some of the Sanskrit versions also appear in a Mahapurana or an Upapurana. Some Tamil Sthala Puranas have been researched by David Dean Shulman.

Kula Puranas: These are mostly caste focused Puranas (the word 'Kula' means 'Family' or 'Tribe' in Sanskrit). They deal with a caste's origin myth, stories and legends. The caste purana is an important source for caste identity and is usually contested by other, rival, castes. This subgenre is usually in the vernacular and might at times be oral.

This subgenre has been little researched. But it is rather well documented in the caste section of the British Census of India Report and the various Gazzeteers.

Other Puranas: There are many other narratives that go by the name of Purana. Most are written in vernaculars and are usually concerned with mythical and historical narrations. These texts, such as the Padma Purana of Bengal and Assam (narrating the story of the goddess Manas), are vast in number and scattered all over the Indian subcontinent.

Non Hindu Puranas: There are many Jain Puranas, dealing with Jain myths, history and legends. Studies and translations of this particular genre are meagre. Arguably, some Buddhist Mahyna Sktras seem to have some characteristics of Puranas.

4

HISTORY OF THE GRAHA AND YUGA

INTRODUCTION

In Hinduism, *Chandra* is a lunar deity. Chandra is sometimes identified with Soma. He is white and rides his chariot (the moon) across the sky every night, pulled by ten white horses. He is connected with dew, and as such, is one of the gods of fertility. He is the father of Budha, (planet Mercury) the mother being either Tara or Rohini. He is also married to Anuradha and Bharani, both daughters of Daksha.

Legend has it that Daksha was livid with Chandra for dating his daughters and hence cursed him to lose all his lustre. Chandra then invoked Lord Shiva who abated the effect of the curse to the extent that Chandra's powers would wane and wax periodically every 14 days.

In another story, Chandra is said to have married twenty seven of Daksha's daughters, but favoured one (Rohini) in particular, neglecting his other wives. This angered Daksha who cursed Chandra to wither away and die. The daughters of Daksha intervened and made Chandra's death periodic.

Other Meanings: Chandra is also the word in Sanskrit, Hindi and other Indian languages for moon. It is the middle name of the Hindu god Rama. This word is named after Nisha Chandra. Chandra Shekara literally refers to the 'Person who wears the moon' which links to Lord Shiva in Hindu Mythology.

It is directed as both evil and good, as it could mean 'Queen of the Moon' or 'Demon of the moon'. It is also a common Indian name, both male and female.

Ketu (Mythology): *Ketu* is the descending lunar node. In Hindu mythology, Ketu is generally referred to as a "shadow" planet. It has a tremendous impact on human lives and also the whole creation. In some special circumstances it helps someone achieve the zenith of fame.

Astronomically, Ketu and Rahu denote the points of intersection of the paths of the Sun and the Moon as they move on the celestial sphere. Therefore, Rahu and Ketu are respectively called the north and the south lunar nodes. The fact that Eclipses occur when Sun and Moon are at one of these points gives rise to the mythology of the swallowing of the Sun by the Moon.

MANGALA

In Jyotish astrology, *Mangala* is the name for Mars, the red planet. Mars is also called *Angaraka* in Sanskrit. He is the god of war and is celibate. He is the owner of the Aries and Scorpio signs, and a teacher of the occult sciences (Rucaka Mahapurusha Yoga).

NAVAGRAHA

"Nava" means "nine". Graha is sometimes translated as "planet", but the Sun, Moon, and Rahu and Ketu are not "planets" according to modern astronomy. "Graha" is sometimes translated as "celestial body", but Rahu and Ketu are not celestial bodies either. A third translation is celestial god or demi-god, but again, Rahu and Ketu are Asuras not Devas. Rahu and Ketu are further believed to be only positions in the planetary paths. A fact common to all navagrahas is that they have relative movement with respect to the background of fixed stars in the zodiac belt.

There is also a stotra in the praise of the Navagrahas.

"Namah Sooryaya, Chandraya, Mangalaya, Budhaya cha, Guruhu, Shukra, Shanibhihi cha Rahuve, Ketuve Namaha"

Some people believe that by chanting this stotra, man is relieved from all his sins and bad effects that may occur due to these grahas on him.

In several parts of India, there are clusters of Navagraha temples. One such cluster is near the town of Kumbakonam, Tamil Nadu; another temple is in Guwahati, Assam.

RAHU

Rahu is the ascending lunar node. In Hindu mythology, *Rahu* is a snake that swallows the sun or the moon causing eclipses. He is depicted in art as a dragon with no body riding a chariot drawn by eight black horses.

According to legend, during the Samudra manthan, the asura Rahu drank some of the divine nectar. But before the nectar could pass his throat, Mohini (the female avatar of Vishnu) cut off his head. The head, however, remained immortal. It is believed that this immortal head occasionally swallows the sun or the moon, causing eclipses. Then, the sun or moon passes through the opening at the neck, ending the eclipse.

Rahu is one of the navagrahas (nine planets). The *rahu kala* is considered inauspicious.

In Buddhism Rahu is one of the *krodhadevatas* (terror-inspiring gods).

Astronomy: Astronomically, Rahu and Ketu denotes the two points of intersection of the paths of the Sun and the Moon as they move on the celestial sphere. Therefore, Rahu and Ketu are respectively called the north and the south lunar nod. The fact that Eclipses occur when Sun and Moon are at one of these points gives rise to the myth of the swallowing of the Sun.

Brihaspati: In Hindu mythology, *Brihaspati* is the guru of the Devas and the chief nemesis of Shukracharya, the guru of the Danavas. He is also known *Ganapati* and *Brahmanaspati*. His name is written in Vedic Sanskrit as *Brihaspati* with two *udtta* accents, probably representing two words *brihaspati*, with the same meaning as his other name *Brahmanas pati*: "the lord of prayer"; *brihas* would be genitive of a noun stem *brihas*.

Brihaspati is also the name of an ancient Indian philosopher who is considered as the founder of the atheistic system of thought *Lokayata*.

A mantras by Vishvamitra from the Rigveda dedicated to Brihaspati declares:

> *Vrsabham charninam vishwarupamdabhyam Vrihaspatim-varenyam*

O Great Men! We sing the praise of Brihaspati (the preceptor of the gods) for the joy of learning and for success in all our good actions. He is the most respectable and the greatest. His wishes are inviolable and we gain in (spiritual) strength by following in His footsteps.

Mention in Hindu Mythology: Brihaspati is the son of rishi Angirasa and Surupa according to the Shiva Purana. He has two brothers named Utathya and Samvartana. He has three wives. His first wife Shuba gave birth to Bhanumati, Raaka, Archishmati, Mahamati, Mahishmati, Sinivalli, and Havishmati, his seven daughters. His second wife Tara gives birth to seven sons and a daughter. Through his third wife Mamata, he has two sons, Kacha and Bharadwaja.

He attained his position as the preceptor of the Devas, by performing penances on the banks of Prabhas Tirtha. Lord Shiva granted him this position, as well as his position as one of the Navagrahas (nine planets). The planet Jupiter in Vedic astrology is known as *Guru, Brihaspati, Cura* and *Devaguru*. According to traditional Hindu astrology, worship or propitiation of Brihaspati or Guru (Jupiter) results in cure from ailments affecting the stomach and helps ward off sins.

Role in Jyotisha: In jyotisha (Hindu astrology), *Brihaspati* is the name for the planet Jupiter, which is one of the navagraha (cosmic influencers) or planets.

It is believed that the great red spot of Jupiter is the piratti of Brihaspati. Much significance is given to the great red spot in Hindu spiritual belief.

BUDHA

In Hindu mythology, *Budha* (not to be confused with Buddha) is the name for the planet Mercury, a son of Chandra (the moon) with either Tara or Rohini.

The planet is associated with Wednesday in Indian timekeeping. In modern Hindi, Telugu, Bengali, and Gujarati, Wednesday is called *Budhvara*; in Tamil and Malayalam it is *Budhan*.

SHANI

Shani (also spelled *Sani*) is one of the nine Navagraha or primary celestial beings in Hindu astrology (that is, Vedic astrology), Shani is embodied in the planet Saturn. Shani is the Lord of Saturday; the word Shani also denotes the seventh day or Saturday in most Indian languages.

The origin of word *Shani* comes from the following: *Shanaye Kramati Sa:*, *i.e.* the one who moves slowly. Saturn takes about 30 years to revolve around the Sun, thus it moves *slowly* enough compared to other planets, thus the Sanskrit name.

He is also known as *Sanaiscarya*, *Shani Bhagavan, Shaneesvara, Saneesvara, Saneesvaran, Shani Deva,* etc...

Shani is actually a demi-god and is a son of Surya, the (Hindu deity of the sun). It is said that when he opened his eyes as a baby for the very first time, the sun went into an eclipse, which clearly denotes the impact of Shani on astrological charts (horoscope).

In Hindu astrology, a favourably-placed Shani on the horoscope of a person stands for a strong career, healthy life and everything positive for that person. In fact, a well-placed Shani in one's horoscope is something every astrology-believing Hindu hopes for, as no other 'graha' can bestow what a favourable

Shani can. Shani placed "unfavourably", on the other hand, denotes troubles in all of the above. Saneesvara is much feared by those Hindus who believe in astrology, as the "malefic" effects of his being unfavourably placed can be quite severe.

However, it is to be remembered that any pleasure or pain that befalls a person during Saneesvara's influence is not Saneesvara's arbitrary doing; rather, it is the result of the person's own karma, now being manifested in the "presence" of Saneesvara. Thus an "unfavourably-placed" Shani brings about the harsh results of one's bad karma, and vice-versa.

Shani is considered to be a stern *teacher* who represents patience, effort, endeavour, and endurance; he is not the one who gets carried away by platitudes like the careless and/or insincere chanting of matras or the performance of rituals without sincerity and/or faith. He forces people to be disciplined, and to understand that one needs to be humble, focused, patient, and hard-working to achieve success.

Since most Hindus fear Lord Shani, they prefer not to approach him alone directly; rather they turn to God, in His various Forms, for relief.

Effects of Shani: According to Hindu astrology, there are nine grahas (including Sun as one of them) and there are 12 rashis or sunsigns. The planet Shani or Saturn revolves around the Sun in about 30 years. That means, it passes through all the 12 constellations in 30 years. Thus Shani spends on an average about 30/12 = 2.5 years, *i.e.* two and half years in each rashi or sunsign. This movement of Shani through the sunsigns has a lot of importance in the Hindu astrology and horoscope predictions. In Hindu astrology, a person has a specific rashi/ sunsign assigned to him which is determined from his birth date, time and location.

The effect of Shani starts when it enters the penultimate rashi/sunsign and the effect stops when it leaves the next rashi/ sunsign. Thus the total period of 2.5 years in the previous rashi + 2.5 years in own rashi + 2.5 years in the next rashi equalling

7.5 years total. This period of 7.5 years is called *Saadesaati*, and the person faces lot of difficulties during this period of his life. It is believed that Shri Shani-maharaj makes sure that the person who faces difficulties and goes through this period comes out as a very wise person indeed very well aware of most of the dire experiences of life. This period teaches that person many things important in his life. This is another way to make that person humble and be respectful rather than otherwise.

This may be the reason why Shri Shani-maharaj is feared by most. The great story of his life is described in *Shri Shani Mahatmya* written several centuries ago and is still read.

Shri Shani Mahatmya: The story of *Shani Mahatmya* is a very fascinating story depicting the importance of Shri Shani-deva and how difficult devotion service is required to please him and get his *krupa* (blessings) on you. The book starts with describing the importance of various planets and their strengths. These are told by the scholars serving king Vikramaditya's court from the city of Ujjain. The description of Shani comes as: He has a dark complexion, his face is beautiful, he is lame (defective feet), his caste is *teli* (Oil vendors) and he prays *Kal-bhairav*. After listening to the birth story of Shani, Vikramaditya laughed and ridiculed Shani for what he did. Shanidev heard the remarks of Vikramaditya and cursed him.

The rest of the story is how Vikramaditya faces difficulties and problems worse than the ones he could imagine. He loses his kingdom, he is charged with stealing, his both hands and legs are cutoff by King *Chandrasen* of *Tamlinda* town. He is helped by a *teli* of that town and this oil vendor brings him home. But Vikramaditya still prays Shanidev without losing his temper or faith in Shanidev, who eventually is satisfied with Vikramaditya's devotion and brings him back all the lost glory. In fact Shanidev makes him even better and greater than what he was or had before.

The last part of the book describes various experiences faced by various gods, demons and sages, including Brihaspati (the Guru of gods) and Shiva et al. The story essentially stresses the values such as, perseverance in difficult times, complete devotion and faith in the values one believes in or one follows and never to lose his/her confidence in life in spite of lot of difficulties. The story is truly marvellously written. The Marathi version of this is possibly written by Shri Tatyaji Mahipati, however, nothing more is known about this author.

Shani and Hanuman: The worship of Lord Hanuman is a panacea for the harsh effects of the 'unfavourable' presence of Lord Shani. In the Ramayana, Lord Hanuman is said to have rescued Shani from the clutches of Ravana and in gratitude, Shani promised Hanuman that anyone who prayed to Him (Hanuman), especially on Saturdays, would be rescued from the "malefic" effects of Saturn, or at the very least, the effects would be softened.

Another version of the encounter between Lord Hanuman and Shani is that once Shani climbed on to Hanuman's shoulder, implying that Shani's influence was beginning on Lord Hanuman. At this, Hanuman assumed a large size, and Shani was caught painfully between Hanuman's shoulders and the ceiling of the room they were in. As the pain was unbearable, Shani requested Lord Hanuman to release him, promising in return, that if a person prayed to Lord Hanuman, he (Shani) would moderate the malefic effects of his influence on that person if not all together have no malefic influence on the person; following this, Lord Hanuman released Shani.

Shani and Lord Vishnu: Shani went everyday to put his ill effects on Maha Vishnu, but Vishnu was busy every time that Shani appeared. Shani was growing restless and asked Vishnu when he was available. Vishnu said tomorrow. Shani wanted to know how Vishnu would remember. Vishnu said write "tomorrow" on the wall and Shani did. When Shani came the next day, Vishnu pointed to the wall with the word "tomorrow". Shani came the next day and the same thing happened. Shani got tired of coming everyday that he left Vishnu alone.

Alternatively, one who prays to *Lord* Vishnu is protected from Shani as he is said to be a great devotee of Vishnu. (It is interesting to note that Hanuman Himself was devoted to Lord Rama, an avatar of Vishnu).

Shrines for Lord Shani: In several parts of India, there are clusters of nine temples/shrines dedicated to the Navagrahas. One such cluster is located near the town Kumbakonam in the state of Tamil Nadu, India. Lord Shani's shrine in this cluster is located at Tirunallar. It is a Temple dedicated to Lord Darbaranyesvara, a Form of *Lord* Shiva, in which Lord Shani is located in a niche in a wall. At this Temple, Lord Shani is considered to be of *benevolent nature.*

Another important Shrine for Lord Shani is in Shingnapur, in Maharashtra, India. The deity self emerged from the earth in form of stone block and was found by shepherds. When they touched stone with a pointed rod the stone began bleeding. The shepherds were astounded and one night one shepherd got a dream that the deity was Lord Shani. To this day, due to fear of Shani, houses within a 1 km radius of the Shani temple do not have locks. No thefts happen in this place. Some who have tried to steal have received punishment (sickness, mental harassment) from Shani.

Another Shani temple is Shani Dhaam, at Fatehpur Beri, about 6 kms from Chhattarpur temple & 16 kms from the Qutub Minar, at Mehrauli, South Delhi, India.

Shani in Jainism: Shani and Lord Munisuvarat (20th jain tirthakar)

One who prays to Lord Munisuvarat is protected from Shani as he is great devotee of Lord Munisuvarat Swami (20th jain tirthankar) as per Jainism and really one can trace from ancient times people worshipping Munisuvarat Swami whose symbol is Tortoise to get protected from ill effects of not properly placed shani in ones horoscope.

Usually Munisuvarat Swamis idol is always found made up of Black colour. Millions of devotees across the world have witnessed miracles of Munisuvarat swami who appeared approx. 10,000 years ago as 20th jain tirthankar.

At Kankali Tila in Mathura a deity of Muni-Suvrat Swami whose insignia is tortoise, was discovered. One of the nude statues in Mohan-Jodaro (Indus Valley) has the tortoise insignia, which indicates that it must be of Muni-Suvrat Swami. In Vedic history there are descriptions of a Muni in the Puran, connected to the tortoise, which throws light on Muni Suvrat. In the Rigved (23, 27, 32) a sage with tortoise insignia has been mentioned which is none other than Tirthankar Muni-Suvrat Swami. It connection with the tortoise the Puran (40, 27, 41) writes that Vishnu appeared in the form of tortoise in Rishabh race (First Tirthakar).

SHUKRA

Shukra is the Sanskrit name for Venus, one of the Navagrahas. It is a male planet for the Hindus and named after the Guru Shukracharya.

SURYA

In Hinduism, *Surya* is the chief solar deity, son of Dyaus Pitar. He has hair and arms of gold. His chariot is pulled by seven horses, which represent the seven chakras.

Surya Namaskara or "Sun Salutation": A well-known Hindu mode of worship of Surya is done at the rising of the Sun, known as Surya Namaskara (Sun Salutation). Ten yogic postures are assumed in successive flowing movements to complete one namaskara. Twelve sacred Hindu mantras uttered and for each mantra one complete namaskara is done. Ancient practice is to do 108 namaskaras a day. It is considered most auspicious by Hindus to do this. The 12 mantras for Surya namaskara:

1. *aum mitrya namah*
2. *aum rvaye namah*
3. *aum skryya namah*

4. *aum bhnave namah*
5. *aum khagaya namah*
6. *aum pushne namah*
7. *aum hiranyagarbhya namah*
8. *aum mrichye namah*
9. *aum dityya namah*
10. *aum svitre namah*
11. *aum rkya namah*
12. *aum bhskarya namah*

The mantra frequently recited to praise the Surya comes from the Rig Veda, Book 1 Hymn 35:

> *Throughout the dusky firmament advancing, laying to rest the immortal and the mortal,*
>
> *Borne in his golden chariot he cometh, Savitar, God who looks on every creature.*

The Gayatri Mantra is also associated with Surya. Another hymn associated with Surya is the Aditya Hridayam, recited by the great sage Agastya to Rama on the battlefield before the fight with Ravana.

Surya's Religious Role and Mythic Relationships: In Hindu religious literature, Surya is notably mentioned as the visible form of God that one can see every day. Furthermore, Shaivites and Vaishnavas often regard Surya as an aspect of Shiva and Vishnu, respectively. For example, the sun is called *Surya* Narayana by Vaishnavas. In Shaivite theology, Surya is said to be one of eight forms of Shiva, named the *Astamurti*.

In the Mahabharata, princess Kunti receives instruction for a mantra from sage Durvasa by which reciting she is able to summon any god and bear a child with him. Unable to believe the power of this mantra she tries to summon Surya. When Surya appears, she is overawed and requests him to go back, but Surya is compelled to fulfil the mantra before returning. Surya magically causes Kunti to bear a child immediately so that she, an unmarried princess, would not be subject to questions from the king or his court. Kunti discards this child, Karna, who grows up to become one of the central characters in the great battle of Kurukshetra.

Surya is the father of the twins known as the Ashwins, divine horsemen and physicians to the Gods. He also fathered the twins Yama Dev (the Lord of Death) and his sister Yami (associated with the river Yamuna). He also fathers Sani Dev (the planet Saturn) and the Monkey King Sugriva, who helped Rama and Laxman defeat Ravana.

TRIVIA

- The intercontinental ballistic missile "Surya" was named after the deity.
- "Surya" is also the Indonesian word for "Sun" Besides "Matahari".

NAKSHATRA

A *nakshatra* or *lunar mansion* is one of the 27 or 28 divisions of the sky, identified by the prominent star(s) in them, that the Moon passes through during its monthly cycle, as used in Hindu astronomy and astrology. Therefore, each represents a division of the ecliptic similar to the zodiac. The mansion associated with a given date corresponds to the constellation which the Moon is passing through at that time. Nakshatra computation appears to have been well known at the time of the Rig Veda (2nd millennium BC). In RV 10.55.3., 34 lights are described, probably the 27 nakshatras and seven Grahas (sun, moon and five planets). The Taittiriya Samhita says that they are connected with the path of the moon.

The starting point for this division is the point on the ecliptic directly opposite to the star Spica called *Chitr* in Sanskrit. (Other slightly-different definitions exist.) It is called *Meshdi* or the "start of Aries". The ecliptic is divided into the *nakshatra*s eastwards starting from this point. The 27 Nakshatras cover 13°20' of the ecliptic each. Each Nakshatra is divided into quarters or *padas* of 3°20'. The nakshatras with their corresponding regions of sky are given below, following Basham's Appendix: Astronomy.

An additional 28th intercalary nakshatra, Abhijit is required to compensate for the sidereal month being eight hours more than 27 days. Unlike the 13°20' range of the 27 proper nakshatras, Abhijit spans 4°14' to reflect the extra span of 7¾ hours.

The list of Nakshatras is found in the Vedic texts (AV 19.7; Taittiriya Samhita) and also in the Shatapatha Brahmana. The first astronomy text that lists them is the Vedanga Jyotisha of Lagadha.

Traditional Hindu Names: Hindu astrologers teach that when a Hindu child is born, they should be given an auspicious first name which will correspond to the child's Nakshatra. Each birthstar has corresponding Sanskrit sounds which would belong at the beginning of such a name. These are available under each Nakshatra, listed above.

ARDRA

- In Hinduism, Ardra is a goddess, and the Nakshatra corresponding to Betelgeuse.

  Under the traditional Hindu principle of naming individuals according to their birthstar, the following Sanskrit syllables correspond with this Nakshatra, and would belong at the beginning of a first name:

Ku (pronounced as in "quicksand")
Gha (pronounced as it appears)
Ng (pronounced as in "tongue")
Chha (pronounced as in "chicken")

ARDRA (NAKSHATRA)

Ardra is the name of a Nakshatra in Indian astronomy that corresponds to the star Betelgeuse.

In Hindu mythology, Ardra is the goddess of good luck and fortune.

ASALESHA NAKSHATRAM

Ashlesha is the name of a daughter of Prajapati Daksha; she is one of the wives of Chandra. She is personified as a Nakshatra, and is best known as that, especially in south Indian astrology: Jyotisha.

Under the traditional Hindu principle of naming individuals according to their birthstar, the following Sanskrit syllables correspond with this Nakshatra, and would belong at the beginning of a first name:

Di (pronounced as in "independant")
Du (pronounced as in "Hindu")
De (pronounced as in "Saturday")
Do (pronounced as in "do re mi")

ASHVINI

Ashvini is the name of a Hindu constellation (the head of Aries, or the first of the 28 Nakshatras). Personified, Ashvini is the wife of the Ashvins (Rigveda 5.46.8), later also considered their mother.

Under the traditional Hindu principle of naming individuals according to their birthstar, the following Sanskrit syllables correspond with this Nakshatra, and would belong at the beginning of a first name:

Chu (pronounced as it appears)
Che (pronouced chay)
Cho (pronounced as it appears)
La (pronounced as it appears)

BHARANI

Bharani is the second nakshatra in Hindu astronomy, corresponding to 35, 39, and 41 Arietis. In Hinduism, *Bharani* is a goddess of bad luck. Like her sister Anuradha, she is a daughter of Daksha, and wife of Chandra. Under the traditional Hindu principle of naming individuals according to their birthstar, the following Sanskrit syllables correspond with this

Nakshatra, and would belong at the beginning of a first name:

Li (pronounced as in "little")
Lu (pronounced as in "look")
Le (pronounced as in "levity")
Lo (pronounced as in "local")

CHITRA

Chitra is a nakshatra. It is also a very common Hindu name for the female child in India derived from the sanskrit word for portrait or picture. Girls born under the star Chitra (Chitirai) are sometimes given this name.

KRITTIKA

Krittika nakshatra corresponds to the open star cluster Pleiades in Indian astronomy and Indian astrology. It is ruled by Kartikeya.

Under the traditional Hindu principle of naming individuals according to their birthstar, the following Sanskrit syllables correspond with this Nakshatra, and would belong at the beginning of a first name:

A (pronounced as "arbor")
I (pronounced as in "invisible")
U (pronounced as in "eunuch")
E (pronounced as in "every")

MAGHA

Magha might be a transliteration for

- The Hindu month Magha
- The nakshatra Magha
- Kalinga Magha a king of Sri Lanka

PUNARVASU

Punarvasu is a Nakshatra in Hindu astronomy, that refers to the two brightest stars in the constellation of Gemini: Castor and Pollux. In Malayalam Punarvasu is termed Punartham.

SHRI RAMA WAS BORN AT THIS NAKSHATRA

Under the traditional Hindu principle of naming individuals according to their birthstar, the following Sanskrit syllables correspond with this Nakshatra, and would belong at the beginning of a first name:

Ke (pronounced as in "Kevin")
Ko (pronounced as in "cocoa")
Ha (pronounced as in "ha ha")
Hi (pronounced as in "Hinterlands")

PUSHYA

Pushya is a nakshatra in Indian astronomy. It corresponds to, and ¸ Cancri, in the Cancer (constellation).

Under the traditional Hindu principle of naming individuals according to their birthstar, the following Sanskrit syllables correspond with this Nakshatra, and would belong at the beginning of a first name:

Hu (pronounced as in "hurry")
He (pronounced as in "heavenly")
Ho (pronounced as it appears")
Da (pronounced as in "Rhonda")

ROHINI

Rohini may refer to any of the following:

1. Rohini as in Rohini Nakshatram, in Hindu mythology a daughter of Daksha and a consort of the moon-God Chandra; symbolised as the star Rohini.

Under the traditional Hindu principle of naming individuals according to their birthstar, the following Sanskrit syllables correspond with this Nakshatra, and would belong at the beginning of a first name:

O (pronounced as it appears)
Va (pronounced as in "vanilla")
Vi (pronounced as in "victory")
Vo (pronounced as it appears)

TIME IN HINDU MYTHOLOGY

In ancient Hindu religion, time tracking was done in the following manner:

The age was divided into four Yugas:

1. Satyuga-4800*360 Human Years
2. Tretayuga-3600*360 Human Years
3. Dwaparyuga-2400*360 Human Years
4. Kaliyug-1200*360 Human Years

The full cycle of all the 4 Yugas was called as a Caturyuga.

That means,

1 Caturyuga = (4800+3600+2400+1200)*360 Human Years

1 Caturyuga = 4,320,000 Human Years

Caturyuga is also called as Mahayuga.

Now that we have defined Caturyuga, let us start with the concept of Kalpa.

One Kalpa is one day in the life of Brahma.

71 Cycle of Caturyuga Makes ONE MANAVANTARA (Time of one Manu). As the name Implies, one manu is associated with a period of 71 caturyugas.

14 Manavantara + 6 Caturyuga makes one Kalpa.

Or in other words

1 kalpa = (14*71+6) Caturyuga = 1000 Caturyuga.

1 Kalpa = 4,320,000,000 Human Years.

The last 6 Caturyuga form the period between the start and ending of each Manavantara.

That precisely means that Four thousand Two Hundred Million human Years forms one day of Brahma. At the end of eack Kalpa, Lord Shiva will destroy the Earth, Pralay.

It is also said that the Brahma will live for 100 Years (1 Brahma Year has 360 days). So there will be a total of 36000 cycles as mentioned above.

By Puranic Calculations, we are currently living in the 28th Caturyuga of the 7th Manavantara of 51st year of brahma.

UTTARAYANA

Uttaryana is the six month period between Makara Sankranti around (January 14) and Karka Sankranti around (July 14), when the Sun travels towards north on the celestial sphere. The period from July 14 to January 14 is known is Dakshinyana. The starting of Uttarayana is celebrated as Makara Sankranti throughout India, which is declared as National festival by Government of India.

ZRUTI

Zruti (Devanagari, "what is heard") is a canon of Hindu sacred texts. They do not date to a particular period, but span the entire history of Hinduism, beginning with the earliest texts known, with some late Upanishads reaching down into modern times.

Zruti is said to have no author; rather, it is believed to be a divine recording of the "cosmic sounds of truth", heard by rishis.

There are several contesting ways to define Zruti. It is most commonly defined along the compositional lines of the four Vedas:

- Rig-Veda Knowledge of Hymns of Praise
- Atharva-Veda Knowledge of Magic Formulas
- Sama-Veda Knowledge of Melodies
- Yajur-Veda Knowledge of Sacrificial Formulas

Some subdivisions within the scriptures, such as the Aranyakas, Brahmanas, and Upanishads, belong to the set of works distinctly labelled as Zruti. In addition, the Mahabharata (an *Itihasa*, or History, also part of the "friendly scripture" class) is considered by some to be Zruti and is sometimes called the 'fifth' Veda. Sometimes the Bhagavad Gita, a chapter within the Mahabharata, is separately considered as worthy of the [ruti status.

SMRITI

Smriti (Sanskrit, "*that which is remembered*") refers to a specific body of Hindu religious scripture. *Smriti* also denotes non-*Shruti* texts generally, seen as secondary in authority to *Shruti*.

Categorization: Classifying the Smriti has been a contentious issue, even the names of proposed categories are debated. One such taxonomy follows:

1. *Dharmashastra or the Laws:* This is represented by 18 books. Each book corresponds to an age of time.
2. *Itihasa or the Histories:* This is by 4 books. It includes the Mahakavyas, or Epics Mahabharata and the Ramayana.
3. *Purana or the Writings:* This is represented by 18 books. They are secondary scriptures that mainly focus on Vishnu or Shiva as the preferred supreme Deity.
4. *Sutras or Proverbs:* This is represented by 6 categories of documents: the Shiksha, Vyakarana, Chandas, Nirukta, Jyotisha, & Kalpa.
5. *Agama or the Doctrines:* There are three major divisions by doctrine: the Vaisnava, Saiva, and Sakta. Another way of grouping them is by Mantra, Tantra, and Yantra.
6. *Darsana (aka Dyasana) or Philosophies:* This is represented by 6 schools of thought: Nyaya, Vaisheshika, Sankhya, Yoga, Purva Mimamsa, and Uttara Mimamsa (aka Vedanta).

YUGA

***Yugas*:** In Hindu philosophy the cycle of evolution of life is divided into four *yugas* (epochs or eras):

1. Satya Yuga or Krita Yuga
2. Treta Yuga

3. Dvapara Yuga
4. Kali Yuga

The Spiritual States of Civilization in each Yuga: In Hindu tradition, the world goes through a continuous cycle of these epochs. Each ascending phase of the cycle from Kali Yuga to Satya Yuga is followed by a descending phase back to Kali Yuga, then another ascending phase and so on. Alternatively, it is sometimes supposed that at the end of the descending Kali Yuga, the world will return to the Satya Yuga, and begin a new decline.

The descent from Satya to Kali is associated with a progressive deterioration of Dharma (righteousness) manifested as decrease in length of human life and quality of human moral standards. In the *Vishnu* Purana, for example, the Kali Yuga is described thus:

"In the Kali Yuga, there will be numerous rulers vying with each other. They will have no character. Violence, falsehood and wickedness will be the order of the day. Piety and good nature will dwindle slowly... Passion and lust will be the only attraction between the sexes. Women will be the objects of sensual pleasure. Dishonest will be the bottom line of subsistence. Learned people will be ridiculed and put to shame; the word of the wealthy person will be the only law."

The traditional virtues accorded highest value in the four epochs are: 1. Satya Yuga or Krita Yuga-dhyana (meditation); 2. Treta Yuga-yajna (sacrifice); 3. Dvapara Yuga-archana (worship); 4. Kali Yuga-daana (alms):

1. In the highest yuga, the great majority of the people can experience spirituality by direct intuitive realization of truth. The veil between the material and the transcendent realms becomes almost transparent. According to Natya Shastra, there is no Natya performances in the Krita Yuga because it is a period free from any kind of unhappiness or misery. Satya Yuga is also called the Golden Age.

2. Treta Yuga is the mental age, mental power is harnessed, men are in power, and inventions dissolve the illusion of time. (Inventions are characteristic of both Dvapara and Treta yugas.)
3. In Dwapara Yuga, science flourishes, people experience the spiritual in terms of subtle energies and rational choices, inventions are abundant, particularly those that dissolve the illusion of distance (between people and between things), and power is mostly in the hands of women. The end of this age is associated with the death of Krishna, and the events described in the Mahabharata.
4. In the lowest phase, Kali Yuga, most people are aware only of the physical aspect of existence, the predominant emphasis of living is material survival, and power is mostly in the hands of men. People's relationship with the spiritual is governed predominantly by superstition and by authority.

Temples, wars, and writing are hallmarks of Dvapara and Kali yugas. In the higher ages (Treta and Satya), writing is unnecessary because people communicate directly by thought; temples are unnecessary because people feel the omnipresence of God; wars are rare but they do occur; one such war is described in the Ramayana.

The traditional timescale of the yugas is as follows:

1. Satya Yuga or Krita Yuga-1,728,000 years
2. Treta Yuga—1,296,000 years
3. Dvapara Yuga—864,000 years
4. Kali Yuga—432,000 years

Upon conclusion of seventy-one circuits of this cycle, there is a period equally long during which the world is inundated; then the cycle begins again.

Sri Yukteswar's Teachings on the Yugas: An alternative view of the yuga cycle and timescale was taught by the 19th/

20th-century Indian yogi Swami Sri Yukteswar Giri, guru of Paramahansa Yogananda.

In his book, The Holy Science, Sri Yukteswar explains that the descending phase of Satya Yuga lasts 4800 years, Treta Yuga 3600 years, Dwapara Yuga 2400 years, and Kali Yuga 1200 years. The ascending phase of Kali Yuga then begins, also lasting 1200 years; and so on. The ascending phase of Kali Yuga began in September of 499 AD. Since September 1699, we have been in the ascending phase of Dwapara Yuga, according to Sri Yukteswar. Evidence exists to support Sri Yukteswar's theory. For example, the average life span is getting longer.

In "The Holy Science", Sri Yukteswar writes that the traditional view is based on a misunderstanding. He says that at the end of the last descending Dwapara Yuga (about 700 BC) "Maharaja Yudhisthira, noticing the appearance of the dark Kali Yuga, made over his throne to his grandson and... together with all of his wise men... retired to the Himalaya Mountains... Thus there was none in the court... who could understand the principle of correctly accounting the ages of the several Yugas."

According to Sri Yukteswar, nobody wanted to announce the bad news of the beginning of the ascending Kali Yuga, so they just kept adding years to the Dwapara date (at that time 2400 Dwapara). As the Kali began to ascend again, scholars of the time recognized that there was a mistake in the date (then being called 3600+ Kali, although their texts said Kali had only 1200 years). "By way of reconciliation, they fancied that 1200 years, the real age of Kali, were not the ordinary years of our earth, but were so many *daiva* (or deva) years ("years of the gods"), consisting of 12 *daiva* months of 30 *daiva* days each, with each *daiva* day being equal to one ordinary solar year of our earth. Hence according to these men 1200 years of Kali Yuga must be equal to 432,000 years of our earth."

Sri Yukteswar also writes that our sun has a 'star for its dual', with an orbit around this star. As our sun moves through this orbit it takes the whole solar system closer to and then further from the "grand centre" of our solar system called 'Vishnunabhi', which is the seat of the creative power, 'Brahma', which... regulates... the mental virtue of the internal world." He states that the proximity to this grand centre determines which yuga it is.

HINDU UNITS OF MEASUREMENT

Old Indian measures are still in use today, primarily for religious purposes in Hinduism and Jainism. They also are employed in the teachings of Surat Shabda Yoga.

Time: The Hindu metrics of time (*Kaala Vyavahara*) can be summarized as below.

SIDEREAL METRICS

- a paramanu is the normal interval of blinking in humans, or approximately 4 seconds
- a vighati is 6 paramaanus, or approximately 24 seconds
- a ghadiya is 60 vighatis, or approximately 24 minutes
- a muhurta is equal to 2 ghadiyas, or approximately 48 minutes
- a nakshatra ahoratram or sidereal day is *exactly* equal to 30 muhurtas (Note: A day is considered to begin and end at sunrise, not midnight.)

An alternate system described in the Vishnu Purana Time measurement section of the Vishnu Purana Book I Chapter III is as follows:

- 15 twinklings of the eye = 1 Kashtha
- 30 Kashthas = 1 Kala
- 30 Kalas = 1 Muhurtta
- 30 Muhurttas = 1 day (24 hours)
- 30 days = 1 month
- 6 months = 1 Ayana
- 2 Ayanas = 1 year or one day (day + night) of the gods

SMALL UNITS OF TIME USED IN THE VEDAS

- a trasarenu is the combination of 6 celestial *atoms*.
- a truti is the time needed to integrate 3 *trasarenus*, or 1/1687.5th of a second.
- a vedha is 100 *trutis*.
- a lava is 3 *vedhas*.
- a nimesha is 3 *lavas*, or a blink.
- a kshanas is 3 *nimeshas*.
- a kashthas is 5 *kshanas*, or about 8 seconds.
- a laghu is 15 *kashthas*, or about 2 minutes.
- 15 laghus make one *nadika*, which is also called a *danda*. This equals the time before water overflows in a six-pala-weight [fourteen ounce] pot of copper, in which a hole is bored with a gold probe weighing four masha and measuring four fingers long. The pot is then placed on water for calculation.
- 2 dandas make one muhurta.
- 6 or 7 dandas make one *yamah*, or 1/4th of a day or night.
- 4 praharas or 4 yamas are in each *day* or each *night*.

Lunar Metrics

- a tithi (also spelled *thithi)* or lunar day is defined as the time it takes for the longitudinal angle between the moon and the sun to increase by 12°. Ti this begin at varying times of day and vary in duration from approximately 19 to approximately 26 hours.
- a *paksa* (also paksha) or lunar fortnight consists of 15 tithis
- a *masa* or lunar month (approximately 29.5 days) is divided into 2 pakshas: the one between new moon and full moon is called *gaura* (bright) or *shukla paksha*; the one between full moon and new moon *krishna* (dark) *paksha*

- a ritu is 2 masa
- an *ayanam* is 3 rituhs
- a year is 2 Aayanas

TROPICAL METRICS

- a *yaama* is 7½ *Ghatis*
- 8 *yaamas* 1 half of the day (either day or night)
- an *ahoratram* is a tropical day (Note: A day is considered to begin and end at sunrise, not midnight.)

Reckoning of Time among Other Entities: Reckoning of time amongst the *pitrs*.

- 1 human year = 1 day of the pitrs
- 30 days of the pitrs = 1 month of the pitrs
- 12 months of the pitrs = 1 year of the pitrs
- The lifespan of the pitrs is 100 years of the pitrs (= 36,000 human years).

The cycle repeats itself so altogether there are 1000 cycles of yugas in one day of Brahma.

- One cycle of the above four *yugas* is one *mahayuga* (4.32 million solar years)
- A *manvantara* consists of 71 mahayugas (306,720,000 solar years). Each Manvantara is ruled by a Manu.
- After each manvantara follows one *Sandhi Kala* of the same duration as a *Krita Yuga* (1,728,000 = 4 Charana). (It is said that during a Sandhi Kala, the entire earth is submerged in water.)
- A kalpa consists of a period of 1,728,000 solar years called *Adi Sandhi*, followed by 14 manvantaras and Sandhi Kalas.
- A day of Brahma equals

  (14 times 71 mahayugas) + (15 x 4 Charanas)

  = 994 mahayugas + (60 Charanas)

= 994 mahayugas + (6 x 10) Charanas

= 994 mahayugas + 6 mahayugas

= 1000 mahayugas

as is confirmed by the Gita statement "sahasra-yuga paryantam aharyad brahmano viduh", meaning, a day of brahma is of 1000 mahayugas. Thus, a day of Brahma, kalpa, is of duration: 4.32 billion solar years. Two *kalpas* constitute a day and night of Brahma

- 30 days of Brahma = 1 month of Brahma (259,200,000,000 human years)
- 12 months of Brahma = 1 year of Brahma (3,110,400,000,000 human years)
- 25 years of Brahma = 1 kalpa (77,760,000,000,000 human years)
- 2 kalpas = 1 parardha (155,520,000,000,000 human years)
- 2 parardhas = 100 years of Brahma, the lifespan of Brahma (311,040,000,000,000 human years)

The Vishnu Purana Time measurement section of the Vishnu Purana Book I Chapter III explains the above as follows:

- 360 days of the gods = 1 year of the gods
- 12,000 years of the gods = 4 Yugas
- 1,000 sets of 4 Yugas = a day of Brahma
- 50 years of Brahma = 1 Pararddham
- 100 years of Brahma = 1 Param
- 4,000 + 400 + 400 = 4,800 years = 1 Krita Yuga
- 3,000 + 300 + 300 = 3,600 years = 1 Treta Yuga
- 2,000 + 200 + 200 = 2,400 years = 1 Dwapara Yuga
- 1,000 + 100 + 100 = 1,200 years = 1 Kali Yuga
- Alternately, the reigns of 7 Rishis, Indra and Manu = 1 Manwantara = 71x12,000+A = 852,000 years of the gods+A (A is not given)

- 14 Manwantaras = a day of Brahma

Our Current Date: We are currently in the 28th kaliyuga of the first day of the 1st year of the shvetavaraha kalpa of the second parardha of Brahma in the reign of the 7th Manu, Manu Vaivasvata. This is the 51st year of the present Brahma and so about 155 trillion years have elapsed since He took over as Brahma.

The current Kali Yuga (Iron Age) began at midnight 17 February/18 February in 3102 BC in the proleptic Julian calendar.

DAY OF BRAHMA

In Hindu esoteric teachings, one *day of Brahma* is a length of time consisting of a thousand cycles of four yugas, or ages: Satya, Treta, Dvapara and Kali. One 'Day of Brahma' then lasts 4,320,000,000 of our years.

- The cycle of Satya is characterized by virtue, wisdom and religion, there being practically no ignorance and vice, and the yuga lasts 1,728,000 years.
- In the Treta-yuga vice is introduced, and this yuga lasts 1,296,000 years.
- In the Dvapara-yuga there is an even greater decline in virtue and religion, vice increasing, and this yuga lasts 864,000 years.
- And finally in Kali-yuga (the yuga we have been experiencing over the past 5000 years) there is an abundance of strife, ignorance, irreligion and vice, true virtue being practically nonexistent, and this yuga lasts 432,000 years.

In Kali-yuga vice increases to such a point that at the termination of the yuga the Supreme Lord himself appears as the Kalki Avatara, vanquishes the demons, saves his devotees, and commences another Satya-yuga. Then the process is set rolling again.

These four yugas, rotating a thousand times, comprise one day of Brahma, and the same number comprise one night. Brahma lives one hundred of such years and then dies. These hundred years by earth calculations total to 311 trillion and 40 billion earth years. By these calculations the life of Brahma seems fantastic and interminable, but from the viewpoint of eternity it is as brief as a lightning flash.

5

MYTHOLOGICAL WEAPONS AND FIGURES OF ANCIENT INDIA

INTRODUCTION

This system take into account the precssion of Vernal Equinox, which result in the relative movement of this astronomical-point against the background of stars in the sky. This movement is very slow, and takes many millania of astronomical observation, to be noticalbe. Ancient Indians aptly took this frame of reference of time, whenever they mention any event, to be remembered. Thus these references are found in Mahabharata and Puranas, while they mention historical events like the Kurukshetra War.

This article tries to compile and classify the prominent personalities of ancient India that finds mention in more than one source of Sanskrit/Vedic literature like the two Hindu epics viz the Mahabharata and the Ramayana, the Puranas and the Vedas with their supplement texts. It also tries to clear the ambiguities arising from the names like Rama and Krishna. The exact date in which these personalities lived is not clear, owing to their antiquity. However it is possible to sequence their life-times based on the Yuga system of time reckoning, which was popular in ancient India. The Yuga system speaks about four Yugas, or epoches of history. The first one being *Krita Yuga*, which was prehistory even to those ancient historians who authored the Sanskrit-Vedic literature. The second Yuga was *Treta Yuga* and the third *Dwapara Yuga*. These two Yugas were contemporary to the ancient historians, in the sense that, they explained events of those epoches as if it was happening during their own time period. This is how the epic Ramayana describes about the reign of Rama and the epic Mahabharata describes about the Kurukshetra War. The last Yuga is *Kali Yuga* which is the period after the Kurukshetra War.

No other Yugas were mentioned, because after this age, those ancinet historians became extinct, and that ancient phsyche no longer exist, except in modern day Hindu traditions, in a transformed state. The mapping of Yuga system into current historic dates (BC & AD) is still under research. The extrimities are those in which the four Yugas have to shrink into a short time span of 1500 BC to 500 AD based on the Indic studies of Max Muller, and those modern studies based on the astronomical, geographical and linguistic evidence, in which it spans from 10000 BC to 500 AD.

The Three Ramas: The name Rama is very common in the ancient Indian literature. There is mention about three district Ramas. They were listed based on the order of their existence.

Bhargava Rama: This Rama was a Brahmin warrior in the lineage of Bhrigus. He was also known as Parasurama.

Raghava Rama: Among all the Ramas of Sanskrit literature, Raghava Rama was the most famous. The epic Ramayana is all about this Rama. The word *Ramayana* means *Rama's travels* in Sanskrit. He was a Kshatriya king, in the Ikshwaku clan, in the lineage of a famous king Raghu, and hence called by the name Raghava Rama.

Bala Rama: This Rama was a Yadava. He was the brother of Krishna, the great political leader during the period of Kurukshetra War. He was also known as Valarama, Sankarshana and as the Son of Rohini.

THE THREE KRISHNAS

Krishna Dwaipayana Vyasa: This Krishna was a great sage, and the author of the epic Mahabharata.

Vasudeva Krishna: This Krishna was the most popular Krishna. He was the author of Bhagavad Gita, the charioteer of Arjuna, during the Kurukshetra War, a great political leader, with divine and ascetic dimensions.

Krishna of Panchala: This Krishna was a women, the wife of the Pandavas, who was also known as Panchali and Draupadi.

THE TWO BHIMAS

The Pandava Bhima: This Bhima was younger brother of the Pandava King Yudhisthira. He was also known by the names Bhimasena, Vrikodara, etc. He was an expert in mace fight and a rival to the Kuru King Duryodhana in mace fight. In Kurukshetra War Bhima killed Duryodhana in mace fight. Both were disciples of Bala Rama.

The Vidarbha King Bhima: Another Bhima mentioned in Mahabharata was Bhima, the king of Vidarbha Kingdom. He was the father of Damayanti, a popular princess and the wife of king Nala of Nishadha Kingdom.

THE TWO ARJUNAS

The Pandava Arjuna: This Arjuna was the second brother of the Pandava King Yudhisthira. He was also known by several names, like Phalguna, Dhanunjaya, Partha, Vijaya, Kiriti, Indrajit, Savyasachi, etc. He was a great friend of Vasudeva Krishna, to whom he expunded the famous philosophy known as the Bhagavad Gita, during the Kurukshetra War. Arjuna was the greatest hero of the Kurukshetra War.

Kartavirya Arjuna of Haihaya Tribe: Haihaya tribe was a brach of Yadavas, who ruled the Haihaya Kingdom. He was the first victim of Bhargava Rama, who destroyed the Kshatriya kings of ancient India. He was the king of Haiheyas, who almost got the status of an emperor. He was a devotee of Dattatreya, now worshipped as a deity, especially in Maharashtra state of India. However, the encounter with the Bhargavas headed by Parasurama (Bhargava Rama) lead to Kartavirya's decline.

THE TWO NAKULAS

The Pandava Nakula: This Nakula, was a Pandava and one among the twin sons of Pandu's second wife Madri. He was well versed in the Science of Horses. He authored a book on horse-training and horce-medicines.

The Tribe called Nakulas: There was a tribe of kings called the Nakulas, as per the epic Mahabharata. They have taken part in the Kurukshetra War.

THE TWO SAHADEVAS

The Pandava Sahadevas: This Sahadeva, was a Pandava and one among the twin sons of Pandu's second wife Madri. He was a great warrior skilled in the use of sword. He also mastered the science of Astronomy and Astrology.

Sahadeva the King of Magadha: The king of Magadha Kingdom, Jarasandha had a son by the name of Sahadeva. After Jarasandha's death by the hands of the Pandava Bhima, Vasudeva Krishna installed Sahadeva on the throne of Magadha. He took part in the Kurukshetra War siding with Duryodhana.

THE JANAMEJAYAS

Janamejaya IV: The most popular figure with the name Janamejaya in Mahabharata is the grand-grandson of Arjuna. The epic Mahabharata is structured as a narration of the history of the Bharatas (the kings of the Bharata Dyasty), told by Vaisampayana, a disciple of Krishna Dwaipayana Vyasa to this Janamejaya. He was the last popular king in the line of the Kuru Kings. His lineage extends from Arjuna as follows:-
Arjuna-> Abhimanyu-> Parikshit II-> Janamejaya IV.

Other Janamejayas in the Line of Puru Kings: *Three more kings with the name Janamejaya were mentioned in the* Lunar Dynasty *of kings. They were designated as Janamejaya I, Janamejaya II and Janamejaya III.*

Janamejaya I: Janamejaya I was the son of Puru, the founder of Paurava Dynasty of kings. (Daksha-> Aditi-> Vivaswat-> Manu-> Ha (Vudha)-> Pururavas (Aila)-> Ayus-> Nahusha-> Yayati-> Puru-> Janamejaya I

Janamejaya II: Janamejaya II was the son of Kuru the founder of Kuru Dynasty. (Samvarana-> Kuru-> *Janamejaya II*)

Janamejaya III: Janamejaya III was born in the race of a Kuru king designated as Parikshit I. Kauravas and Pandavas both descended from him. (Samvarana-> Kuru-> Avikshit-> Parikshit I->... *Janamejaya III*). Janamejaya III's lineage leads to the Kauravas and Pandavas as follows:

JANAMEJAYAS IN UNKNOWN RACES MENTIONED BY DIFFERENT PEOPLE

Janamejaya Mentioned by Bhishma: A king named Janamejaya is mentioned in the 12th volume (Santi Parva) of Mahabharata, by Bhishma in his narration to Yudhisthira. Bhishma describes the conversation between this Janamejaya and a sage named Indrota the son of Sunaka on the subject of expiation from sins. Indrota also assisted a horse sacrifice performed by this king. This narration extends into three chapters (Mbh 12.149, 12.150, 12.151).

Janamejaya Mentioned by Vyasa: Vyasa, mentiones about a king Janamejaya to his son Suka. This conversation, also comes in the 12th volume (Santi Parva) of Mahabharata, within the narration of Bhishma to Yudhisthira.

Mbh 12.233:-King Janamejaya, by giving away his own body, proceeded to high regions of felicity.

Janamejaya Mentioned by Dhrtarashtra: Dhrtarashtra mentions to his son Duryodhana about a Janamejaya who conquered many kingdoms in three days. Mbh.12.123.

JANAMEJAYA MENTIONED BY BHRAMA TO VASISHTHA

Mbh.13.6:- Was not Janamejaya, who followed the foot-prints of Sakra, checked and put down by the gods for killing a Brahmana woman?—Brahma to Vasishtha.

MENTION OF 80 KINGS BY THE NAME OF JANAMEJAYA

Mbh.2.8:- These kings were described to be dead and appear in the court of the lord of death, Yama.

JANAMEJAYA, VANQUISHED BY MANDHATRI

Mbh.7.60:- Mandhatri vanquished, by his bow *Janamejaya* and Sudhanwan and Jaya and Suna and Vrihadratha and Nriga.

Janamejaya Mentioned by Drupada: Drupada, in his list of kings to be summoned to aid Pandavas in Kurukshetra War mentioned about a Janamejaya.

JANAMEJAYA OF SOLAR DYNASTY MENTIONED BY BHISHMA

Mbh.13.137:- King Janamejaya of the solar race, went to the highest heaven by making a gift of earrings, fine vehicles, and cows to Brahmanas.—Bhishma to Yudhisthira

JANAMEJAYA OF HILLY COUNTRY, TOOK PART IN KURUKSHETRA WAR

Mbh.8.6:- Janamejaya of the hilly country, endued with great prowess and accomplished in encounters with the mace, hath, O king, been slain by Dhrtarashtra's son Durmukha.

THE PANCHALA PRINCE, JANAMEJAYA IN KURUKSHETRA WAR

Mbh.8.49:- The Pancala prince *Janamejaya* then pierced

Karna with many arrows. Mbh.8.82:-Felling Janamejaya's driver with broad-faced shafts called Anjalikas, Karna next slew the steeds of that Pancala warrior. Karna then pierced Shikhandi with a dozen keen shafts, and Uttamauja with half a dozen, and Yudhamanyu with three, and then each of the other two, *viz.*, Somaka *Janamejaya* and Dhrishtadyumna with three shafts.

Janamejaya of Nepa Mentioned by Bhima: This Janamejaya is mentioned by Bhima, as a king of Nepa, who caused the destruction of his own race. Mbh.7.74

THE NAGA NAMED JANAMEJAYA

Mbh.2.9:-This Janamejaya was a Naga listed among the Naga Kings who attended the court of Varuna. He was mentioned by Narada to Yudisthira.

MENTION OF AN ASURA KING JANAMEJAYA

Mbh.1.67:-A king Janamejaya is said to be born of the Asura class called Krodhaveshas.

THE PARIKSHITS

Parikshit II: The most popular figure with the name Parikshit in Mahabharata is the grandson of Arjuna. His lineage extends from Arjuna as follows:-Arjuna-> Abhimanyu-> Parikshit II. He was born as a dead child to princess Uttara, the wife of Abhimanyu. Later Vasudeva Krishna revived him and gave him the name, Parikshit. The famous king Janamejaya IV was his son, onto him the epic Mahabharata was narrated by Vasampayana the disciple of Krishna Dwaipayana Vyasa.

THE TWO BHARATAS

Bharata, the Brother of Raghava Rama: Raghava Rama had three brothers, viz, Bharata, Lakshmana and Shatrughna. Bharata ruled the Kosala kingdom, temporarily in the absence of Rama. Bharata also had conquered the Gandhara Kingdom, which was close to Kekaya Kingdom, the native kingdom of his mother Kaikeyi.

Bharata, the Great King of Lunar Dynasty: The Emperor Bharata was the son of the King Dushyanta and Sakuntala. Dushmanta was a king in the line of Puru Dynasty, which itself was a branch of the Lunar Dynasty. The Kuru dynasty as well as the Srinjaya dynasty of the Panchala kings was derived from the Puru Dynasty. After the rule of Bharata, who almost became a great emperor, the dynasty came to be called as the Bharata Dynasty. The name Bhaarata, an official name of India, with equal status, was derived from this dynasty name.

THE TWO LAKSHMANAS

Lakshmana, the Brother of Raghava Rama: Raghava Rama had three brothers, viz, Bharata, Lakshmana and Sathrughna. Bharata was the closest brother to Rama, his companion in all the sojourns, that was described in the epic Ramayana. Lakshmana had undertaken many conquests for the sake of Rama.

Lakshmana the Son of Kuru King Duryodhana: This Lakshmana was the son of Duryodhana the enemy of Pandavas as per the epic Mahabharata. Lakshmana took part in the Kurukshetra War. His main antagonist was Abhimanyu the son of the Pandava, Arjuna.

HINDU DENOMINATIONS

Hinduism encompasses many movements and brahminic schools are fairly organized within *Hindu denominations*. A denomination shares a common ground of beliefs but embraces many different movements and schools inside its philosophical branches.

Basic Overview: Hinduism is a very rich and complex religion. Each Caste is like a denomination with rich religious practices. Professional priestly brahmin castes have denominations like Shaivism, Shaktism, Vaishnavism, and Smartha. Each of these four denominations share rituals, beliefs, traditions and personal Gods with one another, but each denomination has a different philosophy on how to achieve life's ultimate goal (Moksha, liberation) and different views of the Gods.

Each follows different methods of self-realization and worships different aspects of the One Supreme God. However, each respects and accepts all others, and conflict of any kind is rare. Among Hindu followers as a whole, there is a strong belief that there are many paths leading to the One God or the Source, whatever one chooses to call that ultimate Truth.

The presence of different denominations and schools within Hinduism should not be viewed as a schism. On the contrary, there is no animosity between the schools. Instead there is a healthy *cross-pollination* of ideas and logical debate that serves to refine each school's philosophy. It is not uncommon, or disallowed, for an individual to follow one school but take the point of view of another school for a certain issue.

Vaishnavism: *Vaishnavas* worship Vishnu, or his avataras (especially Krishna and Rama) as the supreme deity. This is the largest denomination, with approx. 580 million followers.

Vaishnava sampradayas:

- Madhvas, followers of Madhavacharya
- Shri Vaishnavas, followers of Ramanujacharya
- Rudra Vaishnavas, followers of Vallabhacharya
- Nimbarka Vaishnavas
- Gaudiya Vaishnavism, followers of Chaitanya Mahaprabhu. They are connected to Madhva sampradaya.

Modern Vaishnava groups attached to the main sampradayas:

- Swaminarayan-Ramanuja sampradaya; although they are slanted towards Vaishnavism, Swaminarayan also believed in a Smarta view; he adopted panchadevata system. (Five forms of God, as per Smarta theology.

- International Society for Krishna Consciousness-Madhva/Gaudiya Vaishnava sampradaya
- Sri Krishna Chaitanya Mission-Madhva/Gaudiya Vaishnava sampradaya

Zaivism: Zaivites are those who primarily worship God *Ziva* as Supreme God, both Immanent and Transcendent. There are approx. 220 million followers of Zaivism.

Zaivism embraces at the same time Monism and Dualism. It focuses on yoga, meditation and love for all beings.

Major theological schools of Zaivism include Kashmir Zaivism, Zaiva Siddhanta and Virasaivism.

To Zaivites God Ziva is both with and without form; He is the Supreme Dancer, *Nataraja*. He is the linga, without beginning or end.

- Siddha Yoga
- Lingayats in Karnataka

Shaktism: Shaktas worship Shakti, the divine Mother, in her many forms like (Kali, Durga, Laxmi, Saraswati, etc.).

Shakta form was one of the oldest forms of Hindu religion (evidences even from Indus valley civilisation), but with evolution of civilisation and emergence of various doctrines, various other forms of Hindu philosophy emerged. Shaivism and Shakta forms are really inseparable, as is the description of Shiva and Shakti/Sati/Parvati. Vaishanvism has also its connections with Shakta philosophy as Goddess Durga herself is called Narayani.

Shakta in behaviour are identical to the Shaivites or Vaishanvites in the fundamental philosophy, but they tend to be very liberal in their thinking. Typically in a Shakta family/household, all Ishwar forms are worshipped alongside. Shaktas many times do not identify themselves as Shaktas but as Hindus in general. In India, Bengal, Assam, Orissa and Bihar are the main regions where detailed Devi Pujan or Shakta rituals are followed. Madhya Pradesh (Chamunda Pujan), Maharashtra and Gujarat (Nav Durga) are also equally zealous and various rituals for Devi Pujan and celebration take place in these regions. It is actually unfair and very hard to identify or isolate Shaktas amongst any other denominations. Shaktas do not believe in denominations, and believe that these ideas of classification are a very Christian way of classification. This might be true as Devi Pujan (worship) is actually a nationwide phenomenon.

One of the unique features of Shaktas is that there is immense respect for women as mothers in common household. Young sons and daughters touch the feet of their mother, seeking her blessings on festive/important occasions. Simultaneously mothers typically pray/worship for the well being of their family and children.

To roughly cover the Shakta centres all over India, one could begin with all the Shakti Peeth in India. There are typically 51 Shakti Peeth all over India, which are typically revered as places of pilgrimage. The mythological background behind these temples or Shakti Peeth goes back to the story of Shiva performing "Tandava" (the dance of fury) carrying the dead and burnt body of Sati in immense anger, effectively destroying the entire Universe. Seeing Shiva's rage, Vishnu realised that Shiva's strength emerged from the dead body of Sati/Shakti and decided to cut her dead body to pieces with his Sudarshan chakra, which led to halting of Shiva's wrath. There were 51 pieces of her dead body which fell on earth at 51 places and those are the spots of Shakti Peeth. To name a few are the Kalighat Mandir at Kolkata, the Kamakhya Mandir at Assam, the Vaishnav Devi Mandir at Jammu and many others.

Typically in Shakta philosophy dominated regions, various forms of Hindu religion thrive harmoniously. It is the understanding of Shaktas, that everyone is the son/daughter of the same Divine Mother, and hence harmonious existence is "Mother's" desire. Various stalwarts of Hindu Philosophy *viz.* Sri Ramakrishna Paramhansa Dev and Swami Vivekananda who guided the Hindu world with their depth of understanding of humanity and religion, were Shaktas.

Shaktas celebrate all festivals like Dussera/Durga Puja, Diwali/Kali Puja/Lakshmi Puja, Satya Narayan Puja, Ganesha Puja, Saraswati Puja, Kartik Puja, Janmashtami, Shivaratri, Sankranti, etc. including all possible days. Shaktas never refuse to worship one or the other form of God unlike some Vaishnavites in South India. Shaktas also have diverse philosophy and rituals including Mantra and Tantra. Several Hindu rituals like putting sindoor and bindi and basically the entire attire of Hindu bride has originated from the concept of Goddess Durga and Lakshmi.

Shakta being the oldest form has its origin in Vedas, and Puranas. Durga Puran, Kalika Puran and Skanda Puran are some of the basic sources. Ramayana, Mahabharata and Shrimad Bhagavad Gita also form the basic texts, read and revered by every Shakta. It is very common to see Krishna Pujan and Shiva Pujan in Shakta families. One of the possible explanations could be the fact that Sri Rama the very revered and worshipped avatar of Narayan himself is described to be an ardent Shakti worshipper. It is known that celebration of Durga Puja in Bengal was started, marking the worship performed by Rama himself. In addition, the legends of the demons, Madhu and Kaitabh, also mention the spell cast by Goddess Kali on the demons, which made it easy for Narayan to kill them and save mankind. Apparently, the scriptures and mythology are not classified into such denominations, and after all its those scriptures that still dictate the basic "psyche" of Hindu philosophy.

Smartism: *Smarthas* have free rein to choose whichever deity they wish to worship. They usually worship five deities (pancopasana) or panchadevata as personal formful manifestations of the impersonal Absolute, Brahman. *Smartas* accept and worship the six manifestations of God, (Ganesha, Shiva, Shakti, Vishnu, Surya and Skanda) and the choice of the nature of God is up to the individual worshipper since different manifestations of God are held to be equivalent. It is a liberal and eclectic sect.

different manifestations of God are held to be equivalent. It is a liberal and eclectic sect.

- It is the Smarta view that dominates the view of Hinduism in the West as Smarta belief includes Advaita belief and the first Hindu saint, who significantly brought Hinduism to the west was Swami Vivekananda, an adherent of Advaita. Not till much later, gurus, such as A.C. Bhaktivedanta Swami Prabhupada, and others, brought a Vaishnavite perspective to the West. By contrast with Smarta/Advaita belief, Vaishnavism and Shaivism follows a singular concept of God, or panentheistic monotheism or panentheistic monism.

NEWER DENOMINATIONS

Agama Hindu Dharma: The newest and least numerous denominations are comprised of Balinese Hindus, who make up a sect of Hinduism that once flourished on the nearby island of Java until late 16th century, when a vast majority of its adherents converted to Islam. Theologically, it is closer to Zaivism than to other major sects of Hinduism.

The term "Agama Hindu Dharma" can also refer to the traditional practices in Kalimantan, Sumatra, Sulawesi and other places in Indonesia, where people have started to identify and accept their agamas as Hinduism.

HINDU DEITIES

Ishvara: In Hinduism, when God is thought of as the supreme all-powerful person (rather than as the infinite principle called Brahman), God is called Bhagvan. *Bhagvan* is a word used to refer to the personal aspect of God in general; it is not specific to a particular deity. Bhagvan transcends gender, yet can be looked upon as both father and mother, child, or sweetheart. Most Hindus, in their daily devotional practices, worship some form of this personal aspect of God, although they believe in the more abstract concept of Brahman as well. Sometimes this means worshipping God through an image or a picture. Sometimes it just means thinking of God as a personal being.

Depending on which aspect of Bhagvan one is talking about, a different name will be used—and frequently a different image or picture. For instance, when God is talked about in the aspect as the creator, God is called Brahm. When referred to in the capacity as preserver of the world, God is called Vishnu. When referred to in the capacity as destroyer of the world, God is called Shiva. Many of these individual aspects of God also have other names and images. For example, Krishna and Rama are considered forms of Vishnu. All the various deities and images one finds in Hinduism are considered manifestations of the same God, called Bhagvan in the personal aspect and Brahman when referred to as an abstract concept.

In their personal religious practices, Hindus worship primarily one or another of these deities, known as their "ishta devat," or chosen idol. The particular form of God worshipped as one's chosen ideal is a matter of individual preference. Regional and family traditions can play a large part in influencing this choice. Hindus may also take guidance about this choice from their scriptures.

Although Hindus may worship deities other than their chosen idol from time to time as well, depending on the occasion and their personal inclinations, it is not expected that they will worship—or even know about—every form of God. Hindus generally choose one concept of God (*e.g.*, Krishna, Rama, Shiva, or Kali) and cultivate devotion to that chosen form, while at the same time respecting the chosen ideals of other people.

Devas and Devis: Krishna, an avatra of Vishnu, reveals his universal form to the devotee Arjuna in the *Bhagavad Gita*. This image indicates that all deities are forms of the One God, and that God is everything that exists. The Hindu religion speaks of many individual deities, called Devas. Goddesses are called *dev+s*. The various devas and dev+s are personifications of various aspects of one and the same God (Ishvara). For instance, when a Hindu thinks of Ishvara as the giver of knowledge and learning, that aspect of Ishvara is personified as the deity Saraswati. In the same manner, the deity Lakshmi personifies Ishvara as the giver of wealth and prosperity. This does not imply that Ishvara is the Lord of all the other deities; Ishvara is just the name used to refer to the personal God in general, when no *particular* deity is being referred to.

The *devas* (also called *devats*) constitute an integral part of the colourful Hindu culture. These various forms of God are depicted in innumerable paintings, statues, murals, and scriptural stories that can be found in temples, homes, businesses, and other places. In Hinduism the scriptures recommend that for the satisfaction of a particular material desire a person may worship a particular deity. For example, shopkeepers frequently keep a statue or picture of the Devi Lakshmi in their shops. The elephant-headed deva known as Ganesha is worshipped before commencing any undertaking, as he represents God's aspect as the remover of obstacles. Students and scholars may propitiate Saraswati, the Devi of learning, before taking an exam or giving a lecture.

The most ancient Vedic *devas* included Indra, Agni, Soma, Varuna, Mitra, Savitri, Rudra, Prajapati, Vishnu, Aryaman and the Ashvins; important *dev+s* were *Sarasvat+*, *jc* and *Prithv+*. Later scriptures called the *Purnas* recount traditional stories about each individual deity.

Vishnu and *Shiva* are not regarded as ordinary *devas* but as *Mahdevas* ("Great Gods") because of their central positions in worship and mythology. The *Purnas* also laud other *devas,* such as *Ganesha* and *Hanumn,* and *avatras* such as *Rma* and *Krishna*. Goddesses are worshipped when God is thought of as the Universal Mother. Particular forms of the Universal Mother include *Lakshm+*, *Sarasvat+* and *Parvat+, Durg*, and *Kl+*.

There are some Hindus who consider the various deities not as forms of the one Ishwara, but as independently existing entities, and may thus be properly considered polytheistic to some extent.

Avataras (incarnations of God): Rama (centre), an avatara, shown with wife Sita, brother Lakshmana and devotee Hanuman. Rama is shown with blue skin, symbolizing divinity. Many denominations of Hinduism, such as Vaishnavism and Smartism, teach that from time to time, God comes to Earth as a human being to help humans along in their struggle toward enlightenment and salvation (Moksha). Such an incarnation of God is called an avatara. In some respects, the Hindu concept of avatara is similar to the belief found in Christianity that God came to the earth in the form of Jesus. However, whereas most Christians believe that God has assumed a human body on only one occasion, Hinduism teaches that there have been *multiple* avatars throughout history—and that there will be more in the future. Thus Krishna, an incarnation of God, says:

Whenever righteousness declines

And unrighteousness increases,

I make myself a body;

In every age I come back

To deliver the holy,

To destroy the sin of the sinner,

To establish righteousness.

The most famous of the divine incarnations are Rama, whose life is depicted in the Ramayana, and Krishna, whose life is depicted in the Mahabharata and the Srimad Bhagavatam. The Bhagavad Gita, which contains the spiritual teachings of Krishna, is one of the most widely-read scriptures in Hinduism.

Trimurti: In Hinduism, the Trimurti (also called *the Hindu* trinity) are three aspects of God in His forms as Brahma, Vishnu and Shiva.

- Brahma—the Creator
- Vishnu—the Preserver
- Shiva—the Destroyer

Some other popular Hindu aspects of God include Devi, Krishna, Ganesha, Hanuman, Murugan, Ramachandra and Lakshmi. Smarta Hindus believe that God, in whatever form they prefer, ("Ishta Devata,", *i.e.*, the preferred form of God) can grant worshippers grace to bring them closer to Moksha, end of the cycle of rebirth. The great Hindu saint Ramakrishna studied and embraced other religions, such as Christianity and Islam, and came to the same conclusion proclaimed by the Vedas, "*Truth is one; the wise call it by various names.* (*Ekam Sat Viprah Bahuda Vadanti*)

Denominations of Hinduism: Contemporary Hinduism traditionally has four major divisions, Shaivism, Shaktism, Vaishnavism, and Smarthism.

According to Adherents.com there are 580,000,000 Vaishnavas, 220,000,000 Shaivites and 22,000,000 neo-Hindus and reform Hindus.

However the Shakti sect connects God as Lord Shiva also, as the Aparabrahm while Shakti is the Parabrahm. Further the Saura sect connects itself with Lord Vishnu, one of the 12 Adityas (solar deities.) Ganesha worshippers would connect themselves with Lord Shiva as Lord Shiva is the Father of Lord Ganesha and hence, Lord Ganesha is a Shaiv deity.

Hinduism is a very rich and complex religion. Each of its four denominations shares rituals, beliefs, traditions and personal Gods with one another, but each sect have a same and different philosophy on how to achieve life's ultimate goal (Moksha, liberation). For example a person can be a Shiva devotee and a Vishnu devotee but they can practice the Advaita Vedanta philosophy (Darshana) which believes there is no difference between the Brahman and the Soul. Conversely a Hindu may follow the Dvaita philosophy which stresses that Brahman and the Soul are not the same. But each denomination fundamentally believes in different methods of self-realisation and in different aspects of the One Supreme God. However, each denomination respects and accepts all others, and conflict of any kind is rare.

Vaishnavism, Shaivism and Shaktism, respectively believe in a monotheistic ideal of Vishnu (often as Krishna), Shiva, or Devi; this view does not exclude other personal Gods, as they are understood to be aspects of the chosen ideal (*e.g.*, to many devotees of Krishna, Shiva is seen as having sprung from Krishna's creative force). Often, the monad Brahman is seen as the one source, with all other gods emanating therefrom. Thus, with all Hindus, there is a strong belief in all paths being true religions that lead to one God or source, whatever one chooses to call the ultimate truth.

Even Vaisnavites, like other Hindus, have tolerance for other beliefs because Lord Krishna, avatar of Vishnu, said so in the Gita. Krishna said:

> *"I am in everyone's heart as the Supersoul. As soon as one desires to worship some demigod, I make his faith steady so that he can devote himself to that particular deity. Endowed with such a faith, he endeavors to worship a particular demigod and obtains his desires. But in actuality these benefits are bestowed by Me alone." (Gita: 7:21-22).*

Another quote in the Gita states:

> *"Those who are devotees of other gods and who worship them with faith actually worship only Me, O son of Kunt+, but they do so in a wrong way." (Gita: 9:23).*

Even a Vedic verse illustrates this theme of tolerance. The Vedas are revered in Hinduism, regardless of denomination. For example, a well-known Rig Vedic hymn stemming from Hinduism states that "Truth is One, though the sages know it variously." This is in contrast with some other religious traditions, where one must believe in only one form of God and to totally reject or disdain other beliefs.

Polytheistic Gods: Although the pantheistic system allowed only a subordinate rank to the old polytheistic gods, and the actual religious belief of the people was probably but little affected by their existence, they continued to occupy an important place in the affections of the poet, and were still represented as exercising considerable influence on the destinies of man. The most prominent of them were regarded as the appointed Loka palas, or guardians of the world; and as such they were made to preside over the four cardinal and (according to some authorities) the intermediate points of the compass.

Thus Indra, the chief of the devas, was regarded as the regent of the east; Agni, the fire, was in the same way associated with the southeast; Yama, lord of death and justice with the south; Surya, the sun, with the southwest; Varuna, originally the representative of the all-embracing heaven (atmosphere), now the god of the ocean, with the west; Vayu (or Pavana), the wind, with the northwest; Kubera, the god of wealth, with the north; and Soma with the northeast. (Note: In some traditions, an aspect of Shiva is regarded as the regent of the northeast and Nirrti the regent of the southwest.)

In the institutes of Manu the Loka palas are represented as standing in close relation to the ruling king, who is saki to be composed of particles of these his tutelary deities. The retinue of Indra consists chiefly of the Devas (angels), Gandharvas, a class of genii, considered in the epics as the celestial musicians; and Apsaras, lovely nymphs, who are frequently employed by the gods to make the pious devotee desist from carrying his austere practices to an extent that might render him dangerous to their power. Narada, an ancient sage (probably a personification of the cloud, the water-giver), is considered as the messenger between the gods and men, and as having sprung from the forehead of Brahma.

The interesting office of the god of love is held by Kamadeva, also called Ananga, the bodyless, because, as the myth relates, having once tried by the power of his mischievous arrow to make Shiva fall in love with Parvati, whilst he was engaged in devotional practices, the urchin was reduced to ashes by a glance of the angry god. Two other mythological figures of some importance are considered as sons of Shiva and Parvati, *viz.* Karttikeya or Skanda, the leader of the heavenly armies, who was supposed to have been fostered by the six Knittikas or

Pleiades; and Ganesha (lord of troops), the elephant-headed god of wisdom, and at the same time the leader of the dii minorum gentium.

Smartism: Smartism, a denomination of Hinduism is a monist as well as a monotheist religion that understands different deities as representing various aspects and principles of one supreme entity, Brahman or parabrahman. Teachers such as Swamī Vivekananda, who brought Hinduism to the West, held beliefs like those found in Smartism, although he usually referred to his religion as Vedanta. Other denominations of Hinduism do not strictly hold this belief. A Smartist would have no problem worshipping Shiva or Vishnu together as he views the different aspects of God as leading to the same One God. It is the Smarta view that dominates the view of Hinduism in the West. By contrast, a Vaishnavite considers Vishnu as the one true God, worthy of worship and other forms as subordinate.

Devas in the Vedas: The pantheon in the Zrauta tradition consists of various gods and goddesses. However these entities may not hold the traditional meaning of gods and goddesses in English. Instead the *devas* (which is the sanskrit word used to represent these entities) represent certain forces. For instance, the deva Agni has one aspect as the flame. But this flame symbolises the psychological power associated with Agni namely the power of will. Agni can be called God-will. Similarly Indra is the God-mind; Saraswati is the Power of Inspiration, not merely of learning.

The main devas are (vide 6th anuvaka of Chamakam):

SCHOOLS OF HINDUISM

Hinduism encompasses many movements and schools fairly organized within Hindu *sects*. A sect is a denomination that shares a common ground of beliefs but embraces many different schools inside its philosophical branches.

The many schools and diverse movements of Hinduism trace their origins from as far back as three thousand years to only a few decades. Most are the natural evolution and reinterpretation of old Vedanta and Yoga precepts. Hinduism is recognized as a very dynamic religion, accepting and continuously transmuting new influences from inside and outside with equal ease and remarkable lack of conflict.

The presence of different schools and sects within Hinduism should not be viewed as a schism. On the contrary, there is no animosity between the schools. Instead there is a healthy *cross-pollination* of ideas and logical debate that serves to refine each school's understanding of Hinduism. It is not uncommon, or disallowed, for an individual to follow one school but take the point of view of another school for a certain issue.

Hinduism, as most other major religions, has a great number of schools. The most important are listed below, under the sect in which they find greater expression:

SCHOOLS IN VAISHNAVISM

- Srivaishnavism or Sri-Vaishnava Sampradaya, adheres to teachings of Ramanuja
- Dvaita or Brahma Sampradaya, adheres to teachings of Madhva
- Ramanandi Sampraday, adheres to the teachings of Ramananda
- Shree Swaminarayan Sampraday, adheres to teachings of Swaminarayan
- Pushtimarg Sampraday or Rudra Sampradaya, adheres to the teachings of Vishnuswami/Vallabhacharya
- Kumara Sampraday, adheres to teachings of Nimbarka (Nimbarkacharya)
- Gaudiya Vaishnavism (includes ISKCON, the Hare Krishna movement), adheres to the teachings of Chaitanya Mahaprabhu (Gaurangacharya)
- Mahapuruxiya dharma or Asomiya Vaishnavism, adheres to the teachings of Srimanta Sankaradeva
- Krishna Pranami Sampraday, adheres to the teachings of Devachandra Maharaj

SCHOOLS IN SHAIVISM

- Saiva Siddhanta, adheres to the teachings of Tirumular/ Sundaranatha (Nandinatha Sampradaya, the monistic school) or of Meykandadeva (Meykandar Sampradaya, the dualistic school)
- Adinath Sampradaya or Siddha Siddhanta, adheres to the teachings of Gorakhnath and Matsyendranath
- Shiva Advaita, adheres to the teachings of Nilakantha (Srikantha) and Appayya Dikshitar
- Trika Shaivism or Kashmir Shaivism, adheres to the teachings of Vasugupta and his disciplinic lineage, including Abhinavagupta
- Pasupata Shaivism, adheres to the teachings of Lakulisa
- Veerashaivism or Lingayat Dharma, adheres to the teachings of Basavanna

INDIAN MYTHOLOGICAL WEAPONS

AGNI

Agni is a Hindu and Vedic deity. The word *agni* is Sanskrit for "fire" (noun), cognate with Latin *ignis* (the root of English *ignite*). He is the creator of the Agneyestra a fire weapon. The sacrifices made to Agni go to the deities because Agni is a messenger from and to the other gods. He is ever-young, because the fire is re-lit every day; but also he is immortal.

He is worshipped under a threefold form: fire on earth, lightning and the sun. His cult survived the change of the ancient Vedic nature-worship into modern Hinduism, and there are fire-priests (agnihotr) whose duty is to watch over his worshippers. The sacred fire-drill for procuring the temple-fire by friction—symbolic of Agni's daily miraculous birth—is still used.

Depictions: In Hindu art, Agni is represented as red and two-faced (sometimes covered with butter), suggesting both his destructive and beneficent qualities, and with black eyes and hair, three legs and seven arms. He rides a ram, or a chariot pulled by goats or, more rarely, parrots. Seven rays of light emanate from his body. One of his names is "Sapta jihva", 'seven tongues'.

Family: In Hinduism, he is a deva, second only to Indra in the power and importance attributed to him in Vedic mythology. He is Indra's twin, and therefore a son of Dyaus Pita and Prthivi. While in another version, he is a son of Kashyapa and Aditi or a Queen who kept her pregnancy secret from her husband. He has ten mothers, or ten sisters, or ten maidservants, who represent the ten fingers of the man who lights the fire. He has two parents: these represent the two sticks which, when rubbed together swiftly, create fire (called a fire drill). Some say that he destroyed his parents when he was born because they could not care for him. He is married to Svaha and father of Karttikeya by either Svaha or Ganga. He is one of the Guardians of the directions, representing the southeast.

In some stories about the Hindu gods, Agni is the one who is sent to the front in dangerous situations.

Agni in the Vedas: His name is the first word of the first hymn of the Rigveda:-*agnim +<e purohitam/yajnasya devam Wtvijam/hotraM ratnadhtamam.* (The vowels which are underlined here, carry the Vedic *udtta* pitch accent.)" I praise Agni, the priest of the house, the divine ministrant of sacrifice, the invoker, the best bestower of treasure."

Another hymn runs: "No god indeed, no mortal is beyond the might of thee, the mighty One." He lives among men and is miraculously reborn each day by the fire-drill, the friction of the two sticks which are regarded as his parents. He is the supreme director of religious ceremonies and duties, and even has the power of influencing the fate of each man in the future world. Agni is also representative of the power which digests the food in every person's stomach. He created the stars with the sparks resulting from his flames.

The Rigveda often says that Agni arises from water or dwells in the waters. He may have originally been the same as Apam Napat.

There is a ritual to ignite Agni. This process is called Agni-Mathana. This was the Ancient Hindu way of making fire. Wooden piece from Arani tree (belonging to the family of Ficus religiosa or Urostigma religiosum) is put to vigorous friction, which generates fire.

Agni God as Witness: Although the Vedic fire-sacrifice (yajna) has largely disappeared from modern Hinduism (with the exception of Arya Samaj), Agni with the fire-sacrifice is still the mode of ritual in any modern Hindu marriage, where Agni is said to be the chief sakshi or witness of the marriage and guardian of the sanctity of marriage. Taking Agni (fire) as a witness is a very old tradition-in the Valmiki Ramayana, Rama and Sugreeva swear to help each other and circle the fire thrice as a seal of their bond. Similarly in the Mahabharata, Susarma and his brothers the Trigartas swear by the fire to either defeat Arjuna or die at his hands. Their joint oath earns them the name of "Samsaptaka" as a clan. The tradition stems from the idea that Agni or fire is the purest of all natural elements and is holy as the same.

Agni in Ayurveda: According to Ayurveda, Agni is the biological fire that governs digestion, metabolism and the immune system.

Agni in other Faiths and Religions: In Indo-Tibetan Buddhism, he is a lokapla guarding the Southeast. *Jigten lugs kyi bstan bcos:* which translates, "Make your hearth in the southeast corner of the house, which is the quarter of Agni". He also plays a central role in most Buddhist *homa* fire-puja rites.

BRAHMASTRA

Brahmastra is an arrow created by Brahma. One of the deadliest of weapons that a person can possess (as in Hindu Puranas), it is often speculated in the likeness of a nuclear weapon. It is said that when a Brahmastra is used there will be famine on earth and for 12 years there would be no flora and fauna where it was used, unless the weapon is withdrawn properly following the procedure laid down in the scriptures.

CHAKRAM

The *chakram* is a throwing weapon that was used by the ancient Indians; it is a flat metal ring with a sharp outer edge from 5 to 12 inches (13"30 cm) in diameter.

The word comes from Sanskrit and means round, circle, or wheel. Earliest references come from the Indian epics Mahabharata and Ramayana (here the Sudartana chakram is the weapon of the god Vishnu). It was used by Indian armies, mostly by Sikhs.

It has an effective range of 40 to 50 meters. Because of its aerodynamic shape (similar to an aeroplane wing) it is not easily deflected by wind.

Flying discs and Aerobies are somewhat similar, generally plastic devices for recreational purposes.

A much larger (and purely fictional) version of the chakram has been used in many fantasy and martial arts media. This version, most likely due to its size, is restricted mostly to being a melee weapon instead of a throwing one, with its fighting technique being similar to the acrobatic use of a hula hoop in circus acts.

FILM, TELEVISION, AND ENTERTAINMENT

- Disks are used as weapons in the movie Tron.
- The chakram is featured heavily in the television series Xena: Warrior Princess, as the signature weapon of the title character.
- *Chakram* is also the name of the second episode of the fifth season of *Xena: Warrior Princess*.
- In the movie Krull, the titular character uses a chakram like weapon.
- The character Jango in the anime series One Piece also uses the chakram.

- Oddjob from the James Bond movie Goldfinger uses a chakram-like hat.
- In the movie Predator 2 the Predator has a laser guided Chakram-like weapon.
- Razor-sharp plates are used for self-defense in Stephen King's Wolves of the Calla.
- A chakram weapon is featured in the video game Secret of Mana.
- In Castlevania: Symphony of the Night and Castlevania: Dawn of Sorrow, a chakram is dropped by the enemies Discus Lord and Amalaric Sniper, respectively.
- In the video game Eternal Darkness: Sanity's Requiem, a character, Karim, uses Chakrams on one level.
- In the MMORPG RuneScape, chakrams made of obsidian (known as TokTz-Xil-Ul) can be obtained from defeating TzHaar, or from a shop in the TzHaar city.
- Colette Brunel of the video game Tales of Symphonia fights with two chakrams. She also uses them as melee weapons.
- The character Axel from the *Kingdom Hearts* series uses two fire-based chakrams for his weapons, mostly as melee weapons.
- Chrakram are throwing weapons that return to the thrower like a boomerang in the computer game Arcanum: Of Steamworks and Magick Obscura.
- Kung Lao from the *Mortal Kombat* series has a razor-rimmed hat that can be used as a chakram.
- The reploid Marino can obtain beam chakrams in the video game Mega Man X: Command Mission.
- Sun Shang Xiang in the game series Dynasty Warriors wields a pair of wheel-like blades. They are usually referred to as chakrams, but more accurately resemble wind and fire wheels (a Chinese, rather than Indian weapon). Her moveset does not allow her to throw the weapon like a chakram, but she can throw the wheels

in a wide arc which then return to her.

- In Warcraft 3, the Warden, a Night Elf hero, uses a chakram-like serratted ring-blade (as a melee weapon, not throwing).
- In the Turok 2: Seeds of Evil videogame, the Razorwind weapon is a kind of cybernetic alien chakram, and is one of the most, if not the most powerful weapon.
- In Guild Wars, the Chakram is one of the off-hand weapons usable by the Mesmer class and one of the slashing dagger types used by the Assassin class in Guild Wars: Factions
- In Threads of Fate the character Mint uses a pair of chakrams.
- Sailor Moon uses her tiara as a chakram-like weapon in the popular anime series bearing the same name.
- Wonder Woman has a razor-sharp tiara that she can remove and use as a chakram-like projectile.
- In the manga series Berserk, the character Silat wields chakrams among other weapons of Indian origin.
- Sen of Saturday, the armor piloted by Melissa in the anime Gun X Sword has the chakram as the main weapon and it is also the armors weapon form.
- The character Yakushiji Tenzen uses two Chakram in the 2005 movie SHINOBI Heart Under Blade.
- The character Tira in the video game Soul Calibur 3 wields an oversized Chakram.
- The character Tio in the video game Grandia II attacks using dual Chakrams.
- In Greg Cox's novel, The Eugenics Wars, Khan Noonien Singh rescues Gary Seven from Colonel Anastasia Komananov using chakrams.
- In the video game Nox, the Chakram was a useful ranging equipment that ricochets between the walls and targets and supposedly returns back to the user.
- In the game Fullmetal Alchemist: Curse of the Crimson

Elixir, Edward Elric has the ability to transmute and modify chakrams and use them as a weapon.

- In the video game Suikoden 4 one of the characters named Akaghi uses a chakram as a melee weapon, and in Suikoden 5 two characters named Sialeeds and Sharmitsa use a boomerang type of chakram as a weapon.
- In the video game Baten Kaitos: Eternal Wings and the Lost Ocean, The Great Mizuti uses a single chakram as a melee weapon in addition to spells.
- In the video game Final Fantasy VII, one of the weapons available for Yuffie Kisaragi is a chakram.
- On the television show Ben 10 a new enemy named Charmcaster appears in the episode *Tough Luck*. She takes a few ring chakrams out of her bag and throws them at Ben, and later on she transforms one of her chakrams into a huge chakram and uses it to almost run over Ben's grandpa.
- In the video game Prince of Persia: Warrior Within the Blade Dancer sometimes uses a chakram, and the Prince can wield it as a secondary weapon.
- In the video game Final Fantasy VIII, the character Fujin wields a pair of blue chakrams.
- In the video game Megaman X Command Mission, the character Marino can use Chakram weapons.
- In the PC video game "Lords of Magic" Chakram-like projectile weapons are used by a playable "barbarian huntress" character class.

KAUMODAKI

The *Kaumodaki* is the divine mace weapon of Vishnu. It is believed to be invincible and without parallel.

NARAYANASTRA

The *Narayanastra* is the personal missile weapon of Vishnu in his Narayana form, this astra lets loose a powerful tirade of millions of deadly missiles simultaneously. The intensity of the shower increases with resistance. The only solution is total submission before the missile, given which it will stop.

Ashwathama, a Kuru warrior-hero in the epic Mahabharata unleashes the weapon on the Pandava forces. *Lord* Krishna, who is the Avatara of Vishnu tells the Pandavas and their warriors to drop their weapons and lay down on the ground, submitting completely to the power of the weapon. The secret of the weapon was known by only three warriors, Drona, Aswatthama and Krishna. It was also said that the weapon can be used only once in a war and if tried to use it twice it would devour your own army.

Pandava hero Bhima refuses to do so, thinking it cowardice, and attacks the downpour of fiery arrows. The Narayana weapon concentrates its shower upon him, and he is steadily exhausted. But Krishna and his brothers restrain him in time.

PASHUPATASTRA

The *Pashupatastra* is the irresistible and most destructive personal weapon of Shiva discharged by the mind, eyes, words or a bow. Never to be used against lesser enemies and by lesser warriors, the Pashupata is capable of destroying creation and vanquishing all beings.

SHIVA DHANUSH

Shiva Dhanush in Hindu mythology, was the divine bow of lord Shiva gifted to King Janaka by Sage Parashurama for safe-keeping while the sage performed penances. It was gifted to Parashurama by Shiva for being a great disciple.

In earlier part of her life, Sita while playing with her sisters had unknowingly moved the table over which the "Shiva Dhanush" had been placed; which was something no one in the palace could do. This incident was however observed by King Janaka and he decided to make this incident as the backdrop for swayamvar.

Later, Janaka had announced that whoever wanted to marry Sita had to do so only after lifting (which was itself a difficult job) the bow from its place and stringing it. The bow was broken by Lord Rama when he attempted to string the bow, during the swayamvar of King Janaka's daughter, Sita, whereby he won the hand of Sita in marriage. After the swayamvar, while Rama, Sita and Lakshmana were on their way to Ayodhya, Parashurama confronted and challenged Rama for breaking the bow.

SUDARSHAN CHAKRA

Sudarshan Chakra is a spinning disc like weapon with very sharp edge, which is one of the weapons in the Hindu God Vishnu's hands. Lord Vishnu, also called Narayana, is believed to have four hands.

He holds a Shankha (a conch shell) on one hand, the Sudarshan in the second, a Gada (mace) in the third, and a Padma (lotus) in the fourth.

Lord Vishnu is depicted holding the chakra from a central hole, with his forefinger. Seemingly, the disc simply spins around his finger. According to the Puranas, he could simply release/launch it and it would have the capacity to chop-off someone's head and return back to his finger. It is revered as a divine weapon, which only Lord Vishnu can possess and operate.

The Sudarshan Chakra is mentioned several times in Hindu Mythology, where Lord Vishnu decapitated various rakshasas, asuras and other wicked personalities—one of them being in Mahabharata, where Sri Krishna decapitates Shishupala for his misbehaviour.

The Sudarshan Chakra has lots of abstract imagery as well. It is believed that Lord Vishnu is like the Sun, and the planets of the solar system revolve around him, in a disc-like form..... creating the impression of the Sudarshan Chakra. Lord Vishnu is very commonly worshipped by people having faith in

It is also considered to be a symbol of enlightenment, and hence, in various drawings it is depicted with a brilliant glow.

Lord Vishnu is believed to be the "Protector/Provider" of the universe. He is depicted lying across the entire expanse of the Universe (Vishwadharam) form. The Sudarshan Chakra in his hand depicts the control over the various stars and galaxies, as if they all orbit around him.

Origin of Sudarshan Chakra: According to Hindu mythology the Sudarshan chakra was made by the architect of gods, Viswakarma.

Viswakarma's daughter was married to the Sun. Due to the Sun's blazing power she was unable to go near the Sun and she complained to her father about this. Vishwakarma took the Sun and put him on his workshop and made him less shining and thus his daughter was able to hug the Sun.

The left over Sun-"dust" was collected by Vishwakarma and he made 3 things out of it. The 1st one was the famous aerial vehicle Pushpaka Vimana, the 2nd was the Trident of Lord Shiva, and the 3rd was the Sudarshan Chakra of Lord Vishnu.

Associations with other People: The Sudarshan Chakra was also with the great king Ambarisha, who was a great devotee of Lord Vishnu.

TRISHUL

A *Trishul* is a type of traditional trident in some parts of India, seen as part of traditional religion, but which can also be used as a lethal weapon. This is the weapon wielded by Hindu God, Lord Shiva. The three points are said to represent Shiva's three aspects-creator, destroyer and protector.

- *Trishkla* is Sanskrit for "three-spear". This is the original meaning of the term.
- Trishul is the Pali word for a "Trident". The symbolic weapon of the Hindu god Shiva is a Trishul.

- Trishul can sometimes also designate the Buddhist symbol of the triratna.

Other Affliations: In Hinduism, Goddess Durga also hold the Trishul among seven other weapons in Her hands.

VAISHNAVASTRA

In Hinduism, the *Vaishnavastra* is the personal missile weapon of the God Vishnu. Once fired it cannot be thwarted by any means, except by the will of Vishnu himself.

VAJRA

Vajra is a Sanskrit word meaning both *thunderbolt* and *diamond* and is ritual tool or spiritual implement which is symbolically important to both Buddhism and Hinduism, but is particularly important in Buddhism.

The equivalent word in Tibetan is *dorje* (Wylie: *rdo-rje*; ZWPY: dojê), which is also a common male name in Tibet and Bhutan. Dorje can also refer to a small sceptre held in the right hand by Tibetan lamas during religious ceremonies.

The vajra destroys all kinds of ignorance, and itself is indestructible. In tantric rituals the Vajra symbolizes the male principle which represents method in the right hand and the Bell symbolizes the female principle, which is held in the left. Their interaction leads to enlightenment.

Also the Dorje or Vajra represents the "Upaya" or method Tibetans name Vajra as "Dorje". Made to be worn as a pendant, it reminds the wearer, and the viewer, of the supreme indestructibility of knowledge.

In Buddhism the vajra is the symbol of Vajrayana, one of the three major branches of Buddhism. Vajrayana is translated as *"Thunderbolt Way"* or "Diamond Way" and can imply the thunderbolt experience of Buddhist enlightenment or bodhi and also implies indestructibility, just as diamonds are harder than other gemstones.

In the tantric traditions of both Buddhism and Hinduism, the vajra is a symbol for the nature of reality, or sunyata, indicating endless creativity, potency, and skillful activity. The term is employed extensively in tantric literature: the term for the spiritual teacher is the *vajracarya*; instead of bodhisattva, we have *vajrasattva*, and so on. The practice of prefixing terms, names, places, and so on by vajra represents the conscious attempt to recognize the transcendental aspect of all phenomena; it became part of the process of "sacramentalizing" the activities of the spiritual practitioner and encouraged him to engage all his psychophysical energies in the spiritual life.

An instrument symbolizing vajra is also extensively used in the rituals of the tantra. It consists of a spherical central section, with two symmetrical sets of five prongs, which arc out from lotus blooms on either side of the sphere and come to a point at two points equidistant from the centre, thus giving it the appearance of a "diamond sceptre", which is how the term is sometimes translated.

Various figures in Tantric iconography are represented holding or wielding the vajra. Three of the most famous of these are Vajrasattva, Vajrapani, and Padmasambhava. Vajrasattva (lit. vajra-being) holds the vajra, in his right hand, to his heart. The figure of the Wrathful Vajrapani (lit. vajra in the hand) brandishes the vajra, in his right hand, above his head. Padmasambhava holds the vajra above his right knee in his right hand.

In Hindu mythology vajra is a powerful weapon having the combined features of sword, mace, and spear. It was created out of hard bones of sage Dadhichi who gave up his life willingly for a noble cause so that his spine could be used to build the weapon to be used for a noble cause. This was the weapon Lord Indra used to kill Vitrasur who had conqured heaven and terrorized gods. Due to this supreme sacrifice sage Dadhichi became a legend.

Symbolism: The vajra is made up of several parts: In the centre is a sphere which represents Sunyata, the primordial nature of the universe, the underlying unity of all things.

Emerging from the sphere are two eight petalled lotus flowers. One represents the phenomenal world (or in Buddhist terms Samsara), the other represents the noumenal world (or Nirvana). This is one of the fundamental dichotomies which are perceived by the unenlightened.

Arranged equally around the mouth of the lotus are 2, 4, or 8 mythical creatures which are called makaras. These are mythological half-fish, half-crocodile creatures made up of two or more animals, often representing the union of opposites, (or a harmonisation of qualities that transcend our usual experience).

From the mouths of the makaras come tongues which come together in a point.

The five pronged vajra (with four makaras, plus a central prong) is the most commonly seen vajra. There is an elaborate system of correspondences between the five elements of the noumenal side of the vajra, and the phenomenal side. One important correspondence is between the five 'poisons' with the five wisdoms. The five poisons are the mental states that obscure the original purity of a being's mind, while the five wisdoms are the five most important aspects of the enlightened mind.
Varunastra

The *Varunastra* is the water weapon, incepted by God Varuna, master of the oceans, rivers and lakes.

VAYAVASTRA

The *Vayavastra* is the wind weapon, incepted by the deva Vayu, master of wind.

EXOTIC TRIBES OF ANCIENT INDIA

The classic Indian epics such as the Mahabharata, the Ramayana and the Puranas refer to many *exotic tribes*, describing them as superhuman or subhuman. Narrations about these tribes are often mixed with mythology and fiction. These tribes include Gandharvas, Yakshas, Kinnaras, Kimpurushas, Rakshasas, Nagas, Suparnas, Vanaras, Vidyadharas, Valikilyas, Pisachas, Devas (within them Vasus, Rudras, Maruts, Adityas) and Asuras (within them Danavas, Daityas and Kalakeyas.)

Mythological beings or Humans?: From a historical point of view, these exotic tribes simply may have been tribes that did not interact frequently with mainstream culture so that knowledge of them was very limited, which spurred the invention of fables about them. One extreme and unlikely point of view is that the exotic tribes were mythological beings or even aliens from distant planets; this point of view usually assumes that the exotic capabilities of such tribes, as described in classic literature, are accurate and can be taken at face value.

The exotic capabilities included:

1. the ability to appear and disappear at will
2. the ability to fly in air, with or without the use of an airborn vehicle
3. the knowledge of aircraft (vimana)
4. the ability to change shape at will
5. the ability to read the mind of people
6. the knowledge about other inhabited places like the Earth
7. the ability to influence natural forces

In any case, these tribes had a profound influence on the Vedic culture, but remained separate from the culture due to some reason—perhaps due to their geographic isolation from the rest of the world. The tribes' bases ranged from high mountains (such as the Yaksas and Rakshasas) to deep forests (such as the Vanaras), or they were civilizations beyond the mainstream Indian civilization (as with the Devas and Asuras) which prevailed in the plains of Saraswati, Sindhu and Ganga.

Gandharvas: Gandharvas are described as fierce warriors who could challenge even the great Kshatriya warriors. They were also skilled in art, music and dance. Some Gandharva tribes were allied with the Devas. They inhabited the land to the north of Kailash, close to the Deva territories. The name Gandharva could have been derived from the name Gandhara, since they might originally have inhabited the inaccessible mountains of the Gandhara Kingdom. Later they might have spread to the Saraswati river (seen by Balarama during his pilgrimage over Saraswati). The Ramayana mentions a Gandharva kingdom named Sailusha near the mouth of the river Ganga.

Yaksas: The Yaksas were a tribe living in the area surrounding the Kailash range of the Himalayas. Their king, Vaisravana or Kuvera, was a worshipper of Shiva whose abode is thought to be Kailash.

Kinnaras: The Kinnaras are a tribe often spoken of along with the Gandharvas and Yakshas. There is a district named Kinnaur in Himachal Pradesh which is thought to be the domain of the Kinnara tribes.

Kimpurushas: Kimpurushas were described to be horse headed beings. Puranas mention about an Asura with a horse head, who was known as *Hayagr+va* (which in Sanskrit means *the horse headed one*; *Haya = horse* and *gr+va = head*) This Asura was killed by an incarnation of Lord Vishnu, who took the similar form of a horse headed human figure. In Egyptian sculpures also we see horse headed figures or warriors employing an elongated face mask, which resemble the head of a horse.

The epic Mahabharata and the Puranas describe, regions north to Himalayas as the abode of Kimpurushas. This region was also the abode of a tribe of people called Kambojas. They were fierce warriors skilled in horse ride and horse warfare. Some of them were robber tribes who invaded village settlements, by raiding them using their skilled cavalry forces. The myth of Kimpurushas probably came from these ferocious warrior tribes, who terrorized the Vedic settlements.

RAKSHASAS

Rakshasa's were described to have large bodies, probably due to their continuous life in cold climates over snow covered mountains. One theory says that they were the Neanderthals, the early humans who inhabited Europe and other places in Asia where temperature was very low, like the Himalayan region. The genographic project conducted by National Geographic and IBM, is coming to the conclusion that many species of humans coexisted, all of them in a culturally evolved state.

Thus Rakshasas could be one of these species of humans, reduced to small pockets like the high Himalayas and cool mountains of Sri Lanka, with their social networks steadily shrinking.

This is all speculation. It is very clear in all Indian religious texts of the day that Rakshasas were normal humans who followed a certain religious way (Vyam Raksham, Aggresion and Protection of spiritual life) as opposed to Yakshas (Vyam Yaksham, enjoyment and pleasure ignore spiritual pursuits) and normal or middle path vedic people or even nagas (snake worshippers). There were several other such religious groups aka Dasas ("service and submission", Divodasa and Sudas are called Aryan emporers and even heroes of Rigveda) whose religious beliefs were different.

Many times entire tribes or localities were painted with names. As Vedic Hinduism slowly triumphed over the other ways or paths and they got assimilated, aggressive brahmins started naming underdeveloped or savage tribes with names of their past opponents hence Rakshasas (who originally were all Brahmins) was a term misused as was Dasyu (the priests of dasas) which came to mean savage and is predecessor to modern dacaoit or bandit.

What is astonoshing is that most likely Pleasure, Middle Way and Protection aka Yakshas, Vedics and Rakshasas were contemporary movements where Vedic movement triumphed and many centuries later Ajivikism, Buddhism aka Middle-way and Jainism mimicked the trinity of movements on the Rakshasa side aka aggressive influence of spiritual life. Similar trinity is the Brahma, Vaishnava and Shaiva movements inside the original dasa/vedic movement or the original middle path.

Famous Rakshasas: Ravana was the most famous Rakshasa in Ancient India, who ruled from the Trikuta mountains (Adem's Peak) of Lanka where the climatic conditions were similar to Himalayas. He rose to the status of an emperor who excerted his direct control from Srilanka up to the south of Vindhya ranges in India, and indirectly the kingdoms beyond. Ghatotkacha was a Rakshasa born of the Pandava Bhima and the Rakshasa woman Hidimbi.

Rakshasa Ghatotkacha's kingdom was in Himalaya between Gangotri and Kailash. The forefathers of Ravana also lived here along with the Yakshas. The Yaksha king Vaisravana was the elder brother of Rakshasa king Ravana. Ravana had many sons among Gandharva wives.

The two epics Mahabharata and Ramayana and many Puranas attest that Rakshasas, Yakshas and Gandharvas were related and had inter-marriages.

The famous Rakshasa kingdoms in India were:

1. Lanka Kingdom, ruled by Rakshasa emperor Ravana
2. Danda Kingdom ruled by Khara, Ravana's general
3. Rakhasa Ghatotkacha's kingdom in the Himalayas
4. Other kingdoms in the Himalayas

Nagas: Nagas were a group of Mongoloid people spread throughout India during the period of the epic Mahabharata. The demi-god tribe called *Suparnas* (in which Garuda belonged) were arch-rivals of the Nagas. However, the Nagas near Kashmir seems to be the original abode of all of them. Places like Anantnag attests this theory.

1. Naga Ananta was the first among all the Naga kings.
2. The second Naga chief Vasuki had the kingdom near Kailash (hence the connection of Vasuki with lord Shiva).
3. The third chief Takshaka, in Takshasila both not far from Anantnag.

4. The kingdoms of other Nagas like Karkotaka and Airavata (near river Iravati (Ravi, one among the five rivers of Punjab) were also not far away.

Nagas had kingdoms in Nagaland and Andhra Pradesh. Arjuna's wife Ulupi was from one of such Naga kingdom (in Gangetic Plain) Arjuna's another wife Chitrangada who also was known to Ulupi was from Manipuri (location uncertain). She was probably from a Dravidian tribe. There are now many Naga worshiping places in South India, especially in Andhra Pradesh and Kerala.

Naga race was almost exterminated by Janamejaya, the Kuru king in Arjuna's line, who conducted the massacre of Nagas at Takshasila. This massacre was stopped by Astika, a Brahmin whose mother was a Naga (Vasuki's sister Jaratkaru).

Suparnas: The Suparnas were probably the Falcon worshipping or falcor rearing Iranians who conqured the Naga territories of north west India. They could also be the Dragon worshipping Chinese people. They were arch-rivals of the Nagas. Garuda was a famous Suparna. They had the ability to fly in air without using an aircraft. Some literature tells that they had wings like that of Angels. Some believes that they were birds like the hawk or eagle. Some thinks that they were a race of intelligent Dragons in the family of Dinosaurs, that became extict during the dawn of human civilizations.

Vanaras: Vanaras were a trible who dwelled in the interior of dense forest. During the time of Ramayana, the central part of Indian peninsula was covered by a dense forest by the name Dandaka Forest. Most of the Vanaras lived in this dense forest. Kishindha was their stronghold, that had sway among the whole of the Vanara tribes spread all over the Indian Subcontinent. It was situated in this forest, located now near the Tungabhadra river in Karnataka state of India. Some literature describes them as monkeys, some as apes and some as aboriginal tribes of India, belonging to the Austroloid group.